Collecting the Revolution

Collecting the Revolution

British Engagements with Chinese Cultural Revolution Material Culture

Emily R. Williams

ROWMAN & LITTLEFIELD
Lanham • Boulder • New York • London

Published by Rowman & Littlefield
An imprint of The Rowman & Littlefield Publishing Group, Inc.
4501 Forbes Boulevard, Suite 200, Lanham, Maryland 20706
www.rowman.com

86-90 Paul Street, London EC2A 4NE

Copyright © 2022 by The Rowman & Littlefield Publishing Group, Inc.

All rights reserved. No part of this book may be reproduced in any form or by any electronic or mechanical means, including information storage and retrieval systems, without written permission from the publisher, except by a reviewer who may quote passages in a review.

British Library Cataloguing in Publication Information Available

Library of Congress Cataloguing-in-Publication Data

Names: Williams, Emily R., author.
Title: Collecting the Revolution : British engagements with Chinese
   Cultural Revolution material culture / Emily R. Williams.
Other titles: British engagements with Chinese Cultural Revolution material culture
Description: Lanham : Rowman & Littlefield, [2022] | Includes bibliographical
   references and index. | Summary: "An exploration of British engagements with
   Chinese Cultural Revolution material culture over the period 1966 to the present. It
   examines the ways in which the Cultural Revolution and Chinese Communism was
   more broadly understood, mediated, and represented through its art and propaganda
   and material culture"— Provided by publisher.
Identifiers: LCCN 2021054687 (print) | LCCN 2021054688 (ebook) |
   ISBN 9781538150672 (cloth) | ISBN 9781538150689 (epub)
Subjects: LCSH: China—History—Cultural Revolution, 1966-1976—Public opinion. |
   China—Foreign public opinion, British. | China—History—Cultural Revolution,
   1966-1976—Collectibles. | Material culture—China—Collectors and collecting—Great
   Britain. | Material culture—China—History—20th century. | Public opinion—Great
   Britain. | Great Britain—Relations—China. | China—Relations—Great Britain.
Classification: LCC DS778.7 .W55 2022 (print) | LCC DS778.7 (ebook) |
   DDC 951.05/6—dc23/eng/20220112
LC record available at https://lccn.loc.gov/2021054687
LC ebook record available at https://lccn.loc.gov/2021054688

Contents

Acknowledgements	vii
Introduction	xi
PART I	1
1 Visualising the Cultural Revolution in British Popular Culture	3
2 Idealising the Cultural Revolution: Huxian Peasant Painting and the British Art World	31
3 Experiencing China through Material Culture: The British in China and their Objects	57
PART II	83
4 Individual Collections: The Global Journeys of Cultural Revolution objects	85
5 Public Collections: Collection and Display of Cultural Revolution Objects in British Public Institutions	113
Conclusion: Legacies of Engagements with Cultural Revolution Objects	149
Bibliography	161
Index	177
About the Author	187

Acknowledgements

Like many first books, this book started off as my PhD dissertation, and it has been a long journey since my tentative first research steps in 2011. And yet, the origin of the book goes even further back to my days as an undergraduate studying history at the University of Edinburgh, and my frustrations at what felt like an 'archival fetish' in the approach to historical methodology we were taught. A few lecturers helped me to find that other ways were possible, and in particular Perti Ahonen's final year course on Europe in the 1960s opened my eyes to popular culture as method. My mind was truly opened during my MA in Politics at Goldsmiths College, where I was lucky enough to study with Sanjay Seth and Michael Dutton, who encouraged and perhaps indulged my somewhat wild approaches to intellectual questions. My research interests however finally found an intellectual home at the now defunct London Consortium, a fiercely open-minded, creative and interdisciplinary environment full of interesting people doing ambitious projects.

Crucial to the success of any undertaking are the people that you meet along the way, and I have been very fortunate to encounter the goodwill of a large number of people during my project. I would like to start by thanking my three PhD supervisors Marko Daniel, Harriet Evans and Julia Lovell. Marko's enthusiastic support and somewhat Maoist self-criticism tutorial style helped me search out roots of enquiry I would never have otherwise thought of. Harriet's writing has long been an inspiration to me, and I have been humbled by the support I have received from her both during my PhD and since. I could not ask for a better mentor. I also benefited hugely from the opportunity to work as her research assistant at the University of Westminster Chinese Poster Collection for two years, which gave me unrivalled access to Britain's foremost public collection of Mao-era posters. Julia came on to my supervision team later in the project, but I am immensely grateful for her thorough and thoughtful feedback, and for her generosity with her time and contacts. I'd also like to thank my two PhD examiners, Chris Berry and Louise Tythacott, who managed to turn the potentially terrifying experience of a viva into a stimulating and even enjoyable experience. Their advice on turning the thesis into a book has been indispensable.

This book relies heavily on oral history as a body of primary sources; what building this body of sources meant in practice was a series of immensely interesting meetings with people kind enough to share their time with me (and indeed, often open their homes to me), show me their objects, and recollect their experiences. I am extremely grateful to everyone who took part; I am also grateful to those people who helped put me in touch with potential interviewees: this includes my supervisors, many of my participants, and also my former professor, Colin MacCabe. My interviewees and contacts were Patrick Ainley, Craig Barclay, Guy Brett, Penny Brooke, Terry Cannon, Nicole Chiang, Sara Chiesura, Elsie Collier, Paul Crook, Delia Davin, John Dugger, Christopher Dyer, Harriet Evans, David Fernbach, Gisela Chan Man Fong, Mary Ginsberg, John Gittings, Beverley Hopper, Anna Johnston, Martin Kaufman, Rose Kerr, David King, Richard Kirkby, Beth McKillop, Kevin McLoughlin, Maureen Scott, Michael Sheringham, Neil Taylor, Shelagh Vainker, Helen Wang, George Walden, Aubrey Walter, Scott Watson, Roderick Whitfield, Frances Wood, Zhang Hongxing, and Zheng Shengtian. Some of these individuals also provided me with images of their wonderful objects for this book, which I hope will bring readers the same delight I feel when seeing them. I would like to thank the British Museum's Mary Ginsberg and the National Museum of Scotland's Kevin McLoughlin for taking me to see some of their objects in storage. I would also like to thank SACU's Zoë Reed and Oundle School's Max von Habsburg for their assistance in accessing their institution's unique archives.

I benefited from a number of opportunities to present my research at various stages, and I'd like to thank Anne Witchard, Tracey Fallon, Stephen McDowell and Carol Yinghua Lu for their invitations along the way. Chapters also benefited from close readings by David Goodman, Troy Chen and Malcolm McNeill amongst others.

I was very grateful to receive funding for my PhD in the form of the London Consortium Bursary and for language training in China through the Great Britain-China Educational Trust and the British Council.

A version of chapter 2 was published as Williams, Emily, 'Exporting the Communist Image: The 1976 Chinese Peasant Painting Exhibition', in: *New Global Studies,* 8:3 (2014), pp. 279–305. It is republished here with permission from De Gruyter.

While this book project started in London, it was finished in Suzhou China, where I am based at Xi'an Jiaotong-Liverpool University. I have benefited immensely from the lively intellectual environment of the China Studies department. I am particularly grateful to my Heads of Department, Beibei Tang and Geoffrey Chun-fung Chen, for their constant support and encouragement, and to David Goodman, a fellow Communist material culture enthusiast.

I would like to thank the team at Rowman & Littlefield for their interest in and support for my book, and in particular, my editors, Dhara Snowden, Rebecca Anastasi and Haley White. I'd also like to thank the anonymous peer reviewer for their insightful comments and criticisms, which have helped me to improve the book immeasurably. It should go without saying that any remaining errors are my own.

I was lucky enough to meet not just brilliant minds, but great friends throughout my studies. Rebecca Wright, Andrea Vesentini, Angela Becher, and Malcolm McNeill provided intellectual stimulation, unending support, and perhaps most importantly, the excuse for tea breaks. Friends and family have gotten me through the long days in the libraries and archives, and I am thankful for their support and continued willingness to listen to my new discoveries of the peculiar resting places of Maoist material culture. My parents, Bruce and Cathy, and siblings, Elizabeth and Andrew, have inspired me through their own great achievements. Finally, the final drafts of this book were written throughout my pregnancy and then maternity leave with my first child: I dedicate it, therefore, to my husband Murdoch and my son Torin.

Introduction

The spring of 2016 marked the 50th anniversary of the start of the Cultural Revolution in China. It was marked with extensive media coverage and academic interest in the West and with a steely silence in China. It was also commemorated with a small exhibition in a public library in the provincial English city of Grantham, set up by local Chairman Mao badge collector, Clint Twist.[1] Twist's exhibition was limited to one display case, but contained a multitude of Maoist objects: Mao badges of various styles, Red Guard armbands, copies of *Quotations from Chairman Mao Zedong* (better known as the Little Red Book) in assorted languages as well as other pamphlets and booklets, as well as objects from daily life in the 1960s and 1970s such as children's toys, cups and a clock. In brief didactic panels, Twist introduced library-goers to the major themes of the Cultural Revolution, but also tried to give some sense of daily life in Cultural Revolution China, as well as noting the period's transnational appeal and legacies in contemporary China. Twist rented the space from the local library and transformed what was a relatively dull display cabinet into an intensely red and political space. Grantham is not a city known for its left-wing leanings, and Twist acknowledged that local interest in his exhibition was limited. But this book begins with it because it typifies the complex journeys that Maoist objects have taken since they were produced, as well as the often surprising relationships that have emerged between British individuals and institutions, and Maoist objects, both during the Mao era and after. What would the Chinese producers and consumers of these Communist objects have thought if they had known that 50 years in the future, they would be displayed in a small English town they had likely never heard of, arranged by a middle-class hobbyist?

This book explores these journeys and relationships in order to highlight both the untold story of British engagements with Communist China, and more broadly to explore the ways in which meanings, narratives and identities are formed in the nexus of the person-object relationship. These meanings and identities go well beyond a direct relationship with an ideological position or, to put it more bluntly: it was not just Communists or fellow travellers who owned, engaged with and collected these Maoist objects, and they have meant different things to their various owners. Communist objects, made in Mao's China, found their way to Britain through a number of routes and have ended up in a variety of personal and public collections, often owned by people with no interest – or sometimes even with direct antipathy – to Communist ideology. As such, objects hold the key to unearthing all sorts of relationships between Britain and China that would be overlooked by focusing solely on the British left.

Indeed, Clint Twist is by no means a Communist, much less a Maoist. He had, however, been aware of the Cultural Revolution and its material culture since he was a teenager in the late 1960s. On a day trip to London, he visited the Chinese embassy in order to request a copy of the Little Red Book. He read it and kept it all through his years at the University of Cambridge in the early 1970s, and while he was inclined towards the political left, he was not actively involved in politics, nor did he search out further information on China. He is, however, a lifelong collector, having collected everything from American comic books, to Roman and Chinese coins, to ancient pottery shards. While he is now retired, his career was educationally focused: he worked in museums and as a non-fiction author. For Twist then, objects are a route into knowledge, as well as a fun pastime. As the example of Twist makes clear, the objects one owns are not necessarily a reflection of personal politics; they can instead be avenues into new areas of study, driven by curiosity and the aesthetic appeal of familiar and unfamiliar objects. In this, Twist is like many of the individuals we encounter in this book.

There were Maoists in the United Kingdom in the 1960s and 1970s, although never in large numbers. There have also been exhibitions of Maoist objects at far more prominent locales than Twist's library: at museums, galleries and universities. This book tells the stories of these people, objects and institutions. But the story starts with Clint Twist because his collection allows us to see another side of Sino-British relations than that which might be expected. This book argues that while Britain did not have the extensive 'Maoist' movements that many other countries had in the 1960s and 1970s, Britain had a diverse and complex set of engagements with Mao Zedong's China, and one of the ways this occurred was through China's cultural products. British encounters with this material and visual culture did not end with Mao's death in 1976, but continued in the years that followed, and in recent years, these objects have become visible in a number of different settings: online, in auction houses, in museums and universities, and as before, in people's homes. These objects have a series of afterlives in Britain, as commodities, collectibles, souvenirs, and historical artefacts, which have taken them far beyond their initial status as largely mass-produced government-directed objects. They remind us that while Mao's China may have been considered to have been 'closed' to the outside world at this time, in fact, it played an active role in the 'global sixties', from an ideological, cultural and political perspective, and these influences have had a legacy that have far outlasted Mao himself.

DISCOVERING CULTURAL REVOLUTION COLLECTIONS IN BRITAIN

Research for this book began with the discovery that some of the UK's most prominent cultural institutions – the British Museum, the Victoria and Albert Museum, the Ashmolean Museum, the National Museum of Scotland amongst others – had collections of Maoist material culture. I was surprised to discover Mao badges and propaganda posters sitting in storerooms alongside imperial porcelains and jades. Surely, I thought, the ideological nature of these objects precluded them from inclusion in such august institutions? In reality of course, all objects – all art and culture – reflect the ideologies of the era from which they came: is a Qianlong vase (so called because it dates from the era of the Qianlong Emperor (1735–1796)), reflecting and celebrating the glory of the Qing dynasty, really any less ideological than a Mao bust? And yet, these Maoist objects remained perplexing, not least because they were so infrequently displayed. Despite having collections that reflect China up to the present, British public institutions tended to – at least when this research began in 2011 – display a version of China that reflected only its imperial history. China after 1911 rarely featured in long-term displays at British museums. This prompted me to consider whether this was the case everywhere: were the grand institutions of Chinese art in France, the Musée Guimet or the Musée Cernuschi, also housing collections of propaganda posters in their backrooms? Does the Museum für Asiatische Kunst in Berlin, Germany or the Museum of Fine Arts in Boston, US collect Mao badges as well as neolithic jades and Ming paintings? While there are some exceptions, the answer to these questions is generally a negative: the Mao era remains a lacuna in many museum collections and exhibitions around the world, which focus instead on China's imperial glory, and in some, its re-discovery of traditional cultural forms in the Reform Era. There is, then, something rather unique about British Museum collections of Chinese objects. While they may not always display their Mao-era objects (although this has become much more common since this research began), even the fact that so many public institutions have substantial numbers of Mao-era objects in their collections is itself noteworthy. This prompted consideration of the provenance of these collections: Why do so many British institutions collect these objects when similar museums in other countries do not? What are the routes through which these objects have travelled to get to the museums? Who are the people that have owned, donated, sold or otherwise engaged with these objects? The answer, it turned out, was far more complex than initially expected. The people who donated them and the people who pushed for their inclusion into museum collections (sometimes the same people) did not necessarily always, or even often, come to these objects by way of ideology; instead, they reflected a wide variety of subject positions, of engagements with Mao-era China and Maoist material culture for different reasons, at different times, and with differing levels of sympathy and understanding. Donors to these museum collections ranged from left-wing journalists to right-wing politicians, from Communist fellow travellers to casual tourists.[2] I began, then, to track down these donors and sellers in order to understand the stories of how these objects found their way into these museums.

Public and private collections of Mao-era (and especially Cultural Revolution) objects are, then, the methodological starting point for this project. It is concerned with not just what is in the collections, but also in how they got there and especially, through whom. The collections are seen not just as the archives of the objects, but also as the archives of British engagements with Mao's China. This was developed through oral historical interviews with over forty collectors, donors, curators and others who had an interest in Mao's China and its objects – an experience that has been both intellectually expansive and personally enjoyable. I discovered a surprisingly wide set of views on Mao's China, even for people who still retained and often displayed objects in their own homes. Some people's views on the Cultural Revolution had changed over time, either as new information on the realities emerged, as China itself has changed in the Reform Era, or as people reconsidered their youthful experiences, for some with nostalgia, for others with discomfiture. Others were apathetic or even hostile to Maoism and the Cultural Revolution at the time and have seen no reason to change their appraisal. These diverse views have highlighted the substantial engagements that many people in Britain had with Mao-era China, the plurality of perspectives on it, and the role played by objects in these engagements.

GLOBAL MAOISMS

While this book focuses on Britain's relationship with Cultural Revolution China and Chinese objects, Britain represented one small part of a much broader global interest in China at this time. In recent years, this has become an increasingly developed field of academic enquiry, known loosely as 'global Maoisms', which articulates the widespread engagement many people and groups had with Mao's China (or at least their understanding of it).[3] This research has unearthed the diverse appeal of Mao's China and its ideology for people in various parts of the world. In parts of the developing world, Maoist strategies of guerrilla rebellion and revolution, the concepts of 'surrounding the cities from the countryside' and of the revolutionary potential of the peasants, as well as the inevitability of violence, seemed appropriate to those engaging in struggles against their own or colonial governments. The Maoist organisations in Peru (particularly the *Sendero Luminoso* [Shining Path]) and South Asia (including the Naxalite movement in India or the Maoist guerrillas in Nepal) are perhaps the most famous, due to their often violent strategies, but the engagement went far beyond that, and for some, Mao's China served as an alternative model for development in newly postcolonial countries.[4] China too actively pursued this role, both as a moral and ideological model, and more practically, through its claims to the leadership of the non-aligned movement, particularly after the 1955 Bandung Conference.[5] This involved everything from rhetorical support for the newly independent countries of the developing world, to privileged access to Mao and other top leaders for aspiring revolutionaries, to the provision of weapons, money and training classes for activists and revolutionary leaders. While many of these revolutionary movements were typically not strictly 'Maoist', and few countries explicitly sided with China over either the Soviet Union or the United States, there is no doubt that China had substantial influence in the Global South in the 1950s–1970s.[6]

Individuals and groups in the West were also interested in Mao's China.[7] Some in Europe and North America were interested in the potential for Mao's China to serve as a model for development in Asia, Africa and Latin America, whereas others saw Maoism as an inspiration in their attempts to start a revolution or at least upset the power structures at home. For many, particularly young people in France and America, Maoism and Mao's China was appealing as part of their search for alternatives to the norms of Western society, culture and politics, and also to those of the by-then largely discredited Soviet Union. Within this, the emphasis that Maoism placed on culture and on 'cultural revolution' in the construction of a different social order was particularly illuminating to those interested in social and cultural change, alongside or instead of the more orthodox Marxist interest in politics and economics.[8]

While some of this academic literature has had a tendency to emphasise and even ridicule the 'infantile enthrallment' that young people had with Mao's China, historian Fabio Lanza convincingly argues that Mao's China offered a new critical vocabulary and set of practices to engage with real issues of inequality across the world.⁹ Similarly, art historians Galimberti, de Haro-García and Scott argue that the idea of Mao's China was a 'productive epistemological device to reimagine the world, to reinterpret its hierarchies and to act to change them.'¹⁰ As such, it is worth taking seriously the engagements that people had with Mao's China and the powerful political and emotional impact that the discovery of Mao's China could have on them, even while acknowledging that perspectives on China were often distorted or exaggerated. Collectively, the research on global Maoisms has demonstrated that while the West's impact on China is well known, China too – and the idea of China – has impacted global economics, culture and society. As historian Rebecca Karl has argued, Mao and Maoism are central not just to the history of Chinese and global socialism, but also to the whole history of revolution and modernity in the twentieth century.¹¹ Any effort to come to terms with the impact of ideas on the Cold War and the course of post-Second World War history must include the inspiration provided by Mao's China in shaping ideas about development and social relations.

Britain has been largely excluded from this academic field: while there were 'Maoist' groups in the 1960s and 1970s (Marxist-Leninist groups who aligned themselves with China, rather than with Trotskyist ideas or the Soviet Union), they were always small, peripheral, and unable to affect any real influence, even on the left.¹² Indeed, many significant secondary texts on the British far left omit Maoism and the China-oriented political parties entirely, focusing instead on the Trotskyist and orthodox Communist movement. And yet, Britain did have its own Maoists, even if not in the numbers or force witnessed elsewhere, and Maoism was a facet of the 'cultural revolution' in British social, cultural and intellectual life in the 1960s and 1970s.

British media attention was briefly directed towards the British history of Maoism after the eruption of the 2013 'Lambeth Slavery Case', in which two so-called 'Maoists', Aravindan and Chanda Balakrishnan, were arrested on suspicion of holding three women captive for more than thirty years. The Balakrishnans were key figures in the Workers' Institute of Marxism-Leninism-Mao Zedong Thought in the 1970s, a small political party that aimed to build a 'red base' in London's Brixton and encouraged the Chinese People's Liberation Army to liberate the area, an event they thought was imminent.¹³ A 1978 article called the Workers' Institute 'truly the most lunatic of the lunatic fringe of left politics in Britain,'¹⁴ and the trial made it clear that whatever inspiration the Balakrishnans may have originally drawn from Mao's China, they had long since descended into an outright cult. In 2016, Aravindan Balakrishnan was sentenced to 23 years in prison.¹⁵

Much of the focus of 'global Maoisms' has been on politics (such as the influence on, or even training of, revolutionary groups by Mao's China) or ideology. The search, therefore, has been for 'Maoists'. However, one could engage with, be interested in, even be inspired by Mao's China and the Cultural Revolution without being a 'Maoist'. Unlike in France, where a number of publicly renowned intellectuals explicitly stated their interest in, and at times dedication to Mao's China, British intellectuals were less explicitly influenced by Maoism.[16] However, one of this book's main arguments is that the scarcity of dedicated 'Maoists' in Britain did not equate to a lack of interest in Mao's China. Rather, if the concept of 'global Maoisms' is expanded beyond a focus on the narrowly political or ideological, Britain did, particularly by virtue of its colonial presence in Hong Kong and diplomatic mission in Beijing, have an extensive and diverse set of engagements with Mao's China.[17] One of the mechanisms for this engagement was through objects.

VIEWING CHINA THROUGH OBJECTS

Despite being a country for so long was so difficult to visit, with a language so difficult to master, China has long been a place that has fascinated outsiders: as historian Jonathan Spence has written, 'One aspect of a country's greatness is surely its capacity to attract and retain the attention of others. This capacity has been evident from the very beginnings of the West's encounter with China.'[18] This attraction, however, has never been neutral, and the understandings of China produced by Sino-Western engagements have been both highly changeable and largely contingent on the situation at home: China, over time, has been seen as everything from a model civilisation, ruled by a social and cultural order that perfects human morality; a vast market, overseas access to which would bring untold trading opportunities; a heathen nation, ripe for conversion; or an authoritarian regime given to depravity and cruelty. Indeed, these same views have often been shared about both imperial and Communist China, simultaneously glorifying and demonising the country and the culture, depending on the viewer. In all cases, these descriptions of China reflect ongoing discussions and debates about social, cultural and political developments in Europe and North America: Western views of China always tells us as much, or more, about the West as they do about China. The fact that understandings of China were not necessarily accurate reflections, however, does not mean they should be disregarded: rather they show the ways in which Europeans and others think *through* China. China's difference created a space through which other alternatives became thinkable; in which China or the idea of China served as a platform for discussions that were restricted in a European or American context. This was perhaps never more true than of Maoism in the 1960s and 1970s, when, according to Fabio Lanza, 'China, specifically because of its revolutionary situation, came to constitute a foundation for a transnational discourse of intellectual and political change.'[19] This does not mean, of course, that these views of China were free of misconceptions or 'orientalist fantasies'; indeed, in many ways, these fantasies have long powered China's attraction. And yet, despite this, as Lanza argues, there is much to be gained from acknowledging that people took seriously their understandings of Maoism and other aspects of Chinese culture, even if they contained misconceptions. Moreover, this book argues that in addition to the intellectual space that thinking about Maoist China gave people, it also provided emotional space: Maoist China and the Cultural Revolution became a space through which people's hopes and dreams, and fears and concerns could all find expression. The engagement was intellectual, but also emotional and aesthetic, a reminder that we do not just engage with the world around us rationally, but in an embodied and emotional manner.

For many people in Britain, however, China was only ever at the periphery of their attention: as a country, it was seen as too foreign and too far away for most people to know much about it. Given this, one of the main ways that China has historically impacted the daily lives of people, and consequently the main ways that China became known, was through its arts and material culture. As this book demonstrates, the same remains true in Britain even today.

This has long been the case: for hundreds of years, Chinese porcelain (and the tea that was drunk out of it) helped, in art historian Stacey Pierson's words, 'to define the British conception of China as a place, both as "other" and as part of the fabric of British life'.[20] The vision of China produced from its objects changed over time and reflects as much about the geopolitical balance between Britain and China as it does anything specifically about China. Qing porcelains could be held up for their high craftsmanship, representing a benign and wise moral order or derided as the 'whimsy' and 'triviality' of a static and ultimately declining civilisation.[21] And yet, views of art and of nationality were not always identical: for much of the nineteenth century, Chinese art was admired and appreciated in Britain, even while its people and politics were denigrated and belittled, particularly after the British defeat of China in the First Opium War (1839–1842).[22]

The fall of the Qing dynasty in 1911–1912 produced two Chinas to be visualised through objects: an increasingly nostalgised imperial past and a tumultuous but revolutionary present. These were each displayed in two exhibitions in the 1930s: the International Exhibition of Chinese Art held at the Royal Academy of the Arts in London, which portrayed China as an 'esoteric' culture defined by its dependence on spiritual and symbolic interpretations; and a Contemporary Chinese Woodcuts, Drawings and Cartoons exhibition, which depicted images of Chinese resistance to the invading Japanese and raised money for the China Campaign Committee's 'Aid China' campaign.[23] These two Chinas then, 'traditional' and 'modern' have long competed for the limited mental space the British public has available for China, and certainly from the perspective of objects, the 'traditional' image of Chinese art has frequently dominated.

The victory of Mao Zedong and the Communist Party of China (CCP) over the Nationalists (Guomindang) in 1949 demanded a re-evaluation of China. China were allies during the Second World War, and the dominant British perspective of the Chinese Communists at this time was that they were more akin to agrarian reformers than to hardened Soviet-style Communists.[24] Britain was the first major Western power to recognise the People's Republic of China (PRC) in 1950. The early and mid-1950s saw a new trend for revolutionary and traditional Chinese culture in Britain: there were touring exhibitions of revolutionary woodcuts as well as classical operas; a new Chinese bookstore was established at the central London left-wing bookstore Collet's, and the well-known bookstore Foyles hosted an exhibition of modern Chinese art.[25] At the same time, more negative views of the Chinese Communists also began to form in conjunction with the Korean War (1950–1953) and the Chinese Volunteers' 'human wave' strategy of attack, which brought back the racist 'Yellow Peril' fears of the early twentieth century.[26] Reports at this time of Communist 'brainwashing' and later during the Great Leap Forward (1958–1961), images of vast construction projects powered by identically attired workers, created an idea of a de-humanised society in which individual will was subsumed within the collective.[27]

These varying opinions, and their accompanying images, then were already established when the Cultural Revolution erupted in May 1966, an event which saw an explosion of politically-motivated material culture, some of which was exported around the globe. It was an event difficult to understand, and information coming out of China was limited and often confusing. Was it a civil war between an ageing Mao and his subordinates or was it a genuine revolution in the ideological superstructure?[28] Media coverage from Hong Kong and the limited number of journalists on the mainland tended to paint a rather different picture from the information distributed by the Chinese government itself, which emphasised the participatory and emancipatory elements of the movement, while downplaying the violence and coercion. Chinese official sources included not just government statements, but a whole variety of visual and material culture such as posters, papercuts, paintings, Little Red Books, periodicals and other publications, Mao badges and other small objects. As noted already, these were distributed by the Chinese embassy in the UK, as well as sold by a variety of left-wing bookshops and Chinese stores. This tendency for foreigners to know China through Chinese objects continued, therefore, during the Cultural Revolution. In the imperial period, the global travels of Chinese objects were driven by market forces, not government design, but in the Mao era, the Chinese government realised the potentially potent force of their propaganda, as a form of what would now be called 'soft power.'[29] For many, particularly on the left, these objects were one of the primary ways through which views and images of the Cultural Revolution developed. Indeed, globally, it has been argued that 'art and images were paramount in the dissemination and reception of Maoism's revolutionary ambitions'.[30]

This book argues that just as objects and images have long been central to how foreigners viewed China, this continued to be the case in the modern period. However, while the Chinese designers, producers and distributors of these objects may have had certain ideas about the image of China they intended to communicate to domestic and international audiences, in actuality, they were received in a variety of different ways.

OUR RELATIONSHIPS WITH OBJECTS

The argument that objects have long been part of the way in which Britons have known China is also a reflection of the larger point that our experiences with the world are fundamentally embodied ones, in which visual and material culture shape our experiences, ideas and identities, and in which these experiences also shape how we interact with the visual and material world.[31] It has become commonplace within fields such as Material Culture Studies to accept that our social worlds are as much constituted by materiality as the other way around. And yet, as anthropologist Daniel Miller argues, we also need to go beyond this to acknowledge the diversity of material worlds in order to avoid reducing them to simply maps or models of the social world.[32] This book aims to do this by asking not just how, but *what are the different ways in which* foreign objects shape how we see foreign countries, our own country, and ourselves? In thinking about Cultural Revolution objects in Britain, it must start with the acknowledgement that there are no unmediated contacts with an object: every encounter is situated within the global system of knowledge production, intersected by the singularities of individual positioning and outlook. In the context of the 'global sixties', this means both the Cold War-era fear of Communism *and* the rise of left-wing activist movements seeking alternative socialist modernities beyond the options provided by orthodox Marxism-Leninism and the Soviet Union. Holders of these different visions of the world all encountered the same objects, but read different values from them: depending on the observer, Chairman Mao badges could represent mindless obedience to a tyrannical regime, a coherent society shaped by a unified belief system or the symbolic authority of a revolutionary leader. The views we take towards these foreign objects is then shaped by these larger social and geopolitical forces, and yet, as will become clear through the encounters detailed in this book, our relationships with things go well beyond our and their politics. Our relationships with objects do not purely mirror ideology; the benefit, then, of looking at our relationships with objects is that it allows us to encounter all sorts of engagements with Mao's China or the Cultural Revolution that go beyond simply ideology.

ENGAGING WITH CULTURAL REVOLUTION MATERIAL CULTURE

This book is divided into two parts. Part I (chapters 1–3) focuses on British perceptions of Chinese Communism and the Cultural Revolution during the period of the Cultural Revolution itself, with a particular focus on the role that objects played in shaping views. Part II (chapters 4 and 5) focuses on private and public collections of Cultural Revolution objects, covering the period from the Mao era until the present.

Chapter 1 explores different perceptions of and constructions of Mao's China and the Cultural Revolution in the 1960s and 1970s, with a particular emphasis on material and visual culture. It draws on British popular culture sources to consider how China was constructed, on the one hand, as a 'problem' nation and a danger to world peace, and on the other hand, as an inspiration for the British left, which saw the PRC as constructing an alternative socialist modernity. Both supporters and critics often drew on the same material culture in order to demonstrate these opposing positions, and this chapter looks in particular at the Mao suit. It was developed in China in the early twentieth century as an item of clothing that could be both modern and Chinese, and was associated with the early revolutionary leader Sun Yatsen, from which its Chinese name was derived (中山装 *zhongshanzhuang*).[33] By the late 1950s, however, it came to be associated abroad with the Communist regime, and in particular, with Mao, hence its English name. The Mao suit was an object capable of embodying, for China's critics, the totalitarian nature of the Communist state, in which the masses were reduced to identical 'blue ants', but also conversely, for China's supporters, the anti-capitalist and militant nature of the regime so appreciated by these admirers. The case study of the Mao suit illuminates the ways in which knowledge of and feelings about the Cultural Revolution and the Chinese Communists could be developed and expressed through engagements with Chinese material culture.

Chapter 2 focuses on an exhibition of Chinese art in Britain during 1976–1977 by the Huxian peasant painters. The Huxian peasant painters gained global recognition in the 1970s, popular for being amateur painters who combined manual and creative work and who cheerfully and colourfully depicted the new socialist countryside. It was only a small exhibition, but it received substantial and almost entirely positive coverage in the British mainstream and art press. This chapter positions the success of the Huxian exhibition in the context, firstly, of wider cultural interest in Chinese Communism, in which these paintings were valued because they eschewed some of the more derivative tendencies of socialist realism, and thus seemed less like 'propaganda', but also secondly within the context of the British art world, which at that time was undergoing sustained self-criticism for its perceived elitism and over-specialisation. While interest in the art itself was often superficial, the Huxian peasant painters were held up as embodiments of the possibility of an alternative art system. This case study illustrates the importance of art and visual imagery in creating positive images of China in Britain, in large part because British observers were often willing to take at face value the Chinese government's celebratory narrative about peasant painting, in order to utilise the Chinese model to reflect on domestic issues.

Chapter 3 investigates British experiences in China during the Cultural Revolution and argues that material culture was part of the way that China was knowable to foreigners at the time, in part because it served as an entry point into a society that often remained opaque, even to those in China. It explores the stories of five individuals with very different experiences and perspectives on Cultural Revolution China: a diplomat, a journalist and three students. It demonstrates the key role that material culture played in mediating their experiences: material culture could be a source of information, aesthetic pleasure, an insight into the everyday lives of ordinary Chinese people or an item of entertainment and consumption at this unusual time. The chapter also begins to move towards the present and argues that the ability of these objects to act as 'traces' not only of the Cultural Revolution itself, but of their owner's experiences of this extraordinary period is one reason these objects continue to be found in the homes of individuals whose ideological position put them radically at odds with the politics inherent in Maoist art.

Chapter 4 introduces the collecting stories of British collectors, highlighting the shared and different routes of travel their objects have taken, in the past and present. It considers the concept of collecting as the selective and serial accumulation of objects, and which has been theorised within Western academia as an innately personal process. It adds to this, however, insights from the Chinese tradition of collecting in which collecting is discussed more in terms of the important social role it played. Moreover, the chapter contrasts the idea of collecting as an inherently 'private' and personal endeavour with the global systems of object distribution, value construction and knowledge production that inevitably shapes why, how and who collects. It features five private collections, each of which was formed under different conditions;

a British youth who grew up in China, an English teacher and academic in late Mao-era China; a left-wing British graphic designer and writer, a couple who were professional Chinese antique dealers, and finally, a retiree hobbyist collector. While these are all private collections, each of their owners have made efforts to give their objects a public life too, through their display in university, library or museum exhibitions, through their reproduction in publications or through online display. This highlights, then, the blurred boundary between collectibles as privately owned objects, and the larger social role they continue to play.

Chapter 5 focuses on British public institutional collections of Mao-era objects, the most important of which are the British Museum, the Victoria & Albert Museum, the Ashmolean Museum, the National Museum of Scotland and the University of Westminster. While the British Museum and V&A both independently began collecting twentieth-century objects in the early 1980s, Mao-era objects have largely entered their collections through donation, rather than curatorial purchase. The Ashmolean and National Museum of Scotland only began collecting the Mao era in the 2000s, but have taken more proactive approaches, and have predominantly made purchases from already-formed collections. The University of Westminster has the UK's largest collection of Mao-era objects, with a particular strength in posters; the collection has functioned in different ways over time, reflecting in part the changing attitudes towards the Mao era. The Mao era remains little represented in permanent exhibitions in British museums, but temporary exhibitions have shown some of the different narratives that could be constructed, influenced in part by the institutional histories of the museums. Crucially, this chapter highlights the importance of British individuals who had experienced Mao's China in person as driving many of the museums' acquisitions: these British museum collections can, therefore, be considered as a legacy of British engagement with Mao's China.

The conclusion addresses the question of the legacies of these objects, both in China and in the United Kingdom, arguing that while British collections are small compared to Chinese collections of Communist objects, the continued sensitivities of the Cultural Revolution in China means that British private and public collections are important archives of the period itself, as well, as chapter 5 has argued, of British engagements with Mao's China.

NOTES

1. Information on the exhibition provided to author by Twist.

2. One of the limitations of this methodology is that the British Chinese community has been largely excluded from this book, as they were not a source of objects for public institutions. This heterogeneous community, including – by the 1960s – a large population of recent immigrants from Hong Kong, often had little interest in or sympathy for the Maoist experiment. However, the Cultural Revolution, including the disturbances in Hong Kong, did have an impact on some British Chinese worker's clubs, who organised street protests against British imperialism and put on model operas and films. For more on the British Chinese community, see Gregor Benton and Edmund Terence Gomez, *The Chinese in Britain, 1800-Present: Economy, Transnationalism, Identity* (Basingstoke: Palgrave Macmillan, 2008).

3. Alexander C. Cook, *Mao's Little Red Book: A Global History* (Cambridge: Cambridge University Press, 2014); Fabio Lanza, 'Global Maoism', in *Afterlives of Chinese Communism*, ed. Christian Sorace, Ivan Franceschini, and Nicholas Loubere, (Canberra: ANU Press, 2019), 85–88; Julia Lovell, *Maoism: A Global History* (London: The Bodley Head, 2018).

4. On South America and South Asia, see Michael D. Rothwell, *Transpacific Revolutionaries: The Chinese Revolution in Latin America* (New York: Routledge, 2013); Ina Zharkevich, *Maoist People's War and the Revolution of Everyday Life in Nepal* (Cambridge: Cambridge University Press, 2019); Alpa Shah and Judith Pettigrew, eds., *Windows into a Revolution: Ethnographies of Maoism in India and Nepal* (London & New York: Routledge, 2018).

5. Jian Chen, 'China and the Bandung Conference: Changing Perceptions and Representations', in *Bandung Revisited: The Legacy of the 1955 Asian-African Conference for International Order*, ed. Amitav Acharya and See Seng Tan (Singapore: National University of Singapore Press, 2008), 132–59; See also Christopher J. Lee, *Making a World after Empire: The Bandung Moment and Its Political Afterlives* (Athens: Ohio University Press, 2010).

6. Samantha Christiansen and Zachary A. Scarlett, *The Third World in the Global 1960s* (New York & Oxford: Berghahn Books, 2012). See in particular Scarlett's chapter on the influence of the Cultural Revolution in the Third World.

7. I acknowledge the problematic nature of the term 'the West', as it covers a range of countries with different historical and cultural experiences. I use it, however, because it highlights that Britain's experiences of China were situated within a broader context, and in this the experiences of Western Europe (and primarily (West) Germany, France and Italy) and North America are central to my conception of the West.

8. Influential recent sources include Max Elbaum, *Revolution in the Air: Sixties Radicals Turn to Lenin, Mao and Che* (London & New York: Verso, 2002); Richard Wolin, *The Wind from the East: French Intellectuals, the Cultural Revolution, and the Legacy of the 1960s* (Princeton, NJ; Woodstock: Princeton University Press, 2010); Robeson Taj Frazier, *The East Is Black: Cold War China in the Black Radical Imagination* (Durham & London: Duke University Press, 2015).

9. Fabio Lanza, *The End of Concern: Maoist China, Activism, and Asian Studies* (Durham: Duke University Press, 2017), 6–8.

10. Jacopo Galimberti, Noemi de Haro García, and Victoria H. F. Scott, 'Introduction', in *Art, Global Maoism and the Chinese Cultural Revolution*, ed. Galimberti Jacopo, Noemi de Haro García, and Victoria H. F. Scott (Manchester: Manchester University Press, 2019), 3.

11. Rebecca E. Karl, *Mao Zedong and China in the Twentieth-Century World: A Concise History* (Durham: Duke University Press, 2010), x.

12. Peter Shipley, *Revolutionaries in Modern Britain* (London: Bodley Head, 1976), 151. For the most thorough coverage of Maoist political parties in England, see Sam Richards, 'The Rise & Fall of Maoism: The English Experience', 2013, http://www.marxists.org/history/erol/uk.firstwave/uk-maoism.pdf [accessed 31/07/2020].

13. Workers' Institute Party Committee, 'Workers' Institute Successfully Conducts Vigorous Programme to Uphold Chairman Mao's Revolutionary Line Amidst the Mass Upsurge in Britain - A Report', 31 March 1977, https://www.marxists.org/history/erol/uk.hightide/wi-report.htm [accessed 31/07/2020].

14. anon, 'A Short Guide to Maoists in Britain', *The Leveller*, no. 20 (November 1978), http://www.marxists.org/history/erol/uk.firstwave/shortguide.htm [accessed 31/07/2020].

15. 'Maoist Cult Leader Aravindan Balakrishnan Jailed for 23 Years', *BBC News*, January 29, 2016, https://www.bbc.com/news/uk-england-35443423 [accessed 31/07/2020].

16. Many key French intellectuals of this period were involved in one way or another. While never becoming fully fledged 'Maoists', Jean-Paul Sartre worked with Maoists such as Pierre Victor (Benny Levy) and Serge July in various publishing endeavours, while Michel Foucault worked with Maoists to establish a nationwide prisoners' advocacy group. Intellectuals Philippe Sollers & Julia Kristeva, associated with the journal *Tel Quel*, were more full-throated in their support for Maoism, and undertook a widely publicised tour of China in 1974, with a more sceptical Roland Barthes and others. The 'godfather of French Maoism' was Louis Althusser, even though he never left the French Communist Party. Many of his students called themselves Maoists, at least for a time; the best known of whom is Alain Badiou. For the fullest account of French Maoism, see Wolin, *The Wind from the East*. It could be argued, however, that British intellectuals had a proxy engagement via Louis Althusser, who (along with Antonio Gramsci) was hugely influential in the development of British cultural studies. On Althusser's influence on early British cultural studies, see: Patrick Brantlinger, *Crusoe's Footprints: Cultural Studies in Britain and America* (London: Routledge, 1990), 85; Colin MacCabe, 'Class of '68: Elements of an Intellectual Autobiography 1967-81', in *Theoretical Essays: Film, Linguistics, Literature* (Manchester: Manchester University Press, 1985), 13.

17. The two most important sources on British engagements with Mao-era China are Tom Buchanan, *East Wind: China and the British Left, 1925-1976* (Oxford: Oxford University Press, 2012); Amy Jane Barnes, *Museum Representations of Maoist China: From Cultural Revolution to Commie Kitsch* (Farnham: Ashgate, 2014).

18. Jonathan D. Spence, *The Chan's Great Continent: China in Western Minds* (New York: W. W. Norton & Company, 1999), xi.

19. Lanza, *The End of Concern: Maoist China, Activism, and Asian Studies*, 7.

20. Stacey Pierson, *Collectors, Collections and Museums: The Field of Chinese Ceramics in Britain, 1560-1960* (Bern; Oxford: Peter Lang, 2007), 12.

21. Francesca Vanke, 'Degrees of Otherness: The Ottoman Empire and China at the Great Exhibition of 1851', ed. Jeffrey A. Auerbach and Peter H. Hoffenberg (London & New York: Routledge, 2016), 201.

22. Catherine Pagani, 'Chinese Material Culture and British Perceptions of China in the Mid-Nineteenth Century', in *Colonialism and the Object: Empire, Material Culture and the Museum*, ed. T. J Barringer and Tom Flynn (London: Routledge, 1998), 28.

23. Pierson, *Collectors, Collections and Museums*, 155; Patrick Wright, *Passport to Peking: A Very British Mission to Mao's China* (Oxford: Oxford University Press, 2010), 65.

24. Buchanan, *East Wind*, 107; David E. T. Luard, *Britain and China* (London: Chatto & Windus, 1962), 65.

25. Buchanan, *East Wind*, 142–43.

26. Buchanan, *East Wind*, 122.

27. Robert Jay Lifton, *Thought Reform and the Psychology of Totalism: A Study of 'Brainwashing' in China* (Chapel Hill, NC: University of North Carolina Press, 1989). Lifton's influential study, originally published in 1961, popularised the term 'brainwashing' in English.

28. The literature on the Cultural Revolution is constantly evolving. Some important sources include Roderick MacFarquhar and Michael Schoenhals, *Mao's Last Revolution* (Cambridge, MA; London: Belknap, 2006); Joseph Esherick, Paul Pickowicz, and Andrew G. Walder, eds., *The Chinese Cultural Revolution as History* (Stanford, CA: Stanford University Press, 2006); Weihua Bu, *Zalan Jiu Shijie: Wenhua Dageming de Dongluan Yu Haojie, 1966–1968 [Smashing the Old World: Turmoil and Calamity of the Cultural Revolution, 1966-1968]* (Hong Kong: Chinese University Press, 2008); Joel Andreas, *Rise of the Red Engineers: The Cultural Revolution and the Origins of China's New Class* (Stanford, CA: Stanford University Press, 2009); Andrew G. Walder, *Fractured Rebellion: The Beijing Red Guard Movement* (Cambridge, MA; London: Harvard University Press, 2012); Yang Su, *Collective Killings in Rural China during the Cultural Revolution* (Cambridge: Cambridge University Press, 2011); Yiching Wu, *The Cultural Revolution at the Margins: Chinese Socialism in Crisis* (Cambridge, MA: Harvard University Press, 2014); Guoqiang Dong and Andrew G. Walder, *A Decade of Upheaval: The Cultural Revolution in Rural China* (Princeton, NJ: Princeton University Press, 2021); Jisheng Yang, *The World Turned Upside Down: A History of the Chinese Cultural Revolution*, trans. Stacy Mosher and Jian Guo (New York: Farrar, Straus and Giroux, 2021). There has also been a considerable output in the cultural histories of the Cultural Revolution, which is discussed in more detail in the book's Conclusion.

29. Julia Lovell has emphasised that this was part of a highly choreographed and organized outreach effort designed to raise China's global standing. Lovell, *Maoism: A Global History*.

30. Galimberti, de Haro-García, and Scott, 'Introduction', 3.

31. Throughout this book, I use the seemingly vague word 'object' to refer to these cultural products. This is not to deny their artistic merits (to suggest, in other words, that these are objects *rather than* art), but instead to acknowledge both the diversity of the cultural products and the different functions and meanings they have had for their owners. These objects cannot be reduced to simple categories such as art or propaganda because these terms cannot contain the plurality of what China made and exported, which included things that might be easily categorized as art or propaganda, but also everyday items like enamel mugs, mass-produced textiles or children's toys. Similarly, throughout, I primarily refer to these objects as 'material culture', but I do not see a useful differentiation between visual and material culture. Rather, I follow Gillian Rose and Divya Praful Tolia-Kelly's argument in favour of a 'politics of visual objects', which attempts to avoid reducing 'visuality' to simple observation and 'materiality' to purely 'solid matter'. Gillian Rose and Divya Praful Tolia-Kelly, 'Visuality/Materiality: Introducing a Manifesto for Practice', in *Visuality/Materiality: Images, Objects and Practices*, ed. Gillian Rose and Divya Praful Tolia-Kelly (Farnham: Ashgate Publishing, 2012), 4.

32. Daniel Miller, 'Why some things matter' in Material Cultures: Why Some Things Matter, ed. Daniel Miller (London: UCL Press, 1998), 3.

33. Li Yingjun 李迎军, 'Cong Zhongshan Zhuang Kan Chuangtong Fushi Wenhua de Jicheng Yu Chuangxin 从中山装看传统服饰文化的继承与创新 [The Cultural Inheritance and Innovations of the Chinese Tunic Suit]', *Yishu Sheji Yanjiu* 艺术设计研究 1 (2010): 35.

Part I

Chapter 1

Visualising the Cultural Revolution in British Popular Culture

In 1969, an article in the British *Observer* newspaper discussed the ways in which China was perceived in Britain.[1] It argued that because of China's 'total self-isolation', Britain knew little about the country, but concluded that while knowing the truth about Mao's China was difficult, neither of the extreme pictures many in Britain had of Mao's China were correct:

> It is neither a Yellow Peril of 600 million fanatics setting out to conquer the world with the H-bomb in one hand and Mao's Thoughts in the other. Nor is it a paradise of true Marxist-Leninists who resemble the early Christians not only in their moral fervour and honourable poverty, but also in their reliance on peaceful persuasion.[2]

This quotation, while no doubt intentionally sensationalised, captures something of the tensions inherent in attitudes towards Mao's China in late 1960s Britain. As this chapter will explore, China occupied a number of contradictory positions at this time: it was increasingly prominent as a Cold War enemy, but it was also a point of inspiration for the widespread student movements across the Western world.[3] While the Cultural Revolution has been remembered largely as a disaster, both inside and outside China, at the time there were different ways of viewing it. It was poorly understood and consequently prone to be interpreted in extreme and reductionist ways, and thus was able to stand as proof both of the insanity of the Chinese model and its leader Chairman Mao Zedong, and alternatively, of China's claim to be at the vanguard of the global revolution.

These ideas of China were formed through numerous routes: government policies and statements; popular media including newspapers, films, television shows and novels; academic sources; and accounts written by visitors and residents.⁴ They were also formed through visual and material culture, both produced and exported by China, and sometimes its appropriated or created versions by British individuals and organisations. Indeed in the case of sympathetic perspectives, the British and Chinese sources often built upon each other: Chinese visual culture presented images of a rapidly improving country; these often somewhat fantastical constructions were then legitimised by the enthusiastic accounts of visitors, who often claimed expertise based on short and highly controlled tours of limited areas of China.

The Great Proletarian Cultural Revolution (文化大革命 *Wenhua Dageming*) began in 1966 and was Chairman Mao's attempt to reclaim both political power and the direction of the Chinese revolution by mobilising the youth and the working class.⁵ These Red Guards targeted the supposedly revisionist and certainly increasingly entrenched CCP officials, spurred on by Mao's call to 'bombard the headquarters', but also attacked feudal and bourgeois ideas, habits and individuals that were seen to be preventing China's socialist progress, known as the 'Four Olds'. CCP cadres and government officials as well as former elites and intellectuals were targeted, often with extreme and public violence, and before long the Red Guard groups also began to fight among themselves, with each side convinced they were the true adherents to Mao's word.⁶ This chaos severely impacted the functioning of the government and the economy in the late 1960s, as well as creating long-lasting emotional and societal traumas and tensions. And yet, for some young Red Guards, it was also a time of travel (including for some, to Beijing to see Mao in Tian'anmen square), freedom and optimism.⁷ By 1968, Mao was keen to bring the movement under control, and millions of urban youths were dispatched to the countryside as part of the 'Up to the Mountains and Down to the Countryside Movement' (上山下乡运动 *shangshan xiaxiang yundong*), and order was gradually restored under the guise of 'Revolutionary Committees', a new unit of leadership that combined military officials, vindicated CCP cadres and members of the mass organisations.⁸ The violent phase of the Cultural Revolution was largely over by the 9th CCP Party Congress, held in April 1969, in which the Defence Minister Lin Biao, who had played a central role in the establishment of Mao's cult of personality, was named formally as Mao's successor. He died in 1971 in a plane crash following an alleged coup attempt. Throughout the 1970s, mass campaigns continued periodically, as the radicals centred around Mao's wife, Jiang Qing, battled for political influence with the more moderate members of the political elite under Premier Zhou Enlai. While the Cultural Revolution was typically referred to in the past tense in the 1970s, it was redefined by the new leadership under Deng Xiaoping after Mao's 1976 death as encompassing the whole decade from 1966 until 1976, and that is how it has largely been remembered, both in China and abroad.⁹

This chapter explores the various ways that people and institutions in Britain used Cultural Revolution material and visual culture (or their re-appropriated versions of it), in order to make two arguments. First, that there were competing ideas about and images of China in the late 1960s and 1970s, and that Cultural Revolution material and visual culture were instrumental in constructing these images. Second, that the poorly understood nature of the Cultural Revolution enabled its material culture – posters, Chairman Mao badges, *Quotations from Chairman Mao Zedong* (better known as the Little Red Book) and other written material, and clothing such as the Mao suit (中山装, *zhongshanzhuang*) – to be appropriated and used in a surprisingly diverse number of settings, often in ways that had little to do with China. It investigates the ways in which the Cultural Revolution was experienced in the United Kingdom: how it was known, but also how it was felt and seen. As such, this chapter is not concerned with discerning the 'truth' of the Cultural Revolution or evaluating the accuracy of different perspectives; rather it seeks to unpick the diversity of British representations of the Cultural Revolution in order to reflect on what this reveals about British self-identity in the context of both the Cold War, and the widespread domestic social and cultural changes of 1960s and 1970s Britain.

VIEWING MAO'S CHINA IN 1960S AND 1970S BRITAIN

China as a 'Problem Nation'

Journalist and author Charles Hensman, writing in 1968, was unequivocal as to what the popular image of China was in Britain:

> The overall impression one is left with is that of a China which is a 'problem nation' on a massive, frightening scale. The sense of the dreadfulness of her conduct and ambitions is created and strengthened by the sheer accumulative effects of the news reports, editorial comments, radio and television broadcasts, articles, books, which report, analyse, discuss and warn about China. Most of us only half assimilate the details, but the impression remains with us. [. . .] China has indeed come to be a standard and a criterion of what is bad in the international order.[10]

Hensman suggests that the image of China constructed through the media is one of a 'problem nation', defined by the country's intimidating size and refusal to adhere to international norms. This construction needs to be understood in the context of the Cold War, and particularly, the nature of the Cold War in the 1960s, which saw gradual warming of relations between the Soviet Union and the US, and the collapse of the former alliance between China and the Soviet Union. While the Soviet Union continued to be the central danger in Europe, in the rest of the world, China loomed increasingly large, especially as former European colonies gained independence throughout the 1950s and 1960s. In recent years, scholars have emphasised the importance of Communist China as an inspiration for much of the colonial and newly post-colonial developing world, and the impact this had on American self-positioning in the global sphere.[11] Indeed, Chen Jian has argued that the emergence of Mao's China, a more explicitly 'revolutionary' country than the Soviet Union, helped shift American attention to East Asia, as well as making the Cold War a more explicitly ideological battle between 'good' capitalist democracies and 'evil' Communist regimes.[12]

For a Britain struggling to find its place in the world as its empire came to an end in most of Asia and Africa, and with a remaining colonial holding on China's doorstep in Hong Kong, China was a country to be watched. For most of the British political and media establishment, China was seen as a Cold War enemy, ruled by a totalitarian and inhumane Communist government. It presented a threat to post-Second World War Western-led global institutional and political norms and seemed to threaten Britain's continued influence over much of the newly independent Global South. By the time the Cultural Revolution began in 1966, the trope of the Communist Chinese as identical, brainwashed, soulless 'ants' was well established in popular discourse. This language was perhaps more normalised in mainstream American media publications, but it was also present in the United Kingdom. For example, while he would go on to disagree with its veracity, long-time China watcher Denis Bloodsworth, writing in the *Observer*, noted the common perception of China at the start of the Cultural Revolution, writing, 'To the Western observer, with his inflexible dogma of liberalism, China often appears as a monstrous empire of blue ants in which the crushed, terrified, half-starved millions crawl through their bitter days, wistfully dreaming of democracy.'[13] By the end of the Cultural Revolution in 1976, the same view still held. An article by conservative journalist Auberon Waugh in the British magazine the *Spectator* argued that the Communists had destroyed the humanity of the Chinese people, and he drew on the by-now familiar insect analogy:

> The more I read about China, the more it seems obvious that by a process of ideological indoctrination the socialists have succeeded in creating a race of sub-humans. [. . .] I compared the socialist Chinese with insects because they have destroyed their essential human characteristic of free will and subordinated all intellectual and ethical perception of their own to communal discipline.[14]

The Cultural Revolution, with the extreme promotion of the cult of Mao, the enormous Red Guard rallies in Tian'anmen square, and the stories of rampaging Red Guard violence together privileged the idea of the mindless masses in the Western social imagination. In Britain, the connotations of fanaticism were further influenced by the August 1967 pitched battle between Chinese Embassy officials in London and the local police.[15] Far more serious were the demonstrations, strikes and even bombings in the British colony of Hong Kong, organised by local Communists and leftists, and in August 1967, the burning of the British Mission in Beijing, and the violence experienced by British diplomatic staff and their family members.[16]

The China Model as an Alternative Socialist Modernity

Whilst, however, these may have been the dominant positions on China, they were by no means the only ones. Indeed, the same areas in which China was seen as a threat – its 'revolutionary' nature and its refusal to adhere to established political and socio-economic norms – were also the areas that were celebrated by China's supporters. The struggle to secure the ideological alignment of much of the developing world has been an increasingly acknowledged driver of the Cold War, at political, cultural, economic and military levels.[17] Julia Lovell notes the appeal of the Maoist revolution to newly independent countries who were 'suspicious of American intentions and unwilling to embrace the Europeanised blueprints of Soviet Russia.'[18] Moreover, the hope that the Communist Chinese revolution inspired around the world is well-attested to in memoires from the time. Tariq Ali, growing up in newly independent Pakistan and later a prominent anti-Vietnam War activist in the United Kingdom, recalls the hope that the establishment of the People's Republic of China in 1949 inspired, writing 'the victory of China's communist-led peasant armies was seen by the rural and urban poor throughout Asia as a triumph without parallel.'[19] China was able to simultaneously put itself forward as a new, cooperative force in the non-aligned world, as demonstrated by its actions at the Bandung Conference in 1955, and put itself at the head of the anti-imperialist revolutionary movement.[20]

One of the key aspects of China's revolutionary appeal was the alternative model of development it seemed to offer to the largely newly independent Global South. For all the obvious differences between the Soviet Union and the United States, they shared a similar vision of modernisation, in which technological progress dominated a 'carefully mapped and defined pathway from "tradition" to "modernity".'[21] China, from the period of the Great Leap Forwards onwards, offered a model of development that was people-powered, rather than capital-powered, and thus seemed to present a more viable option for many developing countries.[22] Richard Barbrook argues that Cold War events such as the Vietnam War need to be seen in this context of the battle of alternative paths to development: it was an attempt to discredit rural, peasant guerrillas, and with it, the Maoist prophecy of and support for global peasant revolution.²³ China's attempt to position itself as a natural leader of the so-called Third World put it at odds with Britain's attempts to maintain a post-colonial global role, but for some in Britain, China was the country deserving of support, not Britain. Delia Davin, a historian of China who lived in China between 1963–1965 and 1975–1976, described the importance of China's anti-imperial and anti-colonial positioning to sparking her interest in the country. She recalled:

> China meant 'Third World' above all for me and for [then husband] Bill [Jenner]. It is not altogether irrelevant that my elder sister went to Algeria when I was in my second year [in China] and my younger sister went to Zambia. [. . .] We belonged to a generation when radical people felt the Third World was where it was all at, where interesting things were happening, and where we wanted to be.²⁴

Similarly, sociologist Peter Worsley, who published a book about his 1972 trip to China, saw China as one of the few examples of successful post-colonial development. He commented:

> I was one of a generation reared on Edgar Snow's *Red Star Over China*, published in 1937, and still the best general background book for understanding China. [. . .] I have tried to keep abreast of what has happened within China since, and to relate Chinese development to development (to be strict, to non-development) in the rest of the Third World.²⁵

For Worsley, China's developmental model, which was so different from that prescribed by the American-dominated neoliberal global financial and aid institutions was attractive, as it offered a 'more directly-imitable model for underdeveloped societies'.²⁶ Many within development studies were at this time developing critiques of the dependency created by existing aid models, and for some, like Worsley, China offered a real alternative.

The alternative socio-economic relationship promised by Chinese socialism was also of interest to some on the British left. Much of the left lost faith in the Soviet Union after the invasions of Hungary in 1956 and Czechoslovakia in 1968, and the rise of the New Left within the British academic environment brought about a renewed interest in the Marxist tradition outside Marxist-Leninist or Communist Party orthodoxy.²⁷ This resulted in the exploration of alternative Marxist traditions starting from the late 1950s, as well as the search for political ideologies that avoided both the inertia and sustained hierarchies of parliamentary democracies and the de-humanising bureaucratisation of the Soviet Union.²⁸ Maoism, then, fit within this broader search for alternative Marxist theories, and was appealing because of its focus on cultural, ideological and social change, in contrast to the typical emphasis on economic change and political power associated with Soviet socialism.

The prominent economist Joan Robinson, in her 1967 book on the Cultural Revolution, for example, praised the Chinese system for its ability to avoid the alienation prevalent in both the Western and Soviet economic systems, writing: 'The aim of Chinese socialism is to make use of all the technical achievements of modern industry without the dreary boredom and dehumanisation of personal relationships that accompany it everywhere else.'[29] Within this context, the Cultural Revolution was interpreted by some, not as a violent power struggle, as the media represented it, but rather as a necessary continuation of the revolution into the ideological superstructure. Robinson wrote that the movement was necessarily to prevent the entrenchment of a new elite, arguing: 'The sad lesson of revisionism in the Soviet Union gives us warning that removing property is not enough; the revolution must be carried into the superstructure of the economic system.'[30]

During the late 1960s era of student protests, some students were similarly inspired by this understanding of the Cultural Revolution. David Fernbach, a student at the London School of Economics and radical member of the Socialist Society, recalled the impact the idea of the Cultural Revolution had on him:

> As important as the counter-culture, if not more so, for many radicalised students was the Chinese Cultural Revolution. Although it took us a long time to understand much about it except that it was a great upheaval, that in some ways it was against authority and the entrenching of a new system of privilege and power in post-revolutionary society, [. . .] it had a great effect on us morally.[31]

For some, the upheaval and fight against authority of the Cultural Revolution was seen in light of their own protests. Kim Howells, who was active in the student occupation of Hornsey College of Art in May 1968, saw his own actions in light of those ongoing in China, writing 'I was very keen on storming buildings, [I] really saw myself as a Red Guard when I went in and told the Principal [of Hornsey College of Art] he had to leave his office because the student body had decided we needed it.'[32]

As the title of Richard Neville's influential 1971 book *Playpower* suggests, the counter-culture in the UK was not always was focused on serious revolutionary action, but instead was 'irresistible, fun-possessed, play-powered'.[33] In this context, an interest in Mao and Mao's works did not necessarily communicate a deep engagement with Maoist ideology, but often just an appreciation for the Chairman's ability to coin a good slogan. When, for example, a socialist faction at Oxford tried to force All Souls College to admit undergraduates for the first time, sparking a clash with the College Warden John Sparrow, someone painted a slogan on a college wall reading 'Chairman Mao says, make sparrows into birds-nest soup.'[34] What this demonstrates was not the potential of revolutionary violence against the College authorities, but rather the way British students cleverly and humorously appropriated the leftist language of foreign leaders and philosophers to legitimise their own complaints against structures of authority.

More broadly, historian Adam Lent has argued that in Britain, Maoism was 'one of the most influential strands of Marxist thought for the student left during the 1960s', with Maoist slogans, ideas and objects inspiring many, even if this took a more peripheral role in Britain than in many other Western countries.[35]

By the early 1970s, interest in China expanded beyond just student protestors. Labour politician Roy Jenkins noted the current fascination with China in 1973 after returning from a visit. He commented that many people are 'delighted to seize the opportunity of treading the still-fresh but increasingly clearly marked pilgrims' path. So it was with me.'[36] Most visits to China were organised through the Society for Anglo-Chinese Understanding (SACU), and the SACU journal *China Now* from this period is replete with articles by professionals in education, healthcare, social work and similar fields, all professing the lessons that could be learnt from the Chinese model. The view of China coming from its supporters at the time can be summarised best perhaps in the words of SACU Chairman and well-known historian of Chinese science, Joseph Needham, who argued in a series of talks and articles that China was transforming into a classless society, where 'human values' were in command, not economic requirements. He concluded that while the Cultural Revolution had resulted in tremendous upheaval, 'I would say that in the end almost nothing but good has come out of it.'[37] In education, the more practically oriented curriculum was applauded, while in healthcare, efforts to expand rural and community-based healthcare were welcomed. For some observers, Britain could learn from the Chinese developments. Physician Robin Stott addressed this question directly, and noted, '[Economist John Kenneth] Galbraith and other Western pundits, while applauding the present Chinese system, say that it is not for us. This, I am sure, is erroneous.'[38] He made a number of specific recommendations for Britain, including introducing a system of 'barefoot social workers and doctors', in which housewives would be trained in basic social and medical work in order to provide community care. He concluded that 'None of these concepts is new, but China has shown that all of them, and more, can work.'

There were also some who took the inspiration from Mao's China beyond just the level of vague or rhetorical inspiration, and particularly by the early 1970s, China-oriented Marxist-Leninist political parties and organisations were growing in size and number.[39] While the earliest China-oriented Marxist-Leninist groups had emerged in Britain as a result of the Sino-Soviet split of the early 1960s, the number of adherents grew later on, as parties incorporated expelled members of the Soviet-oriented Communist Party of Great Britain, plus young members radicalised by international events.[40] Throughout the 1970s, there were over twenty different organisations that declared allegiance to Mao's China, even if for some groups, this was a short-term commitment.[41] However, their highly sectarian nature, as well as the authoritarian personalities often at the head of organisations, limited the numbers of recruits they could attract: writing in 1976, Peter Shipley estimated that there were approximately 1,500 members of China-oriented Marxist-Leninist groups, compared to 14,000 Trotskyists and 28,000 members of the Communist Party of Great Britain.[42]

The Affective Power of the Cultural Revolution

One way to understand the impact that the Cultural Revolution and Maoism had in Britain is through a concept of affect. According to William Callahan, this concept seeks to 'shift critical focus from facts to feelings, from stable individual identity to multiple flows of encounter, from texts to nonlinear, nonlinguistic, and nonrepresentational genres, from abstract rational knowledge to embodied forms of experience, and thus from ideology to affect.'[43] As Melissa Gregg and Gregory Seigworth write, 'Affect . . . is the name we give to those forces – visceral forces beneath, alongside, or generally *other than* conscious knowing, vital forces insisting beyond emotion – that can serve to drive us toward movement.'[44] It focuses on emotion, but goes beyond a simple dwelling on feelings to see the propulsion to act that comes from the state of emotion in both individual and social contexts: in Giles Deleuze and Félix Guatarri's understanding it relates to a discharge of emotion that alters a bodily capacity to act.[45] Moreover, going beyond individual emotion, affect 'emerges as a social experience as bodies connect in an "affective economy".'[46] For Sara Ahmed, emotions are neither individual nor social, but produce the boundaries that allow the individual and the social to be delineated.[47] A focus on affect then, forces us to recognise not only that feelings matter, but that they spur action, shape identities and allegiances; they are shaped by individual and cultural histories, and they themselves shape these histories. As Callahan notes in his discussion of affect and visuality, we often respond viscerally to what we see, not rationally to what we understand; visual images can work in non-narrative and nonlinear ways to construct social relations by provoking emotions that are not reducible to either the individual or the social: we are then embedded within 'affective communities of sense'.[48]

Michael Dutton has argued that the Cultural Revolution can be understood as an 'affective revolution': a movement that sought to touch people in their very souls and transform affect into a revolutionary weapon.[49] While the Cultural Revolution made no such claim on the souls of British people, and undoubtedly, the affective power of the Cultural Revolution was lessened in the United Kingdom, one way to understand British reactions to the movement is through the idea that people reacted to their understanding of the movement not purely, or even primarily, rationally or intellectually, but also emotionally. This was no doubt in part because so little information about the Cultural Revolution was available abroad and because of the extreme nature of the information that was available, both positive and negative: a dispassionate, considered response was difficult. But to say that people reacted to what they saw and what they felt does not delegitimise the reactions: they are not lesser because they were propelled by feelings. Instead, they are important because responses to the Cultural Revolution tell us about modes of social and individual change that different people saw as desirable. For critics, the Cultural Revolution was a tragedy for its denial of individuality; for its supporters, it gave faith in the possibility of a different type of society. The reactions we see are emotive and moral as much as they are intellectual, even if the distinction was not necessarily clearly delineated.

The emotional responses to Chinese Communism well precede the Cultural Revolution: they can be seen in the laments about who 'lost' China that wracked American political circles after the Communist victory in 1949. They can also be seen in the language used about Chinese Communism reducing its people to ants, as seen in Auberon Waugh's quote above, or to automatons. One of the early and influential articles on the Great Leap Forward was James Bell's 1959 article in the American magazine *Life*, which argued, 'All over China the family-centred, individualistic Chinese are being reduced to 653 million indistinguishable and interchangeable parts in a vast, inhuman machine. This machine is the commune, the most frightful form of regimentation in history'.[50] This type of language aims not to explain, but rather to scare, to create an atmosphere of fear and foreboding, which precludes approaching Chinese politics with anything other than disgust and the Chinese people with pity. By the time the Cultural Revolution started, therefore, Chinese Communism had already acquired a negative affective force, in which laments about the inhumanity of the Chinese regime or the Cultural Revolution found a ready audience, preprepared emotionally and intellectually to accept at face value more bad news about China. Much of the coverage was presented in a comparative framework, in order to demonstrate how ideological conditioning had produced a society fundamentally different from that of Britain. A 1966 article in the British tabloid *Daily Mail* by twenty-year-old Vivien Clore, the daughter of financier Charles Clore, and a recent returnee from China, for example, lamented the loss of romance and love in revolutionary China, with the blame placed squarely on the country's emphasis on gender equality. She fretted over the children, who to her seemed 'unreal because they never quarrelled or disobeyed', and concluded: 'It looked frighteningly like the ultimate in the control of the minds of a people. No feelings for love. No feelings for anything at all, except the Revolution and the "red, red, reddest sun" in their hearts, Chairman Mao.'[51] The appeal to the fate of the children and the agonising over the loss of love and sex aimed to cement in the readers' minds the feeling that the Chinese had destroyed the basics of humanity, and thus, could not be comprehended in a rational manner: fear and loathing instead take its place.

However, the Cultural Revolution could also have a positive affective pull, as David Fernbach's statement above about the moral effect of the movement makes clear. Sophia Knight, a twenty-one-year old who taught English in Shanghai from 1965 to 1967, developed an almost completely oppositional perspective to that offered by Clore. For Knight, the children were not brainwashed, but rather just understood the progress China had made under socialism. She wrote: 'Chinese kids who never knew what life was like before the Liberation are still influenced by the feelings it produced among their parents and families; the changes here have been so great that it needs very little to make them believe that there is no other way for China and Asia as a whole.'[52] Rather than seeing the loss of feeling like Clore, Knight felt uplifted by what she saw: 'The whole spirit of the place is so happy and self-confident that one can't help but be struck by it and wonder what it is that has succeeded in creating this new kind of people.'[53] She described the Cultural Revolution in terms of the enthusiasm and energy it produced throughout the country, as well its visuality, suggesting

> Shanghai's appearance has changed so much, with bright scarlet banners, slogans in huge red, black and gold characters, red placards everywhere. Every other lamp-post carried a red board with quotations. With the green of summer, the impression as you go down the road is one of immense energy and life.[54]

Her book demonstrated the affective force the visual environment Cultural Revolution China could have and attempted to attach different emotions to the movement: hope, inspiration and vitality take the place of fear and loathing.

In the United Kingdom too, encounters with Maoist material culture, including in combination with other forms of left-wing aesthetics, could have quite an impact. Comedian Alexei Sayle recalled his first encounter with Maoism, in the form of material culture, during an anti-Vietnam War demonstration in Liverpool in early 1967:

There was this extraordinary guy walking along by himself; he had long hair, a straggly beard and a floor-length overcoat. Using both hands, he carried in front of him a large poster of Chairman Mao Zedong attached to a tube of grey plastic piping. As we passed a Chinese restaurant on Lime Street, all the waiters and chefs piled out of the restaurant cheering him and making the 'waving a little red book' gesture.[55]

Sayle, brought up in a Communist household, soon joined this Maoist in a Marxist-Leninist reading group in Liverpool, and later joined the China-oriented Communist Party of Britain (Marxist-Leninist). For him, the affective pull of the counter-cultural appearance of the Maoist came from its divergence from the rigidity and puritanism of his Communist upbringing. In this sense, the impact of Maoism in Britain was as much about feeling and style as it was about ideology, as the next section further elaborates.

CHINESE MATERIAL CULTURE IN BRITISH POPULAR CULTURE AND MEDIA

Understanding Material Culture in Circulation

China and the Cultural Revolution were perceived as meaning, entailing and aiming for very different things to different individuals and groups in Britain. In the media, it was a 'problem nation', whereas for some in the counter-culture, it represented an alternative socialist modernity. So far this chapter has discussed the impact of China mainly in the realm of ideas and feelings. And yet, as William Callahan has argued, politics also have a 'sensible' component: what we think and feel cannot be separated from what we see.[56] The rest of the chapter aims to link this to material and visual culture, in order to argue that part of the way in which Mao-era China was known was through its visual culture. Key to understanding this, however, is the point that the China that was 'knowable' through visual culture was multiple: proponents of the diverse and often contradictory views on China explained above all drew on the same Chinese visual and material culture as 'evidence' of their own view. This chapter uses the Mao suit as a case study to demonstrate this.

As explained in the book's Introduction, the Mao suit (often at the time called a Mao tunic or simply Mao jacket) was a grey, green or blue cotton jacket with four patch pockets, five large buttons and a turned-down collar. It was developed in China in the early twentieth century as an item of clothing that could be both modern and Chinese and was associated with the early revolutionary leader Sun Yatsen, from which its Chinese name was derived (中山裝 *zhongshanzhuang*).[57] By the late 1950s, however, it came to be associated abroad with the Communist regime, and in particular, with Mao, hence its English name. Fashion historian Michael Langkjær summed up the contrasting associations of the Mao suit in the West as 'either you were ideologically "turned off" by its indissoluble ties with Communist totalitarian "worker-ant" egalitarianism, or you were ideologically "turned on" by its associations with the "people's revolution".'[58] And yet, as the previous section has argued, whether you were 'turned on' or 'turned off' by Maoism and its material culture went beyond ideology. The affective charge of Maoism and the Cultural Revolution was experiential as much as it was intellectual; Maoism functioned as a style, a set of visual cues that could be drawn on as shorthand for both China's dehumanised masses and for its revolutionary people power.

Moreover, focusing on the way that Maoist material culture was received and experienced in Britain reminds us that there is no neutral way to engage with an object: engagement is always mediated through layers of conscious and unconscious histories, associations and meanings. When considering uses and representations of the Mao suit in a British context, then, attention must be paid to the specific network of associations present, and it is clear that this network tells us far more about Britain than about China: these objects were Chinese, but the 'China' they represented in a British context was a product of British fantasies, imaginations and fears. In other words, when both supporters and critics of Communist China used the Mao suit as 'evidence' of their views on China, it reflected very little of the reality of China. This inaccuracy does not mean, however, that these views and uses should be simply discounted; rather it shows the way in which China became a platform for the fears, anxieties and dreams about British society and Britain's place in the Cold War world, and how China could be used in this way because of how distant and 'other' it seemed at the time. Objects like the Mao suit, then, became the material and visual embodiment of this 'other', which, when removed from their original Chinese context, left them open to interpretation. As discussed in the book's Introduction, this has always been the case with objects from and ideas about China: they tell us more about Britain than they do about China. But as objects circulate globally with ever greater speed and frequency in the modern world, objects end up in ever more complex networks of meanings, taking on identities and associations that their producers never could have imagined. These new environments in which they entered, meant they were often given associations and meanings that had very little to do with their original identities.

Blue Ants and Bond Villains: The Mao Suit in Television and Film

Communist China was not very frequently represented in television and film in the late 1960s, but when it was, it was almost always portrayed as the enemy. The first episode of the ITV series *The Champions*, for example, begins in Communist China, with the heroes stealing bacterial warfare from the Chinese, on behalf of the British, American and Soviet intelligence services, under the auspices of the United Nations. The heroes' plane crashes in the Himalayas as they attempt to escape, but they are saved and given magical powers by an undiscovered Tibetan civilisation, thus establishing the premise of the show.

The British satirical sketch show *Monty Python's Flying Circus* frequently referenced the Chinese Communists, with Chinese characters indicated through Mao suits and the Little Red Book, as well as racial stereotypes such as slanted eyes and heavy accents. Tomasz Dobrogoszcz argues that national or racial stereotypes in Monty Python were adopted consciously, in order to draw attention to Britain's own stereotypes.[59] Fear of Communism and of China in Monty Python represented, therefore, British perceptions of the growing Chinese threat.[60] For example, Monty Python caricatured the depiction of the Chinese Communists as the enemy in a skit entitled 'The International Chinese Communist Conspiracy', which depicted a 'wave' of tiny yellow Chinese people engulfing a British woman, playing on long-established fears of the size of the Chinese population.[61]

Other shows, while not depicting the Chinese as enemies, portrayed them as little more than Little Red Book-regurgitating drones. The ITV show *Mind Your Language*, which ran from 1977 to 1981, centred on an English-language evening class at a London college. It relied heavily on cultural stereotypes, and the Chinese character spoke almost exclusively in phrases from the Little Red Book.[62]

Similarly, the 1969 Anglo-American film *The Most Dangerous Man in the World* (known outside of Britain as *The Chairman*), directed by British director J. Lee Thompson and staring American actor Gregory Peck, relied on tropes of China as the most pressing global enemy.[63] The film is set in the late 1960s, and opens, in a way not dissimilar to *The Champions,* with a joint British, American and Soviet intelligence project discovering that the Chinese have developed an enzyme that enabled crops to grow under any climatic conditions: we see, for example, satellite footage of pineapples growing on the snowy Tibetan plateau. The Chinese want to use this enzyme to secure the loyalty of the developing world, and the Anglo-American-Soviet alliance are determined to get the enzyme for the same utilitarian purposes. A London-based American Noble Prize-winning scientist named John Hathaway (Gregory Peck) is chosen to go to China to try to steal the enzyme, as he is the former colleague of the Chinese scientist Song Li (Keye Luke) who developed it.

Throughout the film, Cultural Revolution China is portrayed as an entirely alien and 'other' environment, in which the masses have been dehumanised and turned into little more than slogan-shouting, propaganda-waving mobs. The difference of China (and it is a difference portrayed as being entirely negative) is communicated through an over-abundance of material culture (see figure 1.1). The opening credits are a montage of photographs of contemporary China, which emphasise the total saturation of Maoism and Maoist propaganda in Chinese life. It starts with two images of 'ancient' China: the Great Wall and then an imposing imperial-era statue. Agricultural fields comprise the background, empty save for a poor farmer on a donkey-pulled cart, piled high with hay. Initially, then, the image constructed is of a 'timeless China', an impression bolstered by Jerry Goldman's stereotypically 'Chinese'-sounding music. The next photograph shows a poor-looking Chinese village, but here we see the first sign of Communism in the form of a portrait of Chairman Mao. From here, however, the montage immediately jumps to an overlay of a group of people holding red flags. This is followed by a constant succession of photographs of group study, performances of revolutionary drama, and other aspects of collective life. Two techniques are used, therefore, in the opening sequence: there is a montage of images, but these images are also combined within single frames to form collages. What these two techniques together suggest is the total saturation of Maoism in

Figure 1.1 Gregory Peck as John Hathaway in 'The Chairman' (1969), directed by J. Lee Thompson. *Source*: Allstar Picture Library Ltd./ Alamy Stock Photo.

Chinese life: we see fields with slogans erected on billboards; factory workers engaged in group study; People's Liberation Army troops marching with portraits and banners; and even small children marching in unison, wearing badges and holding up the Little Red Book. The Chinese are never depicted as individuals; even if they are alone in the photograph used, it is immediately combined with a photograph of a group, suggesting that actions are never truly the individual's own, but rather are just the manifestation of the larger social group's collective action. The only real colour is from the omnipresent red flags and Little Red Books: China is portrayed as utterly dominated by the Chairman's thought, a point underlined at the end of the title sequence, in which a photograph of Mao himself appears, hovering above another photograph of a huge crowd in Tiananmen square, and accompanied by a rousing crescendo in the music. The title sequence by Paul Brown-Constable is over three minutes long and draws on dozens of colour and black and white photographs of China. The photographs used in Brown-Constable's montage appear very similar to the types of images that *Xinhua* exported to the West, or that appeared in Chinese export publications such as *China Pictorial* or *China Reconstructs*. As such, there is nothing inherently sinister about the images: they had been selected by the Chinese as representatives of the changes underway within China. But it is how they are used in this sequence, particularly in conjunction with the music, which gives an image of China as a sinister, dehumanised 'other', where individuality is suppressed and replaced by a mob mentality.

This is replicated throughout the film, in which Chinese people are rarely seen as individuals, but rather move in large groups: a friendly mob welcomes Hathaway at the airport, holding high Mao portraits and shouting slogans; an unfriendly mob attacks Song Li for his revisionist thinking, holding high Mao portraits and shouting slogans. The depiction of Chinese people immediately recalls the 'blue ant' trope so common in the West and leaves the viewer in no doubt about the reality of China: it is a totally foreign world, peopled not by individuals, but by crowds, subsumed within an ideological framework alien to that of the 'free' West.

The only Chinese characters who get any real character development are those who do not wear the Mao suit: Song Li, the Chinese scientist who developed the enzyme and his daughter, Song Chu, both of whom wear traditional Chinese clothing. These two are humane, individualistic and in touch with a China that the Communists are portrayed as destroying. There is, however, one scene when the scientist's daughter changes in a Red Guard outfit (a military-style jacket, a Mao badge and a Red Guard armband) in an effort to fit into the crowd, and when dressed as such, she criticises her father for his unwillingness to subsume his individual will to the requirements of the revolution. Soon after, Song Li commits suicide, and we see Song Chu back in her traditional silk jacket, lamenting her father's fate and rescinding the responsibility she had so recently ascribed to him. Clothing in the film, then, becomes a marker for ideological positioning, and in it, the Mao suit and Red Guard clothing becomes shorthand for mindless devotion to a totalitarian regime. Hathaway eventually escapes, taking with him Song Li's Little Red Book, and once back in London, Hathaway discovers that Song Li had traced in lead pencil over the letters for the enzyme's molecular formula in the Little Red Book, thus communicating to Hathaway the secret of his discovery, via the medium of the chairman's words. The Cultural Revolution is experienced in the film through a profusion of material culture, with crowds characterised by Maoist objects, but it is this same material culture that provides the means for Song Li to sneak his formula out of the country, and consequently to bring about the plot resolution.

In *The Most Dangerous Man in the World*, socialist material culture, particularly clothing, becomes a shorthand for the madness and inhumanity of the regime, emphasising the repression or even obliteration of individuality beneath the collective will. It draws, therefore, on established tropes about Chinese Communism, but also further entrenches them; while its performance at the box office was mediocre, it still would have played a role in forming or cementing this negative impression of China in people's minds.

There was another more popular series of films, which similarly used the Mao suit as shorthand for evil: the James Bond films. The Bond films were based on books by British author Ian Fleming and starred a British hero, although most analysis of the films has positioned them within the context of the Cold War, in which Bond is fighting for or legitimising American values.[64] Over time, there was a transition in the films from Russians-as-villains to the Chinese Communists-as-villains, a move, according to film critic Drew Moniot, which reflected the shift in international politics and public opinion.[65] However, it is worth noting that while James Bond as the 'hero' represented Western (or even American) interests, the villains were not always so clearly nationalised. The main enemy for much of the 1960s and 1970s was 'SPECTRE' (the Special Executive for Counter-Intelligence, Terrorism, Revenge and Extortion), a shadowy corporation. Many of the villains appeared to be from the Soviet Union or Eastern Europe, but they were not necessarily representing the Communist governments in those territories; indeed, on a number of occasions Bond works with Soviet representatives to fight against SPECTRE, and SPECTRE would attack both the Soviet Union and Communist China. The world of James Bond is clearly classified in Manichean terms of 'good' versus 'evil', but these values were not necessarily mapped precisely onto 'West' and 'East' or even 'capitalist' and 'Communist'. It is significant then, that the main leader of SPECTRE, Ernst Stavro Blofeld typically wears a Mao suit (see figure 1.2). In *Diamonds of*

Figure 1.2 Charles Grey as Ernst Stavro Blofeld in 'Diamonds Are Forever' (1971), directed by Guy Hamilton. *Source*: APL Archive/Alamy Stock Photo.

Forever, for example, it transpires that Blofeld has used plastic surgery to create a series of doppelgangers and Bond must fight a series of identical Blofeld lookalikes. This proliferation of Mao-suited villains recalls and reinforces the Cold War conception of identical Chinese 'ants'. Blofeld clearly is not Chinese, but within the transnational, or even denationalised space of SPECTRE, a corporation run without recourse to human values and dedicated only to power, Blofeld's Mao suit can be seen to draw on already existing ideas about the Chinese – represented through their characteristic clothing – as representing the antithesis of Western values.

In popular culture, the negative connotations of the Mao suit have outlasted Mao himself, and indeed, even the Cold War. In the 1997 Bond film *Tomorrow Never Dies*, media mogul and villain Elliot Carver (Jonathan Pryce) wears a sharply tailored black Mao suit. Pryce acknowledged the continued power of these associations when he called Carver's costume the 'NAR look: no acting required, because the image is so good, it tells you everything.'[66] This use of the Mao suit drew on its association with power-hungry 'evil', but the Mao suit also continues to be associated with robotic conformity. For example, Ridley Scott's 2012 science fiction film *Prometheus* featured a Mao-suited android named David.[67]

Mao's China was repeatedly constructed in the British mainstream media as embodying dehumanising totalitarian evil. This was constructed visually, including through reference to the Mao suit as embodying both the perceived conformity of Chinese society and China's rejection of the norms of international political and social discourse.

Carnaby Street and the Kings Road: The Mao Suit as Fashion

For some on the left and in the counter-culture, other interpretations of the Mao suit and Chinese Communist material culture were possible. The 1960s saw an explosion of new fashion styles, and a new focus, for many young people, in self-expression through fashion.[68] The Mao suit emerged as one of a number of new fashion options in the late 1960s and early 1970s. It was successful because of its specific range of connotations. First, it was associated with the 'East', and thus had meaning within the contemporary interest in Oriental exoticism publicised perhaps most famously through the Beatles. Second, the Mao suit had an implicit militancy (it was based initially on early twentieth-century Japanese military uniforms, but was also associated with Maoist guerrilla warfare), which spoke to the combativeness of many young people. Thirdly, it had proletarian associations which coincided with the revival of Marxism and young people's professed allegiance to the proletariat in the late 1960s.[69] As a result, the Mao suit became a fashion option, and British designers began making their own versions.

Mates by Irvine Sellers, a fashionable store on London's Carnaby Street sold what they called 'Red Guard' suits, in dark blue and green, for men and women.[70] Similarly, an article by Ian Dallas in the radical underground newspaper *IT* (also known as *International Times*), reported that Michael Rainey's boutique Hung On You sold a 'quilted jacket buttoned high in the style of Mao' and called 'The Great Leap Forward', and that this jacket was the store's most popular item.[71] Moreover, in Hung On You, a shop best known for flowery shirts and kipper ties in bold colours, the Chinese influence ran further than just the quilted jackets. According to counter-culture figure Barry Miles, Rainey became inspired by the Cultural Revolution, and installed a huge photograph of Chairman Mao's famous 1966 swim in the Yangtze River in his shop on London's King's Road.[72]

According to Dallas, wearing a Mao jacket was not just about fashion, it was, he wrote, 'an outward sign of an invisible change in the thought structures of young people in this country', as the Cultural Revolution had inspired them to reconsider the basic tenets of their own society.[73] Dallas acknowledged that the situations in Britain and China were fundamentally different, although perhaps not in the way one might expect. He wrote, 'Of course, their situation is not ours. Embedded in a stale run-down capitalist puppet state we can only identify with the exultant youth of China by vicarious gesture, reading Mao's Handbook, wearing the Great Leap Forward [Mao suit].' Owning, wearing or displaying the Chinese objects were, then, a way of constructing a shared experience with the admired Chinese youth. As objects widely associated with the Red Guards, they became 'objects-in-common', a transnational link that symbolised the shared dream of an alternative socialist modernity. As part of this shared experience then, the Mao suit became a symbol of communitarian human relations, and not, as in some interpretations, mindless totalitarianism.

While Dallas suggested a real desire to learn from the experiences of Chinese youth, many in the youth movement were far less serious, and indeed, as suggested above, the British movement was often characterised by a sense of 'play'.[74] Despite the deadly seriousness of the reality of the China's Cultural Revolution, its material culture and rhetorical boldness fit in well with the British movement's creative appropriation of international militancy. While some, therefore, wore more 'standard' Mao suits, others kept the style—or aspects of the style, primarily the buttoned-up, turned-down collar or the patch pockets with the pointed flap design—but changed other aspects (see figure 1.3). Langkjær comments that in France, such was the interest in Maoism and Mao suits that 'anything remotely Chinese-looking would in the loosest possible way be called "Mao"'. Indeed, many of the so-called Mao jackets from the 1960s would be more correctly called 'Nehru' jackets, as they had a short up-turned mandarin collar, a style long pre-existing but popularised by Indian Prime Minister

Figure 1.3 Michael Rainey in a Chinese-inspired jacket and hat, outside his shop Hung on You, 1966. *Source*: Harold Chapman/TopFoto.

Jawaharlal Nehru.[75] The Beatles brought these suits to popular attention by wearing a Nehru-collared jacket with Mao suit-style patch pockets in their 1965 performance at Shea stadium and in the 1965 film *Help*. These are not Mao suits that would be recognised as such in China, but they traded off the contemporary interest in China and Chinese Communism in Britain at the time.

This stylistic ambiguity no doubt reflected an orientalising view of the exotic, but undifferentiated East: it did not really matter that these Chinese suits were not really like what people wore in China to their wearers, because the reality of China was largely unimportant. Rather Mao suits and other Maoist material culture communicated an adherence to contemporary fashion, a general leftism, and an often idealistic view of the possibility of change.

For *Guardian* journalist and academic, John Gittings, the appeal of Maoist attire was similarly about communicating a difference. He bought a number of Mao caps on a SACU-organised trip to China in 1971 and wore one in London for many months upon his return.[76] But the Mao cap was only one part of his 'look', as he frequently paired it with a Chilean poncho.[77] Gittings concluded: 'I think it was more a 1970s alternative culture fashion statement than anything else. Perhaps also I enjoyed the disapproval of more sober China watchers at SOAS [the School of Oriental and African Studies] and Chatham House [the Royal Institute of International Affairs, in London].'[78]

Maoist clothing – jackets and caps – then, were a way of constructing and communicating a left-wing identity, and perhaps a certain sympathy for China, but their iconic importance outweighed their ideological alignment. Maoism then functioned more as style, as affect, than as true ideological inspiration. This was even more so the case with other objects from Mao's China, such as the Little Red Book. Individuals could write to the Chinese Embassy in London or visit it in person and request Little Red Books and other materials.[79] Andrew Marr, later a prominent BBC journalist and author, wrote to the Chinese Embassy in 1970 that he admired the Cultural Revolution and wanted to start one in Britain. He did not mention that he was only at prep school, and the Embassy duly sent a box of Little Red Books and journals, which he passed around at school.[80] Similarly, academic Richard Barbrook recalled a friend at his boarding school writing to the Embassy that his father was a Royal Navy captain and a 'running dog of imperialism' and receiving a box of Little Red Books in return. According to Maureen Scott, a social realist artist and member of the Marxist-Leninist Organisation of Britain, which was briefly aligned with Mao's China, people would acquire Little Red Books from the Chinese Embassy and then wander around Hyde Park selling them.[81] Stalls were also set up near Speaker's Corner and even outside tube stations in London.[82] An article in the *Guardian* in May 1967 covered a story from China's official news agency *Xinhua* that reported that a bookshop in Cambridge specialising in Chinese publications (likely New Era Books) had sold more than 3,000 copies of the Little Red Book and quoted a Cambridge student who said that in his college, 'almost everyone, teachers and students alike, had a copy'.[83]

An interest in Chinese material culture, therefore, did not necessarily align with a political commitment to or even deep knowledge about China. Rather, the diversity of associations attached to China – totalitarian regime, utopian fantasy, developing country and ancient civilisation – meant that Maoist material culture could fit into a variety of environments simultaneously. They could be objects linking British youth with their counterparts in China, they could represent Chinese developments (positively or negatively), they could function as symbolic criticisms of the British situation or they could just be objects of fashion and fun in the British or Western context. Their meaning was largely situationally determined, and they could be used to communicate a wide variety of meanings depending on the user's or viewer's perception of both Mao's China and contemporary Britain.

CONCLUSION

Britain in the late 1960s and 1970s was in a period of flux. It was reconceptualising its global role as its empire wound down and it faced competition for influence, resources and power from new players like China. Domestically, social change followed from a new generation who reached maturity and began to ask difficult questions about the structural inequalities that had not been mitigated by the post-War boom, and who were willing to look outside of capitalist liberal democracies for political and personal inspiration. For both those fearful and supportive of these changes, China was a country with a growing presence throughout the 1960s. As this chapter has demonstrated, while the critics and supporters saw very different things in China, they used the same types of Maoist material culture as evidence of their claims about China's potential to be a threat or a model. Maoist material culture was, then, part of the way in which China was known at this time, but the 'China' that was knowable was multiple, partial and subject to British prejudices and biases. This is, of course, unavoidable: there is no unmediated or neutral engagement with a foreign culture. But the perceived unknowability or 'closedness' of China at this time meant that material culture had a distinct role: British knowledge of knowledge was mediated through Chinese material culture, and at the same time, reception of the material culture was mediated through British attitudes towards China, Communism, and global change. At a time when most people in Britain knew little about China, the positive or negative associations derived from chance or peripheral encounters with Maoist material culture had a significance beyond that which might be expected. The next chapter will demonstrate this in more depth by considering the reception of the British art world of a group of Chinese peasant painters in the late years of the Cultural Revolution.

NOTES

1. anon, 'China: The Greatest Enigma of Our World', *The Observer*, 28 September 1969.
2. 'China: The Greatest Enigma'.
3. By the early 1970s, China increasingly became a power to be courted by the West in the battle between the two superpowers, witnessed most prominently in US President Richard Nixon's much-heralded 1972 visit to China.
4. While this chapter focuses on British impressions and perceptions of China, there was wide circulation of English-language texts in Britain by American and less frequently by European authors. American perceptions, which were often more extreme in both the positive and negative sense, undoubtedly influenced British perceptions. There are, therefore, significant cross-cultural implications to much of this chapter's argument.
5. As discussed in the Introduction, there is a substantial academic literature on the Cultural Revolution, which remains a complex and difficult to understand set of events. As such, only a cursory overview can be provided here. For a basic introduction, see Richard Curtis Kraus, *The Cultural Revolution: A Very Short Introduction* (Oxford; New York: Oxford University Press, 2012).
6. The works of political sociologist Andrew Walder are essential reading on the early years of the Cultural Revolution. On the Red Guard movement, see Andrew G. Walder, *Fractured Rebellion: The Beijing Red Guard Movement* (Cambridge, MA; London: Harvard University Press, 2012); on the collapse of the party state, see Andrew G Walder, *Agents of Disorder: Inside China's Cultural Revolution* (Cambridge, MA: Harvard University Press, 2019).
7. See, for example, Yuan Gao, *Born Red: A Chronicle of the Cultural Revolution* (Stanford, CA: Stanford University Press, 1987).
8. Recent research has emphasised the impact the Cultural Revolution had on rural China, and in particular, the violence inherent in and following from the formation of Revolutionary Committees in the countryside. Yang Su, *Collective Killings in Rural China during the Cultural Revolution* (Cambridge: Cambridge University Press, 2011); Guoqiang Dong and Andrew G. Walder, *A Decade of Upheaval: The Cultural Revolution in Rural China* (Princeton, NJ: Princeton University Press, 2021).
9. Jonathan Unger, 'The Cultural Revolution at the Grass Roots', *The China Journal* 57 (2007): 114–15, https://doi.org/10.2307/20066243.
10. Charles Richard Hensman, *China: Yellow Peril? Red Hope?* (London: SCM Press, 1968), 10–12.

11. Fabio Lanza, 'Making Sense of "China" during the Cold War: Global Maoism and Asian Studies', in *De-Centering Cold War History: Local and Global Change*, ed. Jadwiga E. Pieper Mooney and Fabio Lanza (London: Routledge, 2013), 147–66; Michael Szonyi and Hong Liu, 'New Approaches to the Study of the Cold War in Asia', in *The Cold War in Asia: The Battle for Hearts and Minds*, ed. Michael Szonyi, Hong Liu, and Yangwen Zheng (Leiden: Koninklijke Brill NV, 2010), 1–10.

12. Jian Chen, *Mao's China and the Cold War* (Chapel Hill: The University of North Carolina Press, 2001), 3–4.

13. Dennis Bloodworth, 'How Mao Rides the Dragon', *The Observer*, 11 September 1966, 6.

14. Auberon Waugh, 'Another Voice', *The Spectator*, 21 May 1976, 6.

15. Roderick MacFarquhar and Michael Schoenhals, *Mao's Last Revolution* (Cambridge, MA; London: Belknap, 2006), 224.

16. Anne-Marie Brady, *Making the Foreign Serve China: Managing Foreigners in the People's Republic* (Lanham, MD; Oxford: Rowman & Littlefield, 2003), 162–63; MacFarquhar and Schoenhals, *Mao's Last Revolution*, 224–27.

17. See, for example, Odd Arne Westad, *The Global Cold War: Third World Interventions and the Making of Our Times*, New Edition (Cambridge; New York: Cambridge University Press, 2007); Robert J. Mcmahon, ed., *The Cold War in the Third World* (Oxford; New York: Oxford University Press, 2013).

18. Julia Lovell, *Maoism: A Global History* (London: The Bodley Head, 2018), 460.

19. Tariq Ali, *Street Fighting Years: An Autobiography of the Sixties*, 2nd Edition (London: Verso, 2005), 61–62.

20. Jian Chen, 'China and the Bandung Conference: Changing Perceptions and Representations', in *Bandung Revisited: The Legacy of the 1955 Asian-African Conference for International Order*, ed. Amitav Acharya and See Seng Tan (Singapore: National University of Singapore Press, 2008), 135.

21. Rana Mitter, 'China and the Cold War', in *The Oxford Handbook of the Cold War*, ed. Richard H. Immerman and Petra Goedde (Oxford: Oxford University Press, 2013), 135.

22. The problems with this model, and in particular the disastrous results of the Great Leap Forward, are now clear, but at the time, many of China's supporters were convinced that no famine had taken place. See, for example, Hewlett Johnson, *The Upsurge of China* (Peking: New World Press, 1961), 372.

23. Richard Barbrook, *Imaginary Futures: From Thinking Machines to the Global Village* (London; Ann Arbor: Pluto Press, 2007), 226.

24. Davin, interview with author, 02/03/2014, Ilkley, Yorkshire.

25. Peter Worsley, *Inside China* (London: Allen Lane, 1975), 22.

26. Worsley, *Inside China*, 20.

27. Madeleine Davis, 'The Marxism of the British New Left', *Journal of Political Ideologies* 11, no. 3 (October 2006): 336–37.

28. Ronald Fraser, *1968: A Student Generation in Revolt* (London: Chatto & Windus, 1988), 109.

29. Joan Robinson, *The Cultural Revolution in China* (Harmondsworth: Penguin, 1969), 39.

30. Robinson, *The Cultural Revolution*, 46.
31. Fernbach quoted in Fraser, *1968*, 111.
32. Howells quoted in Fraser, 248. Howells was also one of the 'Maoists' involved in the clashes with police outside the US embassy as part of an anti-Vietnam War demonstration in March 1968.
33. Richard Neville, *Playpower* (London: Paladin, 1971), 209.
34. David Caute, *The Year of the Barricades: A Journey through 1968* (New York: Harper & Row, 1988), 312.
35. Adam Lent, *British Social Movements since 1945: Sex, Colour, Peace and Power* (Basingstoke: Palgrave, 2001), 63.
36. Roy Jenkins, 'How China Sees the World', *The Observer*, 9 December 1973.
37. Joseph Needham, 'A Question of Values Part 1: Be the Man for Others', *China Now*, February 1973, 5. It is worth noting that in private, Needham was far more circumspect about the Cultural Revolution. Tom Buchanan, *East Wind: China and the British Left, 1925-1976* (Oxford: Oxford University Press, 2012), 188; Simon Winchester, *Bomb, Book and Compass: Joseph Needham and the Great Secrets of China* (London: Penguin, 2009), 243–44.
38. Robin Stott, 'New Medical Care', *China Now*, November 1973, 14.
39. On British Maoist parties, see Robert Jackson Alexander, *Maoism in the Developed World* (Westport: Praeger, 2001); Peter Barberis, John McHugh, and Mike Tyldesley, *Encyclopedia of British and Irish Political Organizations: Parties, Groups and Movements of the 20th Century* (London: Pinter, 2000); David Widgery, *The Left in Britain 1956–68* (Harmondsworth: Penguin Books, 1976).
40. Sam Richards, 'The Rise & Fall of Maoism: The English Experience', 2013, 52, http://www.marxists.org/history/erol/uk.firstwave/uk-maoism.pdf.
41. For example, The Marxist-Leninist Organisation of Britain's foundational text in October 1967 explicitly declared support for Mao Zedong Thought and the Cultural Revolution. In January 1968, however, one of the group's key theorist's published a special report which accused Mao of being a revisionist, and upheld Liu Shaoqi as the true revolutionary. Mike Baker, 'The Political Report', *Red Front: For Working-Class Power for a Socialist Britain!*, October 1967; William Bland, 'Report of the Central Committee of the MLOB on the Situation in the People's Republic of China', *Red Front: Special Edition*, January 1968.
42. Peter Shipley, *Revolutionaries in Modern Britain* (London: Bodley Head, 1976), 116.
43. Williams A. Callahan, *Sensible Politics: Visualizing International Relations* (Oxford: Oxford University Press, 2020), 39–40.
44. Melissa Gregg and Gregory J. Seigworth, 'An Inventory of Shimmers', in *The Affect Theory Reader*, ed. Melissa Gregg and Gregory J. Seigworth (Durham & London: Duke University Press, 2010), 1.
45. Gilles Deleuze and Felix Guattari as discussed in Michael Dutton, 'Cultural Revolution as Method', *The China Quarterly* 227 (2016): 718.
46. Callahan, *Sensible Politics: Visualizing International Relations*, 40.
47. Sara Ahmed, *The Cultural Politics of Emotion* (Edinburgh: University of Edinburgh Press, 2004), 10.
48. Callahan, *Sensible Politics: Visualizing International Relations*, 41.

49. Dutton, 'Cultural Revolution as Method'.
50. Bell quoted in Felix Greene, *The Wall Has Two Sides: A Portrait of China Today* (London: Cape, 1963), 138.
51. Vivien Clore, 'When the State Decrees Thou Shalt Not Fall in Love', *Daily Mail*, 29 November 1966.
52. Sophia Knight, *Window on Shanghai: Letters from China, 1965-67* (London: André Deutsch, 1967), 70.
53. Knight, *Window on Shanghai*, 88.
54. Knight, *Window on Shanghai*, 236.
55. Alexei Sayle, *Stalin Ate My Homework* (London: Sceptre, 2010), 227.
56. Callahan, *Sensible Politics: Visualizing International Relations*.
57. Yingjun Li, 'Cong Zhongshanzhuang Kan Chuangtong Fushi Wenhua de Jicheng Yu Chuangxin [The Cultural Inheritance and Innovations of the Chinese Tunic Suit]', *Yishu Sheji Yanjiu* 1 (2010): 35.
58. Michael A. Langkjær, 'From Cool to Un-Cool to Re-Cool: Nehru and Mao Tunics in the Sixties and Post-Sixties West', in *Global Textile Encounters,* ed. Marie-Louise Nosch, Zhao Feng, and Lotika Varadarajan (Oxford & Philadelphia: Oxbow Books, 2014) 235.
59. Tomasz Dobrogoszcz, 'The British Look Abroad: Monty Python and the Foreign', in *Nobody Expects the Spanish Inquisition: Cultural Contexts in Monty Python*, ed. Tomasz Dobrogoszcz (Lanham, MD: Rowman & Littlefield, 2014), 92.
60. Dobrogoszcz, 'The British Look Abroad: Monty Python and the Foreign', 87.
61. Larsen highlights the fascination China seemed to hold for Monty Python, and notes that the Chinese Communists appeared in 8 separate episodes. Darl Larsen, *Monty Python's Flying Circus: An Utterly Complete, Thoroughly Unillustrated, Absolutely Unauthorized Guide to Possibly All the References: From Arthur 'Two-Sheds' Jackson to Zambesi* (Lanham, MD; Plymouth: Rowman & Littlefield, 2008), 409.
62. The show was hugely popular, but it was cancelled after three series because of this negative stereotyping. Sarita Malik, *Representing Black Britain: Black and Asian Images on Television* (London: SAGE Publications, 2002), 97.
63. Director J. Lee Thompson was forced to change the British name as it was decided audience members would think *The Chairman* was a boring film about business. *The Most Dangerous Man in the World* was the name of the 1969 Jay Richard Kennedy novel, on which the film was based. Steve Chibnall, *J. Lee Thompson* (Manchester: Manchester University Press, 2000), p. 317.
64. Shin Byungiu and Gon Namkung, 'Films and Cultural Hegemony: American Hegemony "Outside" and "Inside" the "007" Movie Series', *Asian Perspective* 32, no. 2 (2008): 115–43.
65. Drew Moniot, 'James Bond and America in the Sixties: An Investigation of the Formula Film in Popular Culture', *Journal of the University Film Association* 28, no. 3 (Summer 1976): 27.
66. Langkjær, 'From Cool to Un-Cool to Re-Cool: Nehru and Mao Tunics in the Sixties and Post-Sixties West', 233.
67. Langkjær, 'From Cool to Un-Cool to Re-Cool: Nehru and Mao Tunics in the Sixties and Post-Sixties West', 234.

68. Arthur Marwick, *The Sixties: Cultural Revolution in Britain, France, Italy, and the United States, c.1958-c.1974* (Oxford: Oxford University Press, 1998), 411.

69. British-based American artist John Dugger, for example, visited China through SACU in 1972. He wore a German workers jacket, which, he recalled, got him promptly elected group leader. Whilst in China, he paired the jacket with a Mao cap and badge. John Dugger, personal communication, 21/05/2014.

70. Amy Jane Barnes, *Museum Representations of Maoist China: From Cultural Revolution to Commie Kitsch* (Farnham: Ashgate, 2014), 94.

71. Ian Dallas, 'red guard pointers' *International Times*, no. 11, 21 April 1967, 5, http://www.internationaltimes.it/archive/page.php?i=IT_1967-04-21_B-IT-Volume-1_Iss-11_005&view=text [accessed 04/08/2020].

72. Barry Miles, *London Calling: A Countercultural History of London since 1945* (London: Atlantic Books, 2010), 330. See also Cally Blackman, 'Clothing the Cosmic Counterculture: Fashion and Psychedelia', in *Summer of Love: Psychedelic Art, Social Crisis and Counterculture in the 1960s*, ed. Christoph Grunenberg and Jonathan Harris (Liverpool: Liverpool University Press, 2005), 214; Peter Doggett, *There's a Riot Going on: Revolutionaries, Rock Stars and the Rise and Fall of '60s Counter-Culture* (Edinburgh: Canongate Books, 2008), 168.

73. Dallas, 'red guard pointers'.

74. Neville, *Playpower*.

75. Langkjær, 'From Cool to Un-Cool to Re-Cool: Nehru and Mao Tunics in the Sixties and Post-Sixties West', 229.

76. John Gittings, 'Reporting China since the 1960s', in *China's Transformations : The Stories beyond the Headlines*, ed. Lionel M. Jensen and Timothy B. Weston (Lanham, MD; Plymouth: Rowman & Littlefield, 2007), 288.

77. Gittings had lived in Chile prior to moving to Hong Kong in 1968. By the early 1970s, Chile was of interest to many on the left. The election of the socialist Salvador Allende prompted interest, however Chile really became a cause after General Pinochet's 1973 coup d'etat.

78. Gittings, interview with author, 13/10/2014, Oxfordshire.

79. Richard Neville's 1971 account of the British counter-culture states: 'Mao's Thoughts: free copy from the Chinese Embassy in Portland Place . . . Just ring on the door. Also write to Radio China, Peking, China, and ask for a few details on the cultural revolution [*sic*]. It will come by the ton, all in English, all free.' Neville, *Playpower,* appendix.

80. 'Politicians Interview Pundits: George Osborne and Andrew Marr', *The Guardian*, 26 September 2009, sec. Media, http://www.theguardian.com/media/2009/sep/26/george-osborne-interviews-andrew-marr [accessed 03/08/2020].

81. Maureen Scott, interview with author, 10/06/2014, London.

82. According to a 1967 report by the MLOB, the police had recently arrested sellers of the Little Red Book in Hyde Park and outside Earls Court Underground Station in London. Marxist-Leninist Organisation of Britain, 'More Police Violence Against Chinese', *Red Front: For Working-Class Power for a Socialist Britain!*, October 1967.

83. Victor Zorza, 'Thoughts of Mao Take Root in Britain', *The Guardian*, 30 May 1967, 8.

Chapter 2

Idealising the Cultural Revolution
Huxian Peasant Painting and the British Art World[1]

In early 1977, a review in the art magazine *Artscribe* praised an exhibition that had recently finished at London's Warehouse Gallery. Critic Adrian Rifkin enthused that the works on display had 'presented in a living way the possibility, indeed necessity, of building an alternative to the decaying, anti-people bourgeois and imperialist art which predominates like a deadweight in Britain and the entire capitalist world.'[2] He continued his description of these exciting new works, commenting: 'All this is achieved in opposition to the arid and lifeless "expertise" which is the condition of cultural achievements in capitalist or revisionist countries, and which is the mask of the arid and lifeless content of their art'. Finally, Rifkin made an argument about what the British art world could learn from this exhibition, stating: 'We can learn from this revolutionary art that it is the determined and class conscious political struggle against the old world and old ideas that is the basis for a completely new culture, and not the feeble "innovations" of avant-gardism, made within the confines of old and decadent ideologies.'

The exhibition in question featured paintings by Chinese peasants from Hu county, or Huxian (户县), a rural area near Xi'an that became famous in the 1970s for its art, produced by supposedly amateur artists who combined agricultural labour with spare-time painting. Huxian paintings tended to focus on the everyday activities of the commune: farming and animal husbandry, political study, recreation and family life (see figures 2.1–2.3). In the words of a 1974 Chinese Foreign Languages Press catalogue, the peasants depicted 'the new socialist countryside.'[3] The style was broadly realist, but, influenced both by Soviet socialist realism and Chinese folk art, the paintings presented a romanticised, idealised view of the Chinese countryside under socialism. Their bright and cheerful colouring made them immediately eye-catching, and they portrayed a world of abundance, cleanliness and unity. For Rifkin,

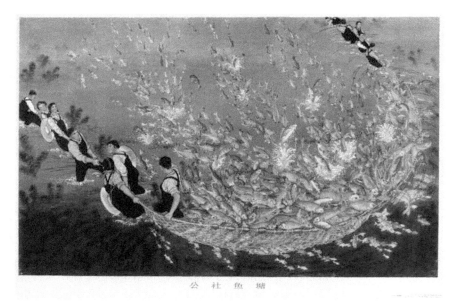

Figure 2.1 Huxian Peasant Painting. Dong Zhengyi 董正谊, 'Commune Fish Pond' (公社鱼塘 *Gongshe yutang*), 1974. *Source*: Reproduced with the permission of the University of Westminster Archive.

they represented refreshingly new cultural principles to those characterising cultural life in Britain.

A year later, in 1978, the 'Art for Whom?' exhibition at the Serpentine Gallery produced a manifesto that touched on many of the same issues raised in Rifkin's review of the Huxian exhibition. The catalogue contained a ten-point collective statement by curator Richard Cork and the participating artists, proclaiming their increasing dissatisfaction with the failure of so much contemporary art to communicate with anyone outside a small circle of initiates.[4] They wrote that they refused to accept that art was an inherently marginal, mercantile and misunderstood activity, declaring instead that art must be transformed into a progressive force for change. They commented that artists ought to engage with working people, who felt alienated from the art world, as this was the only way that art could contribute to creating an egalitarian society.

The works that Cork chose for 'Art for Whom?' bore no visible similarities to the Huxian peasant paintings, but despite this lack of aesthetic parallels, the works reflected a shared interest in the class nature of art. By virtue of being made by peasants, rather than professional elites, the Huxian works implicitly represented an alternative model of artistic production, which foregrounded the importance of the social and political context in which art was made. They

Idealising the Cultural Revolution 33

Figure 2.2 Huxian Peasant Painting. Liu Zhigui 刘知贵 **'Red Flag Brigade/After the Bumper Harvest'** (红旗大队/丰收之后 *hongqi dadui/feng shou zhi hou*), n.d. *Source*: Reproduced with the permission of the University of Westminster Archive.

spoke, then, directly to Cork's question, 'art for whom', but also, importantly, the question 'art *by* whom'? Whereas British art betrayed, in Cork's words, 'a glaring lack of communication with society at large', for Rifkin, these peasant paintings 'reflect all that is best and most positive in the life of the people, which includes the transformation of just about every aspect of their lives.'[5] 'Art for whom?' featured art that was made with a social purpose: art made in collaboration with local communities, and that responded to their concerns. The Huxian paintings took this social aim one step further, as they – in theory at least – dispensed with the guiding hand of the professional artist altogether.

These criticisms about the elitism of the art world were not new: indeed, art colleges were frequent sites for student activism in the late 1960s, most famously Hornsey Art College. Art student, and later Labour MP, Kim Howells, mentioned in chapter 1 as part of the occupation of Hornsey Art College, was unrestrained in his criticism of the art world, writing:

> It is totally irrelevant to the lives and struggles of the great mass of population and it is the inheritance of the years of acceptance of the myth of the 'artist' as being the lone spirit, free from the mundane pursuits that govern most people's lives, and born radical, the free liberal thinker, sitting up high creating his works in an attempt to communicate the ideas of a superior mind to the philistine public.[6]

Figure 2.3 Huxian Peasant Painting. Zhao Kunhan 赵坤汉 'Production Brigade Library' (大队图书室 *Dadui tushishu*), 1975. *Source*: Reproduced with the permission of the University of Westminster Archive.

Artistically, however, the 1960s had been characterised by excitement and innovation; this was followed by a more directly politicised atmosphere in the 1970s. This had diverse implications: stylistically, some artists reacted against conceptualism by returning to figuration and focusing on content, while ideologically, other artists focused on developing the criticism of elitism.[7] Marxism remained an important inspiration for these developments, but provoked quite different responses from different artists: for the Marxist–Leninist group and the League of Socialist Artists, social realism was the only acceptable art form, whereas for other artists like John Dugger and David Medalla, inspiration from China and from Marxist theory was less about formal artistic concerns, and more about the search for an alternative structure of social and artistic relations.[8] There could be tensions, then, between the militant Marxist–Leninist left wing, which supported realism and the production of paintings that were easy for the working classes to understand, and the countercultural left, seeking individual expression and tempted by the exoticism of China.

The responses to the Huxian exhibition therefore need to be seen in light of already existing debates about the state of the British art world. This chapter makes a claim not for a causal link – that the discovery of the peasant painters provoked a re-evaluation of the British art model – but rather that this evaluation and critique was ongoing, and the Huxian peasant painters were used as an external example to demonstrate that alternative models of artistic production were possible. The Huxian peasant paintings were appreciated both for what they supposedly represented about Communist China and for their comparative value in suggesting an artistic alternative to the British art world, which was being criticised by left-wing and socially conscious artists and critics. The Huxian exhibition built upon already existing interest in Chinese Communism, and particularly the Cultural Revolution, and created an image of a utopian rural society that had overcome the divisions between mental and manual labour, men and women, and city and countryside that continued to plague capitalist countries.

THE HUXIAN PEASANT PAINTERS

Peasant painting started in Huxian in 1958, when the County Party Committee set up art classes run by professionals. This was done in the context of the Great Leap Forward, which, along with the better-known communes and rural industrialisation projects, also included attempts to spread arts and culture to rural areas, and initially Huxian was just one of many areas with similar initiatives. Their art aimed to capture the radical transformations of the countryside that were being carried out largely through manual labour, with peasants painting during breaks on the side of agricultural fields and construction projects. Huxian peasants were again mobilised in 1962 during the Socialist Education Movement, during which they painted pictures for an exhibition that showed the differences between old and new Chinese society.[9]

They appeared again during the Cultural Revolution, where they played a dual role: they both contributed to specific campaigns such as the initial campaign against the so-called capitalist roaders and class enemies, and the mid-1970s 'Criticise Lin Biao Criticise Confucius (批林批孔 *piLin piKong*)' campaign, as well as immortalising in paint the successes of the new socialist countryside. In 1966, Huxian works were exhibited in Beijing as part of the 'Beijing Asia-Africa Authors' Conference' and were the subject of a full-page article in the *People's Daily* (人民日报 *Renmin ribao*), called 'Peasants' Revolutionary Paintings'.[10] Their real period of fame began in the early 1970s, when culture became an increasingly important battle ground and one associated with the extension of Mao's wife and key cultural reformer Jiang Qing's influence into the visual arts.[11] When, in 1973, the Huxian painters had a major exhibition at the National Art Gallery in Beijing, it was held under the auspices of the Cultural Group of the State Council, a group in which Jiang Qing had much influence.[12] It was this exhibition that brought the peasant painters to national prominence: the exhibition was seen by over two million visitors and was the subject of a major publicity campaign, with coverage in newspapers and magazines, poster reproductions and postage stamp versions of popular paintings, and a national tour of eight cities.[13]

Chinese periodicals published numerous accounts of and interviews with the Huxian painters. These articles frequently focused on the painters' class status, as well as their amateur status. Indeed, their real-life experience was seen as the primary reason for their success as, according to *China Reconstructs*, 'With their rich experience of life, Huxian's amateur artists produce works that are vivid, natural and unaffected.'[14] Poor and lower-middle-class peasants, according to *China Pictorial*, admired the paintings and mentioned 'they give expression to what we want to say'.[15] Along with the necessity of remaining amateurs so as to stay close to the subjects depicted, the painters' sustained peasant status was what allowed them to be held up as models. The 1974 Foreign Languages Press catalogue claimed:

> The broad masses of poor and lower-middle peasants grasping the artist's brush and wielding power in the cultural as well as in the political field is a deep-going revolution in the superstructure. It shows that the working people are not only the creators of man's social material wealth but are also the creators of man's intellectual wealth, that the working people are indeed the masters of history.[16]

In other words, the very fact that peasants were paintings was seen as revolutionary in itself, and a sign of the transformation of Chinese culture. Peasant painters were seen as the new 'socialist men and women' that Marx had envisioned, proficient at both mental and manual work. The general narrative was of poor peasants who had only been granted the opportunity to paint due to Chairman Mao and the Communist Party. Their paintings were seen as both illustrating and embodying China's changing society and more specifically the ideological revolution in the superstructure, a key issue in the Cultural Revolution, and as mentioned in chapter 1, a topic of interest to some on the British left.

Subsequent research has shown that the promotion of the Huxian works was led by radicals associated with Jiang Qing, looking for positive examples of Maoist collective cultural production, in an effort to stem moves by more moderate leaders like Zhou Enlai to restore conventional educational and cultural policies.[17] The largely unacknowledged context behind the promotion of amateurs, then, were the attacks on intellectuals and professionalism that took place throughout the Mao era, but took most ferocious form during the Cultural Revolution. Moreover, Ellen Laing has demonstrated that despite their reputation as amateurs, Huxian painters were given extensive professional support and training, and some, in effect, became full-time artists.[18] This, however, was all largely unknown to observers in the West when they saw the paintings, and they tended to take at face value these paintings as genuine products of an enlightened cultural system.

HUXIAN ABROAD: BRITAIN AND BEYOND

The Global Huxian Exhibitions

The Huxian paintings' popularity was not unique to Britain; rather, Huxian paintings represented a remarkable success story for China in the international art world as a whole throughout the 1970s. Jiang Qing recognised the potential appeal of Huxian paintings to foreigners, and soon after the exhibition in Beijing, groups of foreigners were permitted to visit Huxian.[19] According to Ralph Croizier, between 1972 and 1983, over 13,000 foreigners visited Huxian, and by the mid-1970s it was a common stop on tourist groups' itineraries.[20] A large art gallery was built to exhibit and sell works, along with poster reproductions and other items. Foreigners who visited China often spoke and wrote positively of their visits to Huxian. Society for Anglo-Chinese Understanding (SACU) General Secretary Janet Hadley visited Huxian on a 1976 tour after two group members, Guy Brett and Innes Herdan, requested it. According to Hadley, their day in Huxian was the highlight of the whole trip, and she wrote in her diary that many group members purchased paintings, posters and cards.[21] They met artists Li Fenglan and Liu Zhide, and had conversations which, according to art critic Guy Brett, allowed them to understand 'the link between the paintings and the everyday life activity of production'.[22] Similarly, art historian Craig Clunas, more interested in imperial art than that of Mao's China, recorded his enthusiastic impressions after an August 1975 visit, writing in his diary, 'This stuff is just the antidote to most Chinese art. When you see what the peasants are actually painting, your faith revives.'[23]

Soon after their rise to prominence in China, Huxian peasants and their works were sent abroad. A delegation, which included the prominent female artist Li Fenglan, was sent to Vietnam in 1973 and Albania in 1974.[24] The paintings first reached the West in 1975, where they appeared at the ninth Paris Biennale by special invitation.[25] The French–Chinese painter Zao Wou-Ki (also known as Zhao Wuji) had noticed them on a trip to China and was so impressed he decided to help them get shown abroad.[26] Some eighty paintings were shown in Paris, where they were very positively received. Upon seeing the paintings, one French reporter is said to have commented: 'After seeing other entries [to the Biennale] one had the feeling that painting was dead and the only really living painting is in People's China.'[27]

After their success in Paris, the Beijing government sent two very similar exhibitions on tour, and in 1976 one arrived in Britain, where it was shown in seven locations over ten months. The exhibition was organised at the last minute by the Arts Council of Great Britain in conjunction with the Chinese Embassy, which had contacted the Great Britain-China Centre offering the exhibition.[28] The Great Britain-China Centre handed over organisation of the exhibition to the Arts Council in May 1976. The paintings were originally meant to stay in Britain from August until the end of December. For reasons primarily to do with the organisation of future legs of the exhibition's tour, the paintings stayed in Britain until the following May, when they transferred to Australia and then Canada.[29]

During the initial leg of the tour, the paintings were displayed as part of the Billingham International Folklore Festival in Stockton-On-Tees, and in Bromsgrove as part of the Fourteenth Arts Festival, sponsored by paintbrush company L.G. Harris & Co. In both locations, organisers noted the popularity of the exhibition.[30] They were also shown in Cardiff, before arriving in London in November 1976, which is where they started to receive national attention. In London, the exhibition was shown at the Warehouse Gallery, although the Institute of Contemporary Arts was originally the intended location.[31] The paintings' popularity can be demonstrated by the fact that at least ten locations requested the exhibition after Beijing granted the extension, and in the end the exhibition was sent to Birmingham, Nottingham, and Edinburgh.[32]

Guy Brett and the Huxian Painters

Art critic Guy Brett was a key figure in publicising Huxian: he spoke and published widely on them in the mid-1970s, both as the art critic for the *Times* until 1975 and in articles for the SACU journal, *China Now*. He wrote the text for the British exhibition catalogue, which was later used to accompany the exhibition in Australia and Canada.[33] Brett first visited China on a SACU trip in 1974 and visited Huxian for the first time in 1976 while the exhibition was in Britain.[34] Brett had risen to prominence as the art critic for the *Times*, and he was particularly keen to promote left-wing international art, as well as new developments in conceptual art, such as kineticism.[35] Brett's description of the peasant painters in these written works reproduced much of the narrative from the Chinese publications already discussed, but he also introduced the comparative approach between the British and Chinese art worlds that other critics would adopt.

Brett's interest in the peasant painting largely centred around firstly, the peasant agency depicted within them and secondly, the alternative art system they represented. While some critics tended to read the paintings as accurate representations of the Chinese countryside, Brett recognised that they recorded both the contemporary self-imagining of the Chinese peasants and their aspirations for the future.[36] The exaggeration inherent in the paintings was what, for Brett, gave the works social power: Brett saw the art as both capturing the improved living conditions of the Chinese peasants and also as contributing to these improvements by encouraging other peasants in their struggle with nature. He mused: 'It is as if, instead of being "figures in a timeless landscape" [. . .] they have re-appraised everything and are themselves deciding what their landscape shall be.'[37]

Brett also argued that Huxian peasant painters played a crucial role in the revolution of the ideological superstructure, arguing that in China, the peasant painters were seen as being at the forefront of the development of a truly popular art, in both a socio-political and aesthetic sense.[38] He framed the peasant painters as representatives of the new socialist men and women:

> By showing that they [the peasants] wanted to paint, to write, to dance, as well as produce the nation's food, they challenged the separation between mental and manual work and they forced an opposite reaction in artistic circles. Professional artists began to spend some of their time working in communes and factories. Their relation with the amateurs became more and more one of mutual learning.[39]

Brett clearly approved of the systemic changes to the Chinese art world, and he made numerous comparisons between the Chinese and Western art systems, many of which can be read in the context of existing debates within the Western art world. He argued that the lack of an art market encouraged the production of art that had relevance to the lives of the people, noting that in China, 'Unlike in our own system, emphasis is placed on the political and social importance of cultural work in general, not on the making and breaking of individual careers.'[40] He similarly commended the collective nature by which art was produced, with individual artists submitting their works to those around them for criticism. Brett saw this process as undermining the concept of the artist as an isolated genius, a concept being criticised by many Western artists and critics at this time. For Brett, this reshaped art world created a closeness between the artist and the people that could be seen in the paintings themselves and that was missing elsewhere.[41]

Brett's framing of the Huxian phenomenon undoubtedly impacted their reception in the United Kingdom, not least through his establishment of a comparative approach between the British and Chinese art systems, which would be mirrored in much of the coverage.

Huxian and the British Art World

There was extensive coverage of the exhibition: the London showing was discussed on three BBC radio programmes,[42] as well as coverage in the

Guardian, the *Observer*, the *Times*, the *Evening Standard*, the *Sunday Telegraph*, *Time Out* (which reproduced the *Sunday Telegraph* review), the *Spectator*, *Studio International*, *Artscribe*, *Art Monthly*, *Art Guardian*, plus coverage in a number of local papers during the other legs of the tour.[43] In his review, Rifkin noted the paintings' popularity in Britain, and he argued that this showed the 'irrefutable strength of this revolutionary peasant art'.[44] The widespread support to which Rifkin referred can be demonstrated firstly, by the large numbers of newspapers and art journals that published reviews of the exhibition, despite its relatively small size and unusual subject matter, and secondly, by the largely positive nature of these reviews.[45] Writing in the *Observer*, for example, William Feaver enthused: 'Only the bleakest Scrooge could avoid being exhilarated by the crop of Chinese Peasant Paintings at the Warehouse Gallery. [. . .] Such energy, such disarming zest. Such rejoicings over improvements carried out [. . .] with sacks stuffed as fat as pumpkins, grain bins overflowing, every harvest is a dream fulfilled.'[46]

Similarly, Caroline Tisdall, writing in the *Guardian*, felt that a pride in human labour was visible in the paintings, and argued: 'It's the sense of directness between effort and result that is enough to make even the most hardbitten Western cynic feel a pang of longing for the collective.'[47] The *Times* also found the art praiseworthy, with Paul Overy commenting that there was much that was admirable in the paintings: the vitality of colour and composition, the depiction of a technology strictly under man's control, and a sense of enthusiasm towards the collective endeavour.[48] John McEwen's short and disparaging review for the *Spectator* made clear his view that the peasant paintings were 'propaganda' and not 'art', but even he acknowledged how widespread attention to the peasant paintings had been, noting that they had been 'so extensively advertised and seriously discussed'.[49]

A closer look at a number of reviews will demonstrate that the paintings were appreciated less for their artistic merit, and more for how they could be juxtaposed with the failings of the capitalist British art world, based on the critics' often very partial understanding of the radically transformed Chinese art world. Michael Shepherd's review in the *Sunday Telegraph* demonstrates these key themes. Huxian paintings, he commented, were not the normal propaganda offerings that one saw in London's Chinese bookstores, but were something different: delightful, lively and confident; all attributes that cast British art into a negative light by comparison. He enthused,

> these paintings are in praise of work, cooperation and radical thought about society; no message could be more relevant to us today, responding as we do to the cry 'I'll never buy British again' by brawling, squabbling or sulking. Nor is the work depicted in the paintings drawing on capital investment, but from the riches of the earth in abundance.[50]

He concluded, 'we can respond and learn from this delightful reflowering of a bright-eyed national art'. Shepherd's interest lay in viewing the ideology behind the art in the context of the British art world, which he suggested was riven with dissension, out of touch with society and dominated by capitalist interests. The colourful simplicity of the paintings and the spirit of cooperation they both depicted and represented constructed an image of China that Western sympathisers could appropriate as holding the antidote to the alienation of Western capitalist society. There is no doubt that an element of condescension can be detected in Shepherd's and others celebration of this 'naïve' art. It seems unlikely that such art would have been similarly celebrated if it had been produced by British artists or working people; again what this demonstrates is less an appreciation of the art itself and more an interest in the system in which the art was produced.

Richard Cork similarly adopted a comparative approach. Cork's review in the *Evening Standard* emphasised what the exhibition told Britain about Communism.[51] He remarked on his

> astonishment at finding out how attractive these paintings are, how much they tell us about a form of communism, which positively encourages workers to think of themselves as spare-time artists able to express the social meaning of their labour in visual terms.

Most importantly, what the exhibition revealed for Cork was:

> The realisation that a reborn nation like China can give art an integral position in its everyday functioning, can replace the hostile division between artists and public in the West with a unified alternative, capable of making the act of drawing or painting into a gesture of support for a system based on Mao's belief that 'there is in fact no such thing as art for art's sake, art that stands above classes, art that is detached from or independent of politics'.

He concluded by suggesting that the Chinese might have found a system that integrated artistic production and social change, writing,

> These pictures are the first fruits of an agricultural society attempting to give the visual imagination a position in its daily life infinitely more central than anything which our fragmented culture has to offer. [. . .] China may yet manage to develop a role for art which offers an adequate way out of our own terminal dilemma.

Most of the positive Huxian reviews marry these dual interests: both what the British art world could take from the exhibition, and the importance of the social, political and ideological contexts in which the paintings were produced. The tension between these positions was never noted: what really lay behind the emergence of the peasant painters was the radical social transformation of Chinese society that resulted from the Communist victory in 1949. It was the overthrow of the very types of elites that were now celebrating them in the British context that created the space for peasant painting to emerge. What was necessary for British art to truly follow in the Huxian peasants' path, then, was the total overthrow of British society, including the overthrow of the very elites within the art world who celebrated Huxian, in order to pass the mantle of artistic creation on to the working class.

What is striking about these reviews is the overlap between the views expressed in them and the ongoing domestic critiques of the British art world. The Huxian exhibition did not initiate commentators' criticisms of Western art, but it did offer a point of comparison, evidence of an alternative system against which the British art world could be critiqued. Many of the critics who so approved of the Huxian exhibition were left wing, but they were not 'Maoist' or Marxist–Leninist. Their admiration for the system in which this art was produced appears to have been quite genuine, although they never spelled out precisely how Britain could fulfil their calls to 'learn from' China. Instead, the reviews can be seen as part of a more general idealisation of China. Indeed, for Richard Cork, part of the appeal of the Huxian exhibition was in getting to see work from China, 'which, until very recently, refused to reveal itself to a Western audience.'[52] Cork's language reflects the idea that China at this time was not just 'closed', but also 'hidden', 'exotic' and maybe even in need of 'opening' by outsiders. China, of course, was not the only place that was idealised by the left: Vietnamese guerrillas, African liberation fighters, and South American peasants were similarly romanticised. But the Chinese peasants had an extra appeal because they demonstrated that an alternative to the capitalist system was possible, not just theoretically, but in a way that was already in practice. Huxian works represented, then, a refreshing alternative to much of the other 'Third World' folk art that was on offer, which was created by exploited groups.[53] The Huxian works appealed because they not only demonstrated an alternative to the capitalist system, but originated in a country where this alternative was in power.

UNDERSTANDING BRITISH CULTURAL INTEREST IN CHINA

British Cultural Interest in Imperial China

Imperial Chinese culture and aesthetics had experienced surges of popularity in Europe since the sixteenth century, often shaped by visitors' tales and imported material culture. This continued to be the case in the 1960s and 1970s, which saw continued interest in Chinese or 'Eastern' religious and philosophical thought: Buddhism, Daoism and Confucianism. The American Abstract Expressionist artists were famously interested in Buddhism and a number of avant-garde composers took inspiration from Confucianism and Chinese classical texts.[54] American composer John Cage drew on the *I Ching* (易经 *Yijing*, Book of Changes), while British composer Cornelius Cardew made music based on Ezra Pound's translations of Confucius in his work *The Great Learning*.[55] These engagements with historical China were often tokenistic, but also reflected a desire to find systems of thought and notions of selfhood and interpersonal relations outside of those available in the capitalist West. They spoke to many of the same desires that led others to turn to contemporary Maoist China.

Articles and books published following visits to China frequently made comparisons between old (feudal, unequal, impoverished, rapacious) China and new (clean, developing, equal) China in order to show the benefits of the Communist government.[56] But these sat in an at-times uneasy relationship with long-established admiration for imperial China's cultural achievements. In 1973–1974, three years before the Huxian exhibitions, London's Royal Academy had hosted the blockbuster 'Genius of China' exhibition. This exhibition featured archaeological discoveries that had been made since 1949 and constructed an image of Chinese civilisation as an unbroken line from the Palaeolithic period to the PRC, when the excavations took place.[57] It suggested that, despite what many people thought about the destruction of cultural heritage carried out during the Cultural Revolution, the Communists had not completely forsaken their country's past. Instead, the RA exhibition presented the PRC as the modern heir and protector of this traditional culture. Moreover, given the long struggle over China's United Nations seat, it was also an attempt to demonstrate that Taiwan was not the last stronghold of traditional Chinese culture and civilisation.[58] Many commentators noted this and gave credit to Beijing for its interest in and preservation of the past, with the *Observer* even titling its review of the exhibition 'Mao's Marvels'.[59]

These types of interest in China were in no way mutually exclusive. In conjunction with the Huxian exhibition, the well-known historian of Chinese science and the SACU Chairman Joseph Needham gave a talk entitled 'Ancient Chinese Science in its Modern Social Context', which as the title suggests, tried to tie the two together. For others, an interest in traditional Chinese philosophy could transform over time into a more contemporary engagement. Composer Cornelius Cardew's interest in China became politicised in the 1970s, and he became a prominent member of a number of Marxist–Leninist political organisations, including the Communist Party of England (Marxist–Leninist), which was, for a time, explicitly Maoist. His ideological transformation also produced a shift in his musical output from experimental music to 'people's liberation music'.[60]

British Cultural Interest in Contemporary China

Contemporary China was also on display beyond just the Huxian exhibition. SACU played a leading role in this, organising talks in branches throughout the country, often by people who had just returned from China, as well as film screenings, language lessons, and for small numbers, trips to China (see figure 2.4).[61] SACU would also set up small exhibitions—usually comprising photographs from *Xinhua*—that would be accompanied by posters, pamphlets and other documents for sale.[62] The Huxian exhibition was also not the first display of art from Communist China: there had been a 1974 exhibition of 130 modern Chinese woodblock prints held at Durham's Gulbenkian Museum of Oriental Art, organised by Phillip Rawson, that later travelled to a number of cities around Britain, and which had also been favourably reviewed.[63]

Contemporary China was also represented on the stage, with the Institute of Contemporary Arts performing David Hare's *Fanshen*, a theatrical adaptation of William Hinton's book of the same name, in 1975 and Roger Howard's play *The History of the Tenth Struggle* (also known as *The Tragedy of Mao in the Lin Biao Period*) in the autumn of 1976.[64] A number of film festivals coincided with the Huxian exhibition in London. The National Film Theatre screened seven contemporary Chinese films in September, while the Other Cinema on Tottenham Street had an even more extensive season of Chinese films or films about China in November and December, centred around the monumental *How Yukong Moved the Mountains* by European filmmakers Joris Ivens and Marceline Loridan.[65] This twelve-hour series of films was shown on rotation from late November until the end of January and was seen by some 15,000 people.[66] Ivens, who once said documentary could only achieve its full potential under socialism, was well known for making films in support of anti-colonial and anti-imperialist struggles (such as in Indonesia and Vietnam), and he and Loridan had spent eighteen months in China while working on the film.[67]

Interest in contemporary China was also reflected in the availability of objects, literature and information in left-wing bookshops and Chinese stores. The chain Collet's included a general left-wing shop and a Chinese Gallery (which subsequently became Collet's Penguin Bookshop), a Chinese shop near the British Museum, and branches in other cities.[68] Another important bookshop for Maoist objects in London was Banner Books on Camden High Street.[69] It was run by an Indian immigrant G.V. Bijur and was staffed by young women dressed as Young Pioneers.[70] Arthur Probstain's, an African and Oriental bookshop, run by the SACU-supporting Sheringham

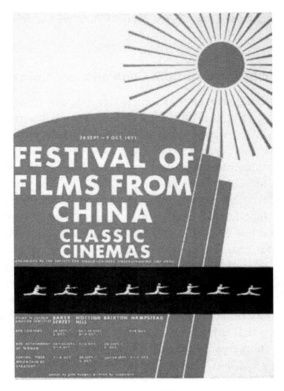

Figure 2.4 Festival Poster for the 'Festival of Films from China' at London's Classic Cinemas, 1971. Poster designed by John Dugger. *Source*: Reproduced with the permission of John Dugger

family, carried Chinese journals, new and second-hand books on China, and of course, the Little Red Book.[71] Chinese-owned bookshops were another option, and Gwanghua in London's Chinatown, established in 1971, was popular as it carried Chinese periodicals, posters, books, as well as art supplies.[72]

Some Maoist or Marxist–Leninist political parties had their own bookshops, or they would set up stalls at local markets and during political events.[73] Art historian Craig Clunas attended an exhibition of books and posters hosted by a group of local Maoists while he was at school in Aberdeen in the early 1970s; he recalled being 'overwhelmed by a desire to possess it all'.[74] Comedian Alexei Sayle was part of a Maoist organisation in Liverpool in the late 1960s; the group's main activity was running a Marxist bookstall every Saturday at the local market.[75]

The idea of China as 'closed', therefore, can be counteracted with the fact that information and images of China were available to those who were

Taking Artistic Inspiration from Contemporary China

For all the positive coverage that the Huxian peasant painters received in the British art world, and all the routes of engagement with contemporary China, there is little evidence that it had much of an impact on the production of art or the organisation of the art world. However, an attempt to rethink art production based on inspiration from Mao's China, as well as traditional Chinese philosophy and Marxist ideology was undertaken by two London-based artists, Filipino David Medalla and American John Dugger. Medalla and Dugger first bonded over a shared interest in Buddhism, as well as Chinese and Indian traditional art. Over the summer of 1968, they performed a series of participatory art works in London's Hampstead Heath, entitled 'Buddha Ballet'. They acted out chapters from Buddhist texts, with the audience invited to bring props and join in the performance.[76] In the late 1960s, the two spent eighteen months travelling in South Asia and Southeast Asia, where they studied Buddhism, but were also increasingly radicalised by what they saw, and from 1969 onwards, they developed an interest in Marxist and Maoist theory.[77] John Dugger visited China on a 1972 SACU tour, becoming, he claims, the first American artist to visit China since 1949 (see figures 2.5 and 2.6 of some of his art from his time there).[78]

The period in which they maintained an interest in Buddhism but were increasingly turning towards Marxism and then Maoism, was captured in the catalogue for John Dugger's 1971 exhibition 'Microcosm', held at the Sigi Krauss gallery in London. The catalogue was small and had a red cover with a star on it: the similarity to the Little Red Book was immediately striking. The frontispiece had two quotes, one from the Buddha, one from Mao Zedong's 'On Contradiction'.[79] Throughout the catalogue, Dugger used the language of 'contradiction' and 'dialectics' in order to explain his artworks, and the catalogue concluded with the manifesto of the 'Artists' Liberation Front', a political organisation that set itself against the elitist, capitalist, imperialist art market and called on artists to make 'a new and liberated art for the peoples' use'.[80]

In the early 1970s, Medalla and Dugger were some of the better-known radical artists in London and were predominantly known for their participatory artworks, a form that allowed them to question established ideas about authorship and intentionality in art by creating works to which the audience members contributed.[81] According to art historian John Walker, this was part of their efforts to 'democratize art by breaking down the barrier between creators and

Figure 2.5 John Dugger, 'Tachai Commune China', 1972. *Source*: Reproduced with the permission of John Dugger.

audiences, between fine artists as specialists/professionals and ordinary people.'[82] Art was to be created collectively, a product of multiple hands, voices and minds, rather than just that of the individual artist. This challenge to authorship was combined with an interest in China most successfully in Medalla's *A Stitch in Time* (1968–1972) which, according to Walker, was inspired by *dazibao* (大字报 big character poster), the handmade wall posters that formed a key part of the visual environment of the Cultural Revolution.[83] In the version of this work used in their 'People's Participation Pavilion' at Documenta 5 in 1972, Medalla suspended long cotton sheets from the ceiling, provided needles and threads of different hues and invited people to embroider designs on the cloth.[84] In China, *dazibao* have long been a means through which individuals could express their opinions. They ranged from a few characters as a slogan to long essays, they could be anonymous or authored; thus, they were an inherently participatory and political artistic product. Medalla tapped into the democratising nature of the *dazibao* by giving the audience an opportunity to contribute to the art, creating a work that beyond the basic parameters set up by the artist (the material, the thread, the needles) was created totally outside of the artist's control. The final product looked nothing like a Chinese *dazibao*, but what mattered was the act of involvement, rather than the outcome itself.

The Maoist influence was also visible more broadly on Dugger and Medalla. Medalla used cut outs from *China Pictorial* in a number of his art works, both

Figure 2.6 John Dugger, 'Yangtze River Bridge', 1972. *Source*: Reproduced with the permission of John Dugger.

of them adopted 'Maoist' clothing, most notably workers' jackets and caps, and they were often seen carrying the Little Red Book.[85] While the actual art of the Cultural Revolution was largely without aesthetic interest to either of them, their interpretation of it as a fundamentally participatory event enabled them to link together their politics and practice. They detached, therefore, what they understood to be the theory from the resulting practice in China, drawing on the former, while largely ignoring the latter. In the late 1960s and early 1970s, then, Dugger and Medalla's political radicalism merged with an already existing interest in China and Chinese systems of thought, in order to produce a period of creation in which they attempted to rethink the relationship between the artist and the viewer.[86] The transformation of Dugger and Medalla's pan-Asian interest into an engagement with Mao's China is a reflection of how distant Asia, and particularly China, was perceived to be at the time, and thus how open it was to personal interpretation.

While the Huxian exhibition represented a moment of particular British interest in Chinese art, it does not appear that, overall, Communist Chinese aesthetics had a big impact on the British art world. And yet, the example of Dugger and Medalla do demonstrate the types of engagements that were possible and the ways in which China was used, not as a model of artistic creation per se, but as a way of approaching art's relationship with its viewers and broader society. In this, the perceived participatory nature of the Cultural Revolution, which the Huxian exhibition embodied, offered a point of comparison to the British art world.

CONCLUSION

In China, the Huxian peasant painters were positioned as being part of the cultural 'battle': the revolutionary 'troops' with brushes as their weapons. This aggressive rhetoric disappeared in Britain, where instead they were held up as a sign that a 'unified alternative' was available to the 'fragmented culture' of the capitalist West.[87] Despite these linguistic differences, their significance in both countries rested on the idea that an alternative to the bourgeois, individualised and rarefied model of art production was possible. While many on the countercultural left appreciated the material culture of Mao's China, and a wide range of people were impressed with its social and economic development, the art world had, until the Huxian exhibition, been largely unimpressed with new China's aesthetic offerings. The delight in the discovery of the Huxian paintings, therefore, appears to be quite genuine. At last, Mao's China, a state founded on a territory possessing a long history of cultural and aesthetic achievements, was producing contemporary art worthy of consideration on the world stage. Charmed by their bright colours, striking graphic designs and optimistic portrayal of new China, British observers seemed more convinced by the Huxian works than by the socialist realism so often associated with Communist Chinese art. These new works seemed to proclaim that Mao's China too had cultural offerings of value to follow in the long line of Chinese civilisational achievements. The Huxian paintings, then, were one of the Communist government's major success stories in terms of global cultural propaganda in the 1970s.

Their success in Britain came down to a particular concurrence of events. Interest in Mao's China grew throughout the 1970s as more information became available; growing numbers of people visited, and frequently published books and articles about their trips once back. There was a substantial desire to see what this new China looked like, and the Huxian paintings provided an insight into the new socialist countryside by its own inhabitants. In contrast to the seeming rigidity of most 'propaganda' offerings, the Huxian paintings seemed spontaneous and authentic. It seems, however, that the Huxian exhibition would not have been one of the 'great cultural event[s] of 1976' if the British art world had not played a crucial role in promoting it in newspapers, magazines and on radio.[88] China's greater accessibility raised its profile in the collective imagination, but its continued aura of distance and exoticism meant that its supporters were able to continue to map their own desires onto it.

The paintings were in Britain when Chairman Mao died in September 1976, and they continued their tour uninterrupted. Within a few years, however, Deng Xiaoping's reforms had radically transformed China, and with it, the art world in which the Huxian painters had come to prominence. Huxian quickly lost its privileged place within the Chinese art world, and the peasant artists' attempts to retain their appeal by removing the political and increasing the decorative content of the paintings was only temporarily successful. However, the appeal of the original paintings from the 1970s has remained for many Britons. The radical changes that have transformed China in the last forty years have left many former supporters and defenders of China in the West disillusioned, and greater subsequent knowledge about the politics of the late Mao era has forced retroactive reappraisals of previous enthusiasms. However, despite research that has proven the existence of the Chinese government's political and artistic interference into the Huxian paintings, they have retained, for many people, much of their original charm. Indeed, they are some of the most common Mao era object that I saw on display in people's homes, either in the forms of prints or paintings.[89] Arthur Probstain's African and Oriental bookstore in London frequently has Huxian prints on display, and in 2014, the Meridian Society held a very well-attended talk by Carol Hughes and Michael Sheringham that celebrated the Huxian paintings. The publicity material for the talk demonstrated the way Huxian's admirers continue to separate the art from the politics, claiming: 'Whatever our view of the politics of those times [. . .] they [the Huxian peasant paintings] are worth revisiting and reviewing as a manifestation and reflection of the idealised lives and aspirations of the rural population during that period.'[90] Thus while the Huxian painters were quickly left behind in the explosion of modern art styles Chinese artists experimented with in the 1980s, and while other memories of personal enthusiasm for Mao's China became tarnished by historical retrospection, the Huxian peasant paintings of the 1970s remain a largely untainted reminder of the hope many Britons once invested in China.

NOTES

1. A version of this chapter was published as Williams, Emily, 'Exporting the Communist Image: The 1976 Chinese Peasant Painting Exhibition'. It is republished here with permission from De Gruyter.

2. Adrian Rifkin, 'The Chinese Exhibition at the Warehouse Gallery', *Artscribe* 5 (February 1977): 17.

3. The Fine Arts Collection Section of the Cultural Group under the State Council of the People's Republic of China, ed., *Peasant Paintings from Huhsien County* (Peking: Foreign Languages Press, 1974), 1.

4. Richard Cork, *Art for Whom?* (London: Arts Council of Great Britain, 1978), 3–4.

5. Cork, *Art for Whom?* 5; Rifkin, 'The Chinese Exhibition at the Warehouse Gallery'.

6. Richard Neville, *Playpower* (London: Paladin, 1971), 40.

7. Edward Lucie-Smith, *Art in the Seventies* (Oxford: Phaidon, 1980); Frances Spalding, *British Art since 1900* (London: Thames and Hudson, 1986); John A. Walker, *Left Shift: Radical Art in 1970s Britain* (London: I.B. Tauris, 2002).

8. Maureen Scott and Mike Baker, *Essays on Art and Imperialism* (London: League of Socialist Artists, 1976); League of Socialist Artists, *Manifesto & Theses on Art* (London: League of Socialist Artists, 1977). Caroline Tisdall, 'Avant-Garde to All Intents', *The Guardian*, 25 August 1972; Caroline Tisdall, 'Chinese Agitscape', *The Guardian*, 15 December 1972; Caroline Tisdall, 'Art Controversies of the 70s', in *British Art in the 20th Century: The Modern Movement*, ed. Susan P. Compton (Munich; New York: Prestel-Verlag, 1986), 83–88.

9. anon, 'Peasant Paintings of Huhsien', *China Reconstructs*, 1974, 17.

10. Ralph Croizier, 'Hu Xian Peasant Painting: From Revolutionary Icon to Market Commodity', in *Art in Turmoil: The Chinese Cultural Revolution, 1966-76*, ed. Richard King (Vancouver: UBC Press, 2010), 141.

11. Ellen Johnston Laing, 'Chinese Peasant Painting, 1958-1976', *Art International* 27, no. 1 (1984): 7.

12. Yin-ki Cheung, 'Iconography of Socialist Revolution: Construction of an Optimistic Imagery in Maoist China, 1949-1976', *G-SEC WORKING PAPER No.20*, 2007.

13. Croizier, 'Hu Xian Peasant Painting: From Revolutionary Icon to Market Commodity', 143; Michael Sullivan, *Art and Artists of Twentieth-Century China* (Berkeley; LA; London: University of California Press, 1996), 148.

14. anon, 'Peasant Paintings of Huhsien', 20.

15. anon, 'Peasants' Paintings', *China Pictorial*, 1966, 37.

16. The Fine Arts Collection Section of the Cultural Group under the State Council of the People's Republic of China, *Peasant Paintings from Huhsien County*, 2.

17. Croizier, 'Hu Xian Peasant Painting: From Revolutionary Icon to Market Commodity', 142.

18. Laing, 'Chinese Peasant Painting, 1958-1976'.

19. Croizier, 'Hu Xian Peasant Painting: From Revolutionary Icon to Market Commodity', 144.

20. Croizier, 'Hu Xian Peasant Painting: From Revolutionary Icon to Market Commodity', 144.

21. School of Oriental and African Studies (SOAS) Archive MS 380899, Records of a visit to China by the Society for Anglo-Chinese Understanding, July 1976. Janet Hadley, Visit to China, July–August 1976.

22. Guy Brett, 'Talking with Huhsien Painters', *China Now*, December 1976, 9.

23. Craig Clunas, 'Souvenirs of Beijing; Authority and Subjectivity in Art Historical Memory', in *Picturing Power in the People's Republic of China: Posters of the Cultural Revolution*, ed. Stephanie Donald and Harriet Evans (Lanham: Rowman & Littlefield Publishers, 1999), 53.

24. Brett, 'Talking with Huhsien Painters', 8.Croizier, 'Hu Xian Peasant Painting: From Revolutionary Icon to Market Commodity', 144; Laing, 'Chinese Peasant Painting', 9.

25. 'Invités spéciaux: Les Peintres Paysans Du District de Houhsien, République Populaire de Chine', *Biennale de Paris Archives*, 1975 http://www.archives.biennaledeparis.org/fr/1975/artistes/invites_speciaux.htm [accessed 26/09/2015].

26. Maria Galikowski, *Art and Politics in China, 1949-1984* (Hong Kong: The Chinese University Press, 1998), 155.

27. Unnamed reporter quoted in Croizier, 'Hu Xian Peasant Painting: From Revolutionary Icon to Market Commodity', 144.

28. The Arts Council of Great Britain Archive, File ACGB/121/863, Peasant Paintings 1976 (hereafter ACGB/121/863), Exhibitions Sub-Committee Meeting, 25/05/ 1976. The Great Britain-China Centre was set up by the Foreign Office (under the name the Great Britain-China Committee) in 1972 and helped organise the 1973–1974 'Genius of China' exhibition at the Royal Academy.

29. ACGB/121/863, Letter: Hugh Shaw to Jeff Watson, 25/01/1977, Letter: Joanna Drew to Hugh Shaw, 18/03/1977. It is also noteworthy in this context that a far more ambitious exhibition about contemporary China was initially planned by the Arts Council, involving a number of artists, curators and art critics. The plan was eventually dropped altogether after the Huxian exhibition was offered by the Chinese Embassy. ACGB/121/863, Chinese Exhibitions: History of Projects, 01/03/1976.

30. The Billingham Art Gallery exhibition dispatch stated that the attendance was 15,410 (between 12 August and 25 September), while Bromsgrove reported an attendance of 2000–3000 for the exhibition between 2 and 10 October. ACGB/121/863, Exhibition dispatch: Billingham 11/10/1976; Exhibition dispatch: Bromsgrove 15/10/1976.

31. A problem arose because the ICA was planning on showing Roger Howard's play *The History of the Tenth Struggle*, to which the Chinese Embassy took offence. When the ICA would not change the dates of the play, a last minute venue had to be sought; the Warehouse Gallery in Covent Garden, run by the co-operative, the Artists' Market Association, was found as a suitable alternative. ACGB/121/863, Arts Council Internal Memo, 29/07/1976; Letter: Hugh Shaw to Hsieh Heng 20/10/1976.

32. ACGB/121/863, Letter: Joanna Drew to Hugh Shaw, 22/12/1976

33. ACGB/121/863, Letter: Hugh Shaw to Joanna Drew, 18/03/1977.

34. Brett, 'Talking with Huhsien Painters', 8.

35. Guy Brett, 'Internationalism among Artists in the 60s and 70s', in *The Other Story: Afro-Asian Artists in Post-War Britain*, ed. Rasheed Araeen (London: Southbank Centre, 1989), 111–15; Guy Brett, *Through Our Own Eyes: Popular Art and Modern History* (London: GMP, 1986).

36. Guy Brett, 'Chinese Painters Celebrate the New Way of Life', *The Times*, 11 September 1974; Guy Brett, 'China's Spare-Time Artists', *Studio International*, February 1975; Brett, 'Talking with Huhsien Painters'.

37. Guy Brett, 'In Millet, the Peasant Is a Heavy Figure, Bowed down by Toil, Earth-Bound. These Chinese Picture Themselves Lightly, They Step Lightly', *Arts Guardian*, February 1976.

38. Guy Brett, *Peasant Paintings from Hu County, Shensi Province, China* (London: Arts Council of Great Britain, 1976), 5.

39. Brett, *Peasant Paintings from Hu County*, 6.

40. Guy Brett, 'Spare Time Art Workers', *China Now*, 1975.

41. Guy Brett, 'Peasant Paintings from Huxian, Shensi Province, China', *Art Monthly*, no. 1 (October 1976).

42. ACGB/121/863 lists the radio programmes: 'Critics Forum', 11/12/76; 'Kaleidoscope' 17/11/76, 'BBC Evening Programme' 17/11/76.

43. Caroline Tisdall, 'Record of Achievement', *The Guardian*, 17 November 1976; William Feaver, 'China at the Double: ART', *The Observer*, 21 November 1976; Paul Overy, 'A Stroll Round Pompeii', *The Times*, 23 November 1976; Richard Cork, 'Painting the Village Red', *Evening Standard*, 9 December 1976; Michael Shepherd, 'East and West', *Sunday Telegraph*, 29 November 1976; Brett, 'China's Spare-Time Artists'; Rifkin, 'The Chinese Exhibition at the Warehouse Gallery'; John McEwen, 'Art', *The Spectator*, 4 December 1976'.

44. Rifkin, 'The Chinese Exhibition at the Warehouse Gallery'.

45. There was some negative feedback, particularly in the visitor's comments. In particular, some of the visitors' comments from the Bromsgrove festival compared the Huxian work negatively both to the Ming and Qing porcelain and to the work by local schoolchildren that were also on display! ACGB/121/863 Collated comments on exhibition.

46. Feaver, 'China at the Double: ART'.

47. Tisdall, 'Record of Achievement'.

48. Overy, 'A Stroll Round Pompeii'.

49. McEwen, 'Art'.

50. Shepherd, 'East and West'.

51. Cork, 'Painting the Village Red'.

52. Cork, 'Painting the Village Red'.

53. In 1976, for example, the Artists for Democracy organized an exhibition of works by the American Indian Movement, while in 1978, an exhibition of Chilean peasant patchworks was shown at the AIR Gallery. Walker, *Left Shift*, 125, 209.

54. Valerie Hellstein, 'Abstract Expressionism's Counterculture: The Club, the Cold War, and the New Sensibility' (Museum of Modern Art Conference New Perspectives in Abstract Expressionism, 2011), http://www.moma.org/momaorg/shared/pdfs/docs/calendar/Hellstein2.25.11MoMApaper.pdf [accessed 05/08/2020].

55. Marc G. Jensen, 'John Cage, Chance Operations, and the Chaos Game: Cage and the "I Ching"', *The Musical Times* 150, no. 1907 (1 July 2009): 97–102; Revolutionary Communist Party of Britain (Marxist-Leninist), 'Cornelius Cardew His Life and Work', Encyclopedia of Anti-Revisionism On-Line, 5 November 1986, https://www.marxists.org/history/erol/uk.hightide/cardew-2.htm [accessed 05/08/2020].

56. For a small selection of the type of comments made on this issue, see: Michael Croft, *Red Carpet to China* (New York: St. Martin's Press, 1958), 30, 98; Sophia Knight, *Window on Shanghai: Letters from China, 1965-67* (London: André Deutsch, 1967), 173–79; Hewlett Johnson, *Searching for Light: An Autobiography* (London: Joseph, 1968), 307–9, 313, 356; Ross Terrill, *800,000,000: The Real China* (Harmondsworth: Penguin Books, 1971), 20; Barbara W. Tuchman, *Notes from China* (New York: Collier books, 1972), 3.

57. William Watson, *The Genius of China: An Exhibition of Archaeological Finds of the People's Republic of China Held at the Royal Academy, London* (London: Times Newspapers, 1973).

58. Chen Huan, 'Political Exhibitionism', *The Guardian*, 27 September 1973, 3.

59. Nigel Gosking, 'Mao's Marvels', *The Observer*, 30 September 1973, 36.

60. John Tilbury, *Cornelius Cardew (1936-1981): A Life Unfinished* (Matching Tye, Essex: Copula, 2008).

61. See the journal *China Now* for monthly listings of events.

62. A 1974 article in the SACU journal *China Now* described an exhibition put on by the Cambridge SACU branch, entitled 'Art and Life in China from 2000 BC to 1973 AD'. It featured photographs of recently discovered antiquities as well as photographs from *China Pictorial*. A group of photographs matching this description is currently in the SACU photo archive. It is likely either from that exhibition, or from a similar one. Oundle School, SACU Photo Archive; Frida Knight, 'Exhibition in Miniature', *China Now*, February 1974, 11–12.

63. Guy Brett, 'The Changing Face of Chinese Art', *The Times*, 21 May 1974, 11; John Gittings, 'A Thousand Cuts', *The Guardian*, 2 May 1974, 14; Herta Christie, 'Astonishing Diversity', *China Now*, 42, December 1974, 9.

64. David Hare, *The Asian Plays* (London: Faber & Fab, 1986), 3; Roger Howard, *The Tragedy of Mao in the Lin Piao Period and Other Plays* (Colchester: Theatre Action Press, 1989); Nicholas de Jongh, 'Tenth Struggle', *The Guardian*, 20 September 1976, 8.

65. ACGB/121/863, Letter: Hugh Shaw to G.F. Chance 14/09/1976; ACGB/121/863, The Other Cinema Schedule, 1976. *Comment Yukong déplaça les montagnes (How Yukong Moved the Mountains)*, dir. by Joris Ivens and Marceline Loridan (Capi Films/Institut National de l'Audiovisuel, 1976).

66. Guy Brett, '"We Give You What We Saw"', *China Now*, Winter 1977, 2.

67. Thomas Waugh, 'How Yukong Moved the Mountains: Filming the Cultural Revolution', *Jump Cut: A Review of Contemporary Media* 12, no. 13 (December 1976): 3–6.

68. The Radical Bookshop History Project, for example, has a whole section on Collets, highlighting its importance. It was also frequently mentioned in interviews. It was owned by Eva Collet Reckitt, a long-time funder of the Communist Party of Great Britain, whose substantial wealth derived from the Reckett & Colman household products manufacturing empire. Dave Cope, 'Radical Bookshop History Project', Left on the shelf, 28–29 [accessed 3/06/2014], http://www.leftontheshelf-books.co.uk/images/doc/Radical-Bookshops-Listing.pdf [accessed 05/08/2020].

69. Numerous interviewees recalled shopping here, including: Patrick Ainley, interview with author, 29/11/2013, London; David Fernbach & Aubrey Walter, personal communication, 26/01/2015.

70. Cope, 'Radical Bookshop History Project', 41.

71. Michael Sheringham, interview with author, 27/11/2013, London.

72. Academic Richard Barbrook recalled buying a number of Chinese posters from Gwanghua in the late 1970s. Richard Barbrook, interview with author, 02/12/2014, London.

73. Cope, 'Radical Bookshop History Project', 30–49.

74. Clunas, 'Souvenirs of Beijing; Authority and Subjectivity in Art Historical Memory', 48.

75. Alexei Sayle, *Stalin Ate My Homework* (London: Sceptre, 2010), 233–35.

76. Nicholas Philip James, *John Dugger: Ergonic Sculpture and Other Works* (London: Cv Publications, 2011), 21–22.

77. John Dugger, personal communication, 21/05/2014; Guy Brett, *Exploding Galaxies: The Art of David Medalla* (London: Kala Press, 1995), 83.

78. James, *John Dugger*, 43.

79. 'On Contradiction' was one of Mao's most influential texts in the West. French philosopher Louis Althusser, for example, clearly draws on it in his 1962 essay 'Contradiction and Overdetermination'.

80. John Dugger, *Microcosm* (London: Sigi Krauss Gallery, 1971), 20.

81. Brett, 'Internationalism among Artists in the 60s and 70s', 113.

82. Walker, *Left Shift*, 47.

83. Walker, *Left Shift*, 47.

84. Walker, *Left Shift*, 47.

85. Brett, *Exploding Galaxies*, 85.

86. Dugger, personal communication, 21/05/2014; Brett, *Exploding Galaxies*, 93.

87. Cork, 'Painting the Village Red'.

88. Rifkin, 'The Chinese Exhibition at the Warehouse Gallery'.

89. Of people interviewed for this book, Huxian paintings or posters were still on display in the following homes: Terry Cannon, Elsie Collier, Paul Crook, and Delia Davin.

90. The Meridian Society, 'Reminder: The Story of the Huxian Peasant Paintings - Talk by Carol Hughes and Michael Sheringham', 2014, http://us2.campaign-archive2.com/?u=978bcf853dda1dfc25cd1f9a3&id=65b0cadb21 [accessed 26/09/2015].

Chapter 3

Experiencing China through Material Culture

The British in China and their Objects

The first two chapters of this book explored some of the different ways Mao's China and the Cultural Revolution were viewed in Britain in the late 1960s and 1970s, and in particular, detailed the support for and interest in China by wide segments of the left. However, in carrying out oral historical interviews while writing this book, one of the surprises was how often I saw Cultural Revolution objects on display in the homes of my interviewees, nearly forty years after Mao's death; clearly, then, these objects continued to have meaning even after the end of the Cultural Revolution. Moreover, what was striking was that this was not limited to the homes of those who had ideologically supported the Cultural Revolution. My interviewees spanned the ideological spectrum, and their current position on the Cultural Revolution ranged from the overwhelmingly negative to the more guardedly positive. What many of them shared, however, was the continued possession, and for some, display of Cultural Revolution material and visual culture.

The presence of similar objects in the homes of very different people in a country far away from these objects' place of origin highlights the often surprisingly diverse identities and routes of travel that objects can take. Influential scholar of consumption Daniel Miller has argued that 'a quest to understand the specific consumption of an object is often most effectively addressed by demonstrating the diversity of that consumption.'[1] In other words, object identities are produced through patterns of consumption as much as through methods of production. Object identities, just as human ones, are reducible not their materiality, but rather are a product of their social positioning; as Victor Buchli writes, 'materiality is by no means a non-negotiable and unquestionable empirical reality, it is a produced social one.'[2] Tracking the paths of objects, and viewing these objects within the visual and political environment of both Cultural Revolution China and

Britain demonstrates the changing associations of Cultural Revolution material culture and highlights the differing ways Britons attempted to make sense of China through engagement with these things. This chapter, then, draws on memoirs and oral historical accounts by Britons in order to demonstrate precisely this diversity.

This chapter focuses on the nature of engagements with Chinese objects in China by Britons in the 1960s and 1970s, as well as some of the personal legacies of these engagements. It makes two main arguments. The first is that focusing on engagements with material culture opens up stories and encounters that would be excluded if the search was only for ideological engagements. The second is a continuation of the argument made in previous chapters, which is that material culture is part of the way in which China was 'knowable'. In particular, Chinese objects were valued as a way of engaging with the everyday lives of Chinese people to which foreigners in China often had little access. The objects were appreciated as markers of a shared experience and served as an entry point into a society that often remained opaque even to those on the ground. Moreover, the objects also tied the British individuals to China at a unique moment in its modern history and represented 'authentic' traces of China once back in Britain.

PAPERCUTS IN FULHAM AND OXFORDSHIRE

A Diplomat in China: George Walden

On a stairwell in George Walden's south London home hangs a large red papercut. The papercut depicts a young Mao: it is an artistic reproduction of American journalist Edgar Snow's famous 1936 photograph of Mao in northern Shaanxi (see figure 3.1).[3] Snow rose to fame for introducing Mao to the world (and indeed, to many within China) in his 1937 book *Red Star Over China*.[4] His photograph of Mao came to even greater prominence in China in 1964, when it was used prominently in the song and dance epic 'The East is Red' (*Dongfang hong*东方红),[5] and it has been used widely in visual representations of Mao ever since. Walden's papercut is a vibrant red colour, and the size of a standard poster. It is part of a set of twelve images of Mao's life made in 1968 and that Walden purchased while he worked for the British Mission in Beijing from 1967 to 1969.[6] He was, and remains, unconvinced by most of the art offerings of that time, but was impressed by these papercuts. In his autobiography, he wrote that artistically speaking, 'they were superb; poster-sized cut-outs whose craftsmanship and intricacy of design made them comparable, in their way, to the Russian poster art of the 1920s.'[7] Walden has, at various times, hung a number of the different papercuts in his home, and indeed some of them bear witness to it, the bright red colour faded

Figure 3.1 A papercut of a young Mao, with the slogan 'Long Live Chairman Mao' (毛主席万岁, *Mao zhuxi wan sui*), 1968, owned by George Walden. *Source:* The George Walden Collection.

through exposure. But it was the 1936 Mao that hung on my October 2013 visit to his home, in a stairwell to prevent exposure to sunlight, with the rest framed and stored in another room.

Walden's papercut is a striking piece of art: confidently executed and highly detailed; it stands as a reminder that subtlety and skill continued to have a role in Cultural Revolution art. Walden bought the papercut while he was living in China: it hangs in his house, then, as a reminder of his presence there during that unique period in Chinese history. He bought other Communist objects too in addition to the Mao papercuts, including squeezedolls in the shape of Red Guards, papercuts with anti-Imperialist themes, scraps of *dazibao* and pamphlets, and other such ephemera. Walden was later a Conservative Member of Parliament and has long been critical of Cultural Revolution China and its Western sympathisers. He called late 1960s China a period of 'mass credulity, brutality, chauvinism, ugliness, mendacity, a gang mentality, violence', which left a lamentable impression on those who witnessed it in person.⁸ His memories of the period centred on the destruction of individuality, a familiar criticism from the right. He wrote

> It is not easy to shake off the memory of the semi-crazed faces and chants of Maoist marchers, the transformation of millions of human beings into malignant-eyed robots. [. . .] Outside North Korea it was difficult to imagine an entire people behaving in such a zombie manner, of the human personality being reduced to nothing.⁹

Walden's largely critical perspective on Mao's China was rooted in an ideological antipathy to Marxism and Chinese socialism, as well as a profound aversion to the behaviour of crowds in the parades and demonstrations he witnessed while in China. It was likely partially the result of the Cold War atmosphere of the time, especially given that Walden had worked in the Foreign Office's Soviet Union department before transferring to the China desk.¹⁰ Walden found the papercut aesthetically interesting, but given its origin in the politicised culture of the Cultural Revolution, politically repulsive. However, its value for him lay not in its relation to these politics, but to his personal experience. He has written:

> There is an unacknowledged rule in life that a residue of affection exists for whatever you have been a part of, in my case the cruel and sordid events in late '60s China. For me at least these were adventurous times. I have an agreeable memory of setting out on my poster reading, scene-observing round in my extra-duty overcoat and fur hat on icy days, when the air seemed as bracing as the tingling political atmosphere.¹¹

Walden arrived in China not long after the 1967 attack on the British Mission in Beijing, a moment of great tension for the small British community in China, and, more broadly, for Sino-British relations.¹² Walden's role was second secretary (political), with additional responsibility for several attaché roles, including press, culture, and information.¹³ His main task, however, was simply trying to find out what was happening in China, and his main source of information for this came from paying close attention to the visual and material environment, and particularly to the *dazibao* (大字报 big character posters) and other posters stuck to the walls throughout Beijing.¹⁴

When Walden first arrived, he and other Chinese-speaking embassy staff were able to mix with the crowds who were reading and writing the posters, and they would copy the text down for later analysis.¹⁵ In the spring of 1968, security forces made it clear that poster reading was off-limits to foreigners, a change which made gathering information much more difficult.¹⁶ Walden and others from the embassy would have to try to memorise poster content as they walked past them or alternatively try to casually pick up slips of paper—pamphlets, newspapers, torn down posters—for later analysis. Percy Cradock, the political counsellor (1966–1968) and later Chargé d'Affaires (1968–1969), recalled his wife Birthe cycling around the city, and returning 'well padded, with several layers of newsprint beneath her coat.'[17] While acknowledging that the banners and newspapers were often written by students, not officials, the British diplomats recognised that they could be reliable sources of information. The first time Cradock heard that Liu Shaoqi was a possible target of attack, for example, was at a diplomatic dinner, and the information had come from a foreign student studying at Beijing University, who had seen Liu's name on posters.[18] Cradock saw the value of the posters and other written material as representing and reflecting the political struggle at a more elite level:

> Reports were appearing critical of government or Party leaders and apparently drawing on privileged or secret material. Though the immediate authors were Red Guards, the leaks clearly came from much higher, presumably from the Cultural Revolution Group itself, and were deliberate. Allowing for some distortion, the reports were probably accurate. In a tightly closed society, where any information, however harmless, was secret, such revelations were pure gold.[19]

Engaging with the particular and peculiar material culture of the Cultural Revolution occupied a significant part of Walden's time in Beijing, and so it is not surprising that they feature heavily in his recollections. They constituted the source material of his professional life, in which they were read as 'texts', regardless of their aesthetics, but by virtue of their profusion throughout the city, they inevitably coloured his personal life too, and his memories of his time in Beijing.

It was this profusion, however, the seeming omnipresence of Mao's visage and Maoist imagery that prompted a search for its opposite: for some 'traditional' China and Chinese art hidden beneath the politics of the present. For Walden, this took the form of scroll-buying. While Walden made light of some of the British Mission's more audacious plans to collect information, his autobiography also made clear that it was a highly stressful environment, and he recalled escaping the tensions of the Cultural Revolution by spending time at a scroll shop run by monks.[20] While buying 'traditional' art would not have been possible for most Chinese people, and the monks were subject to struggle sessions by Red Guards, a number of government-owned and regulated scroll shops remained open, and Walden purchased around a hundred scrolls during his time in China.[21] Over time, his relationship with the monks developed, as did his knowledge of Chinese art, and he bought pieces by both modern and imperial masters. These too hang on the walls of his home, creating a somewhat surprising juxtaposition: on my visit, a Fu Baoshi (a modern master of Chinese ink painting) hung not far away from the Mao papercut already described. His main sitting room embodied, it appeared, his aesthetic choices: the Fu Baoshi was complemented by a number of other Chinese ink paintings as well as antique Chinese furniture, much of which he bought during his time in China. But the continued presence of the Mao papercut, and the careful way he treats the remaining pieces of the set, highlight the complex relationship that often exists between material culture and identity construction.

Watching China from Hong Kong: John Gittings

John Gittings' Oxfordshire home similarly has a Cultural Revolution papercut hanging on one of its walls.[22] It too is poster-sized and red and depicts a group of students taking part in the 'Up to the Mountains and Down to the Countryside Movement' (上山下乡运动 *shangshan xiaxiang yundong*), of the late 1960s, which resulted in millions of young people (so-called educated youth, 知识青年, *zhishi qingnian*) being sent to live and work in often distant rural areas. It is a highly intricate image, depicting scenes of agricultural life, animal husbandry and the collection of an abundant harvest, as observed by the newly arrived young people (see figure 3.2). Gittings bought this poster while living in Hong Kong in 1968, where he worked as a journalist for the *Far Eastern Economic Review*. He bought it from a China Products store: stores known to expatriates in Hong Kong as 'Communist stores' as they sold products from the mainland. The papercut was likely made in Foshan, a papercutting centre in Guangdong province, and, given its theme, it was likely made in 1968.

This was Gitting's first purchase at a 'Communist store', and it sparked his interest in Chinese political art and ephemera, but his interest in China was long established by this point.[23] He had collected Chinese stamps as a child, read Chinese at Oxford University, and then worked for Collet's Chinese bookshop in London in the early 1960s.[24] He catalogued Chinese books, and became acquainted with modern Chinese paintings, as the gallery attached to the bookshop imported and sold Chinese scrolls. Gittings also began to purchase scrolls at this time, including one by Fu Baoshi, which hung in his home during my visit.[25] The paintings that Collets imported were typically ink paintings done by Chinese artists in China, Hong Kong, Taiwan, or elsewhere, and they tended to eschew the political influences visible in much of the art done by artists on the mainland at that time. It was not until he relocated to Hong Kong that Gittings' interest in politicised images of contemporary China really began to develop, and he started to purchase

Figure 3.2 A papercut depicting the 'Up to the Mountains and Down to the Countryside Movement' (上山下乡 *shangshan xiaxiang*) (c.1968–1969), owned by John Gittings. *Source*: The John Gittings Collection.

a variety of objects. He bought, for example, children's toys, such as Red Guard rubber dolls and a puzzle depicting Vietnamese soldiers shooting down an American plane.[26] Also available in Hong Kong were good quality reproductions of ink paintings made by the Rongbaozhai studio in Beijing, some of which Gittings purchased. He long displayed a Song dynasty reproduction painting in his home, until it became too worn out to remain on display.

Gittings' interest in contemporary China and in Chinese Communism, then, was just one element of his broader interest in Chinese arts and culture. Gittings first visited China in 1971 through the British-Chinese friendship group, the Society for Anglo-Chinese Understanding (SACU), and it was there that he began to purchase objects in greater numbers. He bought papercuts, woodblock prints, posters, books such as cartoon books and political manuals, as well as clothing like Mao caps, which he wore upon his return to Britain.[27]

Like George Walden, Gittings was highly sensitised to the importance of visual imagery and text. As a 'China watcher' and a journalist in Hong Kong, Gittings became practised in interpreting the limited amount of material that came out of China. During the Cultural Revolution, China watchers in Hong Kong endeavoured to understand what was really happening on the mainland: there were very few Western journalists actually in China in the early years of the Cultural Revolution, and the only British journalist in China for much of the late 1960s, Reuters correspondent Anthony Grey, was put under house arrest in Beijing for twenty-six months from 1967 to 1969.[28] The early years of the Cultural Revolution resulted in a period of greatly reduced Western presence in China. Many foreign residents left, very few new foreigners were given visas, and few Western delegations were allowed to visit.[29] As a result, China watchers had to be creative in finding source material. Red Guard documents were particularly highly sought after, because as explained above, they often represented and reproduced ongoing debates at the highest levels of politics. Some Red Guard publications managed to acquire and publish 'classified documents', such as speeches by leaders and internal policy disputes.[30] With so few Western journalists in China itself, China watchers were reliant on these documents finding their way to Hong Kong, usually smuggled out either in the post or carried by refugees, who hoped to sell them to journalists and diplomats.[31]

With relatively little coming out of China, through official and unofficial means, China watchers became experts at noticing slight changes of policy or personnel through constant close attention to the visual and textual material that was available. As a result, Gittings was well prepared to continue this sort of analysis when he visited China in 1971 with SACU. On that trip and on a subsequent delegation in 1976, he recalled that he and the other delegates paid close attention to the visual environment.[32] Posters, *dazibao*, and blackboards at work units, which contained a mixture of written text and artistic imagery, were scrutinised closely. The broader visual environment, and particularly the slogans and images were also carefully observed. The practice was called 'reading the walls' and at the end of the day, Gittings and other delegates would compare what they had seen.[33] They were also able to visit the local New China Bookstore (新华书店 *xinhua shudian*) in many cities, where they paid close attention to both the poster and book themes, and made their own purchases. When observed carefully, the visual and material environment often gave insight far beyond what their guides would tell them or what was being said and written officially.[34] The visual environment thus gave Gittings an insight into political and cultural change that he would have otherwise lacked:

> Deprived for most of the time of the normal contacts that help build up understanding in a foreign culture—the casual strolls, chance encounters, and random

conversations—we searched for other reference points among the abundance of visual images on display. These ranged from stark slogans in black or red characters to colourful posters on billboards, or smaller printed versions on sale in bookshops.[35]

Gittings returned to China in 1976 as part of a scholars' delegation, and he again purchased objects: together these formed the foundation of what is now the University of Westminster's China Visual Arts Project Archive, but some of his objects have also been gifted to the Victoria & Albert and Ashmolean museums. The objects functioned for him both as art, aesthetic objects which gave him pleasure, and as texts, which would be read for insight into the political and cultural situation in China. They were, then, objects with professional, political and also personal value. Over the years many of his objects were displayed in his home, but the only one remaining on my 2013 visit was the 1968 papercut.

Unlike George Walden, Gittings was, in the 1970s, sympathetic towards Chinese Communism. He was part of the broader British left, which had lost faith in the Soviet Union and was looking for other revolutionary models. Like many on the left, Gittings was critical of the official narrative on the Vietnam War and the Cold War, and as a result, was sceptical of what he perceived to be the mainstream portrayal of the Cultural Revolution as little more than a violent power struggle.[36] Rather, he engaged with theoretical portrayals of the Cultural Revolution that saw it as fundamental to the establishment of socialism in China. He took seriously the attempts to introduce greater equality to healthcare and education, to breaking down the rural-urban divide, and to encouraging people at all levels of society to become engaged in politics and culture. While he has since written that he did have concerns about the excesses of the Cultural Revolution, he has acknowledged that little of this came through in his writing at the time.[37] While George Walden wrote that the Cultural Revolution was an 'attack on the human spirit and in making automata of themselves the Chinese threatened to reduce themselves to nothing, and us with them',[38] Gittings' impressions after his 1971 visit were radically different. In an article for the *Guardian*, he wrote:

> It is the sense of a collective spirit which is, perhaps, most impressive [. . .]. And the thought of Mao Tse-tung, itself a rather off-putting concept for eclectically-minded visiting Western intellectuals, begins to make sense as the cement which holds the whole system together. [. . .] It is not so much a cult of personality, but more a collective way of life, which provides the moral imperatives for the youth of China who will inherit Mao's revolution.[39]

Gittings was clearly sympathetic to the Maoist project, but a career of living in and writing on China as both a journalist and an academic has left him today with a more neutral view. The continued presence of the papercut in his home was not necessarily, then, a political statement. Rather, it remained because of its connection to his life story: it was his late wife Aelfthryth who initially spotted it and encouraged him to buy it, and it was a memento both of their time together in Hong Kong and of a period of his life in the 1970s when he had looked at China with great hope. As he gradually gave his collected objects away to public institutions, the papercut has remained a symbol of his long-term fascination with Mao-era material and visual culture.

These two lengthy personal narratives have been recounted because each individual represented the two ends of British perspectives on the Cultural Revolution, even if Gittings' views in particular have mellowed with time. Despite these ideological differences, however, they both continue to display very similar objects in their homes. Searching only for political interest in Mao's China would necessitate excluding Walden's engagements, but as this section has demonstrated, interest in and engagement with the material and visual culture of Mao's China was not limited to China's supporters. Both Walden and Gittings used these objects as sources of information for their professional careers, but the objects have also played a part in their personal lives over the past fifty years. Turning our attention to engagements with material culture, therefore, allows consideration of a range of encounters that would otherwise be excluded.

ENCOUNTERS WITH OBJECTS IN CHINA

The previous section's personal narratives have established a number of key themes for analysing the material that follows. Firstly, they highlight that while it was indeed very difficult for foreigners to access China at this time, and that there was a perception that China was 'closed' to the outside world, there remained a small diplomatic and professional presence throughout, and that from the early 1970s, foreign residents and groups of visitors returned in greater, albeit still very limited, numbers. Secondly, these personal stories demonstrate the role that material and visual culture played in initiating engagements with a country that was hard to understand, even for those who spoke Chinese and studied China. These engagements with material culture could have meaning both professionally and personally, and these dual reasons likely go some way in explaining the continued presence of these objects in the individual's lives even today. The rest of this chapter further explores the role that material and visual culture played in mediating the experience of foreigners in China during the 1970s.

Foreigners and Their 'Chinas'

Alongside the foreign diplomatic presence, a small group of the regime's foreign supporters also continued to reside in China throughout the Mao-era, most of whom were based in Beijing and worked either as English-language teachers or as translators and 'polishers' for the Foreign Languages Press.[40] During the mid-1960s, and again from the early 1970s, short-term contracts were also offered to foreigners for these tasks, with less attention paid to their ideological allegiance.[41] People who were given work visas did not have to be politically aligned with the regime, but certainly, many of the individuals who went were sympathetic to the government and interested in what was happening in 'New China'.

From 1973, the British Council began to send groups of students to study in Beijing, for one or two years, and while other nations similarly sent groups of students, the British contingent—of ten students per year in the mid-1970s—was frequently amongst the largest of the Western nations.[42] The larger size of the British contingent brought with it a greater diversity in the nature of the students' interest in China. While certain individuals were politically interested—such as Harriet Evans, who was part of the 1975 cohort—many had more traditional sinological concerns. Another 1975 student, Beth McKillop, was initially interested in developments in Chinese education, but over her time there, developed a more substantial interest in imperial culture and art.[43] Rose Kerr had studied classical and modern Chinese at SOAS before going to China in 1975, and her interests were always linguistic and cultural, rather than political.[44] These interests were not necessarily mutually exclusive. Frances Wood was working on her doctoral thesis while in China, which looked at traditional domestic architecture.[45] At the same time, she recalled being interested in the experiments underway to bring about the 'new socialist men and women', in the barefoot doctors, and in changes to women's conditions, without seeing a need to expand this interest through a study of Marxist or Maoist texts. While difficult to prove, it can be suggested that the British students groups were, by virtue of their larger size and the classical emphasis of British sinology,[46] more diverse than many of the other national groups, many of which had students who had been part of the Maoist movements in their home countries. Craig Clunas, part of the 1974 cohort, recalled that the 'tiny British student community ranged itself along a spectrum of scepticism and hope regarding the ideal new civilization portrayed in the posters.'[47]

While this book is primarily interested in those objects that were created during the Cultural Revolution, it is worth noting that objects like antiques, imperial-era paintings and traditional clothing continued to be desired by many of the visitors to Mao's China, sometimes instead of, sometimes alongside more explicitly 'political' objects. Indeed, such was the perceived overabundance of political and modern material and visual culture that some individuals were more interested in the search for traces of the imperial past as an escape.[48] What the search for 'traditional' Chinese objects often reflected was a search for an authentic 'traditional China'. This could be true in a narrow academic sense, in the search for source materials, but it could also be part of an Orientalizing search for some hidden, 'true' China beneath its modern Communist and partially 'modernised' or 'Sovietised' present. Albert Honig, an American who visited China in 1976, recalled, for example, a history professor on his trip who would remark happily 'This is the real China' every time they visited a temple.[49] This mindset was implicitly mirrored in British public institutions for many years, as chapter 5 will note, with permanent exhibitions of China ending with the downfall of the Qing dynasty. Objects were, then, not just inanimate 'stuff', but a way of constructing or engaging with the idea of 'China' that interested a given individual: objects were representatives of different 'Chinas'. For George Walden, as described earlier, scrolls and the act of purchasing them were a way of escaping from Cultural Revolution China to a more traditional concept of Chinese civilisation. For others, objects were valuable for precisely the opposite reason: for their ability to represent and embody contemporary China.

OBJECTS IN COMMON: BRITISH STUDENTS IN CHINA

Acquiring Meaningful Objects: Harriet Evans

Harriet Evans, a British student in China from 1975 to 1977, and later a professor of Chinese Cultural Studies at the University of Westminster, still owns a ceramic yoghurt cup from her time there, treasured because of the novelty of finding a familiar taste from home in mid-1970s Beijing (see figure 3.3).[50] It was purchased on a shopping outing in Wudaokou in Beijing, and while a yoghurt pot may seem to be a fairly ordinary object, the obvious attention put into its design, as well as the appeal it has long held for Evans is a reminder of the significance that everyday objects can have, particularly in an environment in which consumerist desires remain largely latent. Even though Evans lived in China for two years and spoke fluent Chinese, she, like many others, was aware of the distance between herself and the Chinese people with which she came into contact. Indeed, the issue of isolation from ordinary Chinese people features in many of the autobiographies and recollections of the time by Western students and residents in China. Beverley Hooper, an Australian student who arrived in Beijing in 1975, commented:

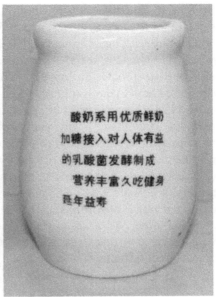

Figure 3.3 A ceramic yoghurt pot (c.1970s), made by the Xi'an Municipal Red Star Dairy Product Plant (西安市红星乳品厂 *Xi'an shi hongxing rupin chang*). The reverse of the pot explains the health benefits of yoghurt. Owned by Harriet Evans. *Source:* The Harriet Evans Collection.

> 'I want to get to know the people' was a common, if naïve, expression heard amongst recently-arrived students. Before long the 'people'—in Peking, over eight million of them—were reduced chiefly to the Chinese students and teachers at the [Beijing Language] Institute.[51]

Frances Wood similarly recalled that foreign students 'had so little communication with ordinary people and such a sense of otherness'.[52] Richard Kirkby, an English teacher in late 1970s China recalled, 'Any normal human contact with Chinese people was out of the question. Whether inside or outside our guarded compounds, communication with the great Chinese masses was limited to curt transactional exchanges.'[53] While it was easier for residents to speak with ordinary Chinese people than it was for visitors on the highly controlled tours, many residents were cognisant of how uncommon unmediated contact was. For Evans, her yoghurt pot contained both the memory of a specific experience, but more importantly, it was a reminder of the everydayness of lives to which she lacked access.[54]

Shared use of material culture was, therefore, one of the ways to overcome the separation between foreigners and Chinese people. While yoghurt may have been something of a novelty to the average Beijinger at this time, the surprise for Evans was at least in part finding a taste of home, and one that she could share with those around her, at this most unusual time. It was an object which tied her to a specific experience of living in a foreign country, and moreover, it stood as an 'object-in-common' with ordinary Chinese people, connected both to the specific event in which she purchased it, and as an icon, symbolically representing her larger experience in China.

Evans accumulated a wide variety of objects during her two years in China, most of which were everyday objects, including enamel plates and mugs, handkerchiefs, pieces of fabric and textiles, second hand clothing, rural pottery, sewing kits, pencil boxes, small mechanical toys, as well as a number of posters (see figure 3.4).[55] She did not purchase or acquire objects systematically, but rather opportunistically, and based on experiences that had some meaning to her. This was not, then, collecting for the sake of collecting, as with others that this book will encounter, but rather the accumulation of objects with meaning.

Figure 3.4 Children's toy of a woman with a mechanised plough (c.1970s), owned by **Harriet Evans.** *Source:* The Harriet Evans Collection.

Susan Stewart's theorisation of the 'souvenir' can shed some light on the continued relevance of these objects, many of which are inexpensive and mass-produced, to their owners' lives. Stewart argues that with the development of an exchange economy, the search for authentic experiences, and correlatively, the search for authentic objects becomes critical.[56] As experience is increasingly mediated and abstracted, Stewart contends, the lived relation of the body to the real world is replaced by a nostalgic myth of contact and presence.[57] The souvenir, then, represents the domestication or internalisation of external experience, a process that relies upon the ability of objects to serve as 'traces' of authentic experience. The souvenir's value comes from its ability to connect the owner to its original context, in this case, Cultural Revolution China. Stewart suggests this is particularly true of 'exotic' objects, which Cultural Revolution objects certainly were and indeed are.

Stewart expounds on the power of the exotic object, noting,

> To have a souvenir of the exotic is to possess both a specimen and a trophy; on the one hand, the object must be marked as exterior and foreign, on the other it must be marked as arising directly out of an immediate experience of its possessor.[58]

In other words, to function as a souvenir, an object must be removed from its original context spatially, temporally, or both. Only once removed from its original context is the exotic object able to serve as an authentic trace of it, but in becoming a souvenir, it functions through a new and different type of narrative: the narrative of its owner.[59]

The use of the term 'souvenir' may seem pejorative, given the term's connotations of cheap, tacky, and kitsch. However, etymologically, the term lacks these associations. The word comes from the Latin *subvenīre*, which means 'to come into the mind', via the French *souvenir* which refers to memory and keepsake. What the etymology of the word hints at, therefore, is the ability of small, potentially meaningless objects to act as memory prompts, as in Proust's famed madeleines. They are objects that retain a connection to their origin through, in Stewart's words, 'a language of longing'; a connection maintained through their ability to generate a narrative which reaches 'behind' in time, and perhaps 'sideways' in space, connecting their owners to different times and places.[60]

Evans' yoghurt pot and her other Cultural Revolution objects have a value irrespective of their financial worth. The value comes not just from the connection to this unique time in China's recent past, but equally importantly, from the owner's connection to that time period. The object functioned at the time as a way of connecting the owner with the foreign culture being experienced and functioned later as a testament to that connection. As such, it is not surprising that souvenirs tend to assume an importance in individual's lives and memories unrelated to their financial value.

Ethnographic Acquisitions: Frances Wood

Another student, Frances Wood, later lead curator of the Chinese collection at the British Library, amassed a substantial collection of objects, including dozens of enamel mugs, around a dozen posters, and other objects, such as enamel and porcelain dishes, stationery, and a bamboo pram, which she used to transport her acquired goods home in 1976.[61] As noted above, she was pursuing her own research on domestic architecture alongside her university coursework while in Beijing, and frequently spent her afternoons cycling around the city taking photographs of Beijing's distinctive domestic architecture – the *hutongs* – and other buildings. But she would also, on these explorations, look into hardware or daily good stores when she came across them. She recalled that this was at least partly because there was not much for foreign students to do. Moreover, while some antique shops and other such markets had remained open throughout or had re-opened by the late 1970s, many of these objects would have been beyond the means of students.

In any case, for Wood, what was interesting were not the elite objects, but rather the everyday ones, which, by 1975–1976, were demonstrating increasing decorative diversity. She developed the habit of stopping in hardware stores she came across, just to see what was inside, and sometimes made her own purchases. She initially purchased enamel mugs with revolutionary slogans on them, but as these became less common, she began to acquire those with any sort of Chinese writing on them, which was at least partially a reflection of the fact that she was in China studying the language. But within this seemingly narrow category – enamel mugs with Chinese characters – Wood found a huge and unexpected diversity. She bought mugs with agricultural themes (such as celebrating a bumper harvest), with revolutionary history themes (such as Mao's hometown Shaoshan, which was a popular tourist destination), as well as those with conventionally 'touristy' themes (such as the Great Wall or the Guilin landscape) (see figure 3.5).

While finding mugs aesthetically and materially interesting, Wood was also drawn to the experience of shopping itself, in particular watching Chinese people shopping, and the complex process through which they negotiated new purchases. As the Chinese economy improved throughout the 1970s and with inflation staying very low, individual families often had slightly more money to spend. Much of this would be put towards saving for larger items such as a bicycle or a radio, but it also resulted in the renewal of some daily use objects. Wood remembered enamel washbasins being particularly

Figure 3.5 An enamel mug with text (c. Early 1970s), including 'a Single Spark can Start a Prairie Fire' (星星之火,可以燎原 *xingxingzhihuo, keyi liaoyuan*), a famous quote by Mao Zedong. Owned by Frances Wood. *Source*: The Frances Wood Collection.

decoratively diverse, and recalled watching families debating extensively which one to purchase. She did not purchase basins – they were too large – but recalled how important this ever-greater degree of choice seemed to be to people. This was not about a shared experience *per se*, as the level of Wood's engagement with the Chinese purchasers was minimal, but for Wood, the growing availability of decorative everyday objects communicated to her something of the nature of changes already underway in Chinese society, even before Mao died. Moreover, her purchasing of mugs also implicitly mirrored this new ability of Chinese consumers to diversify their own household goods. Shopping, then, was part-leisure, part-ethnography: a way of both passing time and gaining insight into the country in which she was living.

Wood's use of objects to understand or deepen her engagement with China is a reflection of two things. First, it is a reflection of the isolated nature of the British experience in Cultural Revolution China. Craig Clunas has written about the difficulties of engaging with people whilst in Beijing, and concluded, 'In these conditions, it is not surprising that much of my engagement with the city was strongly visual', even if he was not personally interested in many of the contemporary artistic offerings.[62] Second, while academic and historical writing is more often concerned with political or ideological engagements, it is a reminder that our experience of the world is a fundamentally embodied one. Indeed, as Elizabeth Grosz has noted, we cannot but perceive the world in terms of objects, and engaging with things is our way of dealing with a world in which we are enmeshed rather than over which we have dominion.[63] As a result, objects inevitably play a role, in Ian Woodward's words, 'in forming or negating interpersonal and group attachments, mediating the formation of self-identity and esteem, and integrating and differentiating social groups, classes or tribes.'[64] Indeed, as Woodward notes, 'the actual qualities of these objects do not always matter greatly for sociality, and may be secondary to its possession.'[65] Engaging with objects, then, provided entry points into Chinese society at a time when many Westerners were keenly aware of their isolation.

Leisurely collecting: Penny Brooke

Frances Wood's purchasing was described as part-ethnography, part-leisure. For a third student, buying objects functioned as a conduit to a certain type of experience: leisure, entertainment and the search for novelty. Penny Brooke, a British student in China from 1973 to 1975, and later the deputy director of the Great Britain-China Centre, described shopping as a leisure activity, and as one of the few forms of entertainment available to foreigners at the time.[66] She bought dozens of Chairman Mao badges, but never wore them: the act of shopping was as important as the object purchased. For Brooke, buying Mao badges was a form of consumption-as-leisure. It was a way of exploring a culture that was difficult to access for foreigners, but the practice was also, somewhat paradoxically, a continuation of Western bourgeois shopping habits in the very different socio-political context of late Mao-era China. The primary aim was not forming a 'collection' of badges, although that could be seen as one outcome; rather, it was primarily an attempt to carve out a sphere of leisure outside of the activities mandated by the university. On outings in Beijing and travels around the country, Brooke searched for new and different badges: her aim was to get as varied a selection as possible. She bought bamboo, ceramic and plastic badges, alongside the more common aluminium ones. There was a pleasure, then, in the search and discovery of new designs or new materials. Many objects, including badges, were made locally and were not available for purchase elsewhere. One of the attractions of travel was finding locally produced objects, and Brooke recalled that foreigners living in China used to exchange news about the best things to buy in different locales: acquiring objects then became a way of engaging with each locale and a form of localised knowledge. Brooke bought, for example, a set of three bamboo badges at Mao's hometown Shaoshan, each with a different image on it. The content on them was less important than their difference: they were unusual, and therefore, of interest.

These objects clearly functioned differently for Brooke than they did for Evans. When Brooke returned to the United Kingdom after finishing her studies in China, she put them in storage and rarely looked at them until 2008, when she donated some of them to the British Museum. They may be, in Stewart's words a 'specimen', but they were not a 'trophy'.[67] They have not been remembered as important markers of her experience of China, and so have not functioned as a souvenir. Stewart suggests that the opposite of the souvenir is the collectable.[68] Whereas the souvenir aims to recall the past, the collection replaces history with classification, in which objects are identified by their seriality. As such, their value comes less from their ability to function as memory triggers, and more from their relation to the other objects in the series. As Brooke was purchasing badges, she was choosing them for their ability to fit within the larger category of Chairman Mao badges, or Cultural Revolution art/propaganda, rather than to commemorate specific experiences, even if her experiences in China were also mediated through these objects. With reference to Stewart, therefore, the collected Cultural Revolution object functions as a representative of China or the Cultural Revolution or some other category through which the collection is organised, whereas the souvenir lacks the same claim to representativeness, and instead functions as an extension of its owner's personal history.

Theories of collecting typically see the collection as a form of 'world-building', in which objects' original identities are discarded and redefined relative to the set of series established by the owners. Jean Baudrillard argues, 'It is because he feels himself alienated or lost within a social discourse whose rules he cannot fathom that the collector is driven to construct an alternative discourse that is for him entirely amenable.'[69] Baudrillard sees the collection as the creation of an alternative discourse, which seeks to create independence from the world. It could be suggested that Brooke collected in part out of alienation from the Chinese society that she was kept out of. But I suggest that a more productive way to see Brooke's actions is not as a 'way to control the outside world' as Baudrillard suggests, and more as an effort to engage with this outside world through one of the small number of options available to her. These three students' acquisition habits were not, then, a defensive and inward-looking reaction to this alienation, but an outward-looking attempt to overcome it through material engagements. In this context, it is noteworthy that other traditions of collecting, including that of China, positions collecting as a fundamentally social act, rather than an individual one as theorised by Baudrillard.[70]

There might implicitly appear to be a value differentiation between the souvenir and the collection. Souvenir buying may seem to lack the cultural capital inherent in collection formation. It is not my intention, however, to attach such value judgements to either of these terms.[71] Rather, both can be seen as subjective and inherently personal processes. The difference comes from how the process of acquisition impacts upon the object. The souvenir becomes defined by reference to the owner's experience, whereas the collected object becomes defined by the set or series into which the owner has inserted it.

While theorists like to draw sharp lines between souvenirs and collectables, in reality, many acquisitions and acquiring habits blur the line. Frances Wood's acquisition of enamel mugs and Penny Brooke's Mao badges were implicitly guided by seriality – the desire to add another similar object to a group – but the process through which that happened (through shopping, travel, and so on) and the unique context of being acquired in Cultural Revolution China, added an extra layer of personal meaning to the objects. Frances Wood at times used her mugs for drinking, as we might with a souvenir, but once back in Britain put the majority of them away in storage, rather than putting them on display in her home as a memory trigger. She treated them, therefore, more as collectables. Brooke's objects were defined by seriality, but they were acquired opportunistically in a way that seems quite different from Baudrillard's somewhat neurotic collector. Rather, like with Evans and Wood, Brooke was searching for ways to engage with China at a difficult time and found a way to do so through objects. The status of these objects as souvenirs or collectables is, therefore, never fixed, but rather is subject to change, and the transnational movement of objects from China to the very different context of Britain undoubtedly had some impact on this. The majority of objects brought back by Britons in China initially functioned as souvenirs (even though their owners may have called them a collection), but over time this could change. As we will see in chapter 5, many of the objects now found in Britain's public institutions were originally brought back as souvenirs by residents or visitors to Mao's China. While they were once souvenirs, they are now undoubtedly collectables, their identities defined by their proximity to similar objects within the legitimising space of the museum archive.

CONCLUSION

The experience of living in China could often be difficult. There were few foreigners there, and few Chinese people spoke English. Even those that could would moderate their contact with foreigners, as protection against criticism. Many books and articles in the 1970s claimed that one had to be in China in order to understand it, but it was clear to those on the ground that presence in the country did not necessarily translate into comprehension of the culture or even the space through which to develop this understanding.

Instead, each individual was trying to make sense of China through their own ideas and experiences. The Chinese objects they encountered and sometimes acquired can be seen as part of that process: a relational process in which their ideas, perceptions, and material experiences combined in the numerous constructions of 'China'.

Objects were valued both as objects in their original sense – as a piece of propaganda, art, or as an object of everyday life from China – and also because they represented the owner's experience of 'China', conceptually and experientially. The object's meaning was therefore transformed once acquired by the foreigner, as it became tied to their personal experience. This double layering of meanings invested in Cultural Revolution objects confirms anthropologist Christopher Tilley's supposition that 'through the artefact, layered and often contradictory sets of meanings can be conveyed simultaneously.'[72] For the Western purchaser, the Cultural Revolution object had a diverse range of potential connotations; it was Chinese, Communist, contemporary, political, kitsch, a gift, a marker of a specific experience or a reminder of a specific person or event. The object's identity, therefore, was not fully established at the moment of its production, but rather, could take on new associations through patterns of consumption. As Tilley observes, 'Things change their meanings through their life cycles and according to the way they are used and appropriated and in the manner in which individuals and groups identify themselves with them.'[73]

Once back in Britain, owners did a number of different things with their objects. Journalist Michael Rank, a student in the mid-1970s China who brought a number of posters back with him, has written that he showed them off when he first got back, but then quickly forgot all about them.[74] Penny Brooke put her badges in a small box, and they sat, largely undisturbed, in a cupboard until 2008, when she donated a number of them to the British Museum.[75] For others, objects were thrown away, gifted to friends and family or just lost over the years. Some people, however, chose to display them in their home, and indeed, even today some of these objects remain on display. Our engagements with material culture are often more complicated than we might assume, precisely because we often buy, obtain, keep, and display objects in our homes without being conscious of the different readings that others might bring to them. In the late historian of China Delia Davin's Yorkshire home for example, a number of (in her estimation, likely fake) paintings by twentieth-century master ink painter Qi Baishi lined the staircase up to the first floor, while prints of Huxian peasant paintings lined the adjoining hallway.[76] They might seem to be in stark contrast to each other, as one represented a theoretically apolitical aesthetic expression, while the other represented precisely the opposite. But in Davin's home, what they both represented was not their specific ideological standpoints, but their own connection with her deep intellectual and personal engagement with Chinese culture and her experiences of living in Beijing in the 1960s and 1970s. They were objects that appealed on an aesthetic level – the Qi Baishi paintings' reflecting the elegance of *guohua*, the Huxian prints the cheerful appeal of graphic Chinese folk art – but also on a personal level, functioning as a reminder of a time when China held much appeal to the British left, and of a time when Davin was one of the few foreigners there.

Moreover, as later chapters of this book will develop, objects that foreigners brought back from China became important in a different sense because in many cases they have entered the collections of British public institutions. Most museums and other institutions that collect Mao-era art have received or purchased objects brought back by tourists and residents in Mao's China. Being purchased by foreigners, then, was not the last stage in the life cycle of some objects; rather, over time, many thousands of objects have been incorporated into public British collections.

NOTES

1. Daniel Miller, 'Consumption', in *Handbook of Material Culture*, ed. Christopher Y. Tilley (London: SAGE, 2006), 349.
2. Victor Buchli, 'Introduction', in *The Material Culture Reader*, ed. Victor Buchli (London: Routledge, 2020), 15.
3. Author's visit to Walden's London home, 19/09/2013.
4. Edgar Snow, *Red Star over China* (London: Victor Gollancz, 1938).
5. Daniel Leese, 'Mao the Man and Mao the Icon', in *A Critical Introduction to Mao*, ed. Timothy Cheek (Cambridge: Cambridge University Press, 2010), 221.
6. George Walden, interview with author, 19/09/2013, London. All of the details of Walden's experience that is not referenced to his written works comes from this personal communication.
7. George Walden, *Lucky George: Memoirs of an Anti-Politician* (London: Allen Lane, 1999), 125.
8. George Walden, *China: A Wolf in the World?* (London: Gibson Square, 2008), 9, 11.
9. Walden, *China*, 11.
10. Walden, *Lucky George*, 69.
11. Walden, *China*, 32.
12. Crowds attacked the British Mission and its occupants in 1967 in response to crackdowns by British colonial authorities in Hong Kong. See Cradock's autobiography for a personal account of the burning of the British Mission. Percy Cradock, *Experiences of China*, New ed. (London: John Murray, 1999).
13. Walden, *Lucky George*, 105.
14. Walden, *Lucky George*, 105–6.
15. Cradock, *Experiences of China*, 44–45; Walden, *Lucky George*, 107.

16. Walden, *Lucky George*, 108.
17. Cradock, *Experiences of China*, 45.
18. Cradock, *Experiences of China*, 41.
19. Cradock, *Experiences of China*, 44–45.
20. Walden, *Lucky George*, 111.
21. Walden, *Lucky George*, 115.
22. Author's visit to Gittings' house, 15/10/2013, Oxfordshire.
23. John Gittings, interview with author, 15/10/2013, Oxfordshire; John Gittings, personal communication, 13/10/2014. All of the details of Gittings' experience that is not referenced to his written works comes from these personal communications.
24. John Gittings, interview with author, 15/10/2013, Oxfordshire.
25. Gittings, personal communication, 13/10/2014.
26. These objects are now housed in the University of Westminster China Visual Arts Project Archive, a collection founded by Gittings and discussed in chapter 5.
27. John Gittings, 'Reporting China since the 1960s', in *China's Transformations : The Stories beyond the Headlines*, ed. Lionel M. Jensen and Timothy B. Weston (Lanham, MD; Plymouth: Rowman & Littlefield, 2007), 288, Gittings, personal communication, 13/10/2014.
28. Lorelies Olslager, 'On the Reporters Anthony Grey Leaves Behind', *Daily Mirror*, 8 October 1969, 15.
29. The Scottish Communist John Collier, for example, arrived in Guangzhou in April 1966 to take up a teaching position at Sun Yatsen University. His wife Elsie and their children, due to join him a few months later, were told that their visas had been cancelled after the outbreak of the Cultural Revolution as no more foreigners were to be allowed to enter. After much negotiation, they were eventually allowed to join John in Guangzhou, where they stayed until 1968. John Collier and Elsie Collier, *China's Socialist Revolution* (London: Stage 1, 1973). Elsie Collier, interview with author, 25/02/2015, Edinburgh.
30. Gittings, 'Reporting China since the 1960s', 288–89.
31. Gittings, 'Reporting China since the 1960s', 288–89.
32. John Gittings, 'Excess and Enthusiasm', in *Picturing Power in the People's Republic of China: Posters of the Cultural Revolution*, ed. Stephanie Donald and Harriet Evans (Lanham: Rowman & Littlefield Publishers, 1999), 27–28. Gittings, interview with author, 15/10/2013, Oxfordshire.
33. Gittings, interview with author, 15/10/2013, Oxfordshire.
34. Gittings, personal communication, 13/10/2014.
35. Gittings, 'Excess and Enthusiasm', 27.
36. Gittings, interview with author, 15/10/2013, Oxfordshire.
37. Gittings, 'Reporting China since the 1960s', 289–90.
38. Walden, *Lucky George*, 127.
39. John Gittings, 'The World Is Their Prize', *The Guardian*, 8 May 1971, 2.
40. For an overview of some of the key names see: *Living in China: Twenty Authors from Abroad* (Beijing: New World Press, 1979). Two key secondary sources are: Anne-Marie Brady, *Making the Foreign Serve China: Managing Foreigners in the People's Republic* (Lanham, MD; Oxford: Rowman & Littlefield, 2003);

Beverley Hooper, *Foreigners Under Mao: Western Lives in China, 1949-1976* (Hong Kong: Hong Kong University Press, 2016).

41. For a small selection of personal accounts of living in Mao-era China by Britons, see: Joshua Samuel Horn, *Away with All Pests: An English Surgeon in People's China, 1954-1969* (London: Paul Hamlyn, 1969); Delia Jenner, *Letters from Peking* (Oxford: Oxford University Press, 1967); Sophia Knight, *Window on Shanghai: Letters from China, 1965-67* (London: André Deutsch, 1967); Muriel Seltman, *What's Left? What's Right?: A Political Journey via North Korea and the Chinese Cultural Revolution* (Kibworth Beauchamp, Leicestershire: Matador, 2014).

42. Despite the improvement in diplomatic relations that followed President Richard Nixon's 1972 visit, American students were not sent to China until 1979.

43. Beth McKillop, interview with author, 13/07/2015, London.

44. Rose Kerr, personal communication, 19/06/2015.

45. Frances Wood, interview with author, 29/04/2014, London.

46. A number of individuals expressed to me their opinion that at this time British university-level Chinese language and history education was very classically focussed. Harriet Evans, interview with author, 23/04/2014, London; John Gittings, interview with author, 15/10/2014, Oxfordshire; Beth McKillop, interview with author, 13/07/2015, London, Frances Wood, interview with author, 29/04/2014, London.

47. Craig Clunas, 'Souvenirs of Beijing: Authority and Subjectivity in Art Historical Memory', in *Picturing Power in the People's Republic of China: Posters of the Cultural Revolution*, ed. Stephanie Donald and Harriet Evans (Lanham: Rowman & Littlefield Publishers, 1999), 49.

48. Beverley Hooper, personal communication, 21/09/2014, London; Clunas, 49.

49. Albert M. Honig, *China Today: Sin or Virtue?* (Hicksville, NY: Exposition Press, 1978), 24.

50. Harriet Evans, interview with author, 17/12/2014, London.

51. Beverley Hooper, *Inside Peking: A Personal Report* (London: Macdonald and Jane's, 1979), 13.

52. Frances Wood, *Hand-Grenade Practice in Peking: My Part in the Cultural Revolution* (London: Slightly Foxed, 2011), 98.

53. Richard Kirkby, *Intruder in Mao's Realm: A Foreigner in China during the Cultural Revolution* (Hong Kong: Earnshaw Books, 2016), Foreword.

54. Harriet Evans, interview with author, 17/12/2014, London.

55. Harriet Evans, interview with author, 11/04/2013, London.

56. Susan Stewart, *On Longing: Narratives of the Miniature, the Gigantic, the Souvenir, the Collection* (Durham, NC: Duke University Press, 1993), 133.

57. Stewart, *On Longing*, 133.

58. Stewart, *On Longing*, 147.

59. Stewart, *On Longing*, 150.

60. Stewart, *On Longing*, 135.

61. Frances Wood, interview with author, 29/04/2014, London. The following description of Wood's purchasing activities comes from this interview.

62. Clunas, 'Souvenirs of Beijing: Authority and Subjectivity in Art Historical Memory', 48.

63. Elizabeth Grosz, 'The Thing', in *The Object Reader*, ed. Fiona Candlin and Raiford Guins (London; New York: Routledge, 2009), 126.

64. Ian Woodward, *Understanding Material Culture* (Los Angeles: SAGE Publications, 2014), 135.

65. Woodward, 135.

66. Penny Brooke, interview with author, 02/04/2012, London; Penny Brooke, personal communication, 12/04/2012. The following description of Brooke's purchasing activities comes from this interview and email exchange.

67. Stewart, *On Longing*, 151.

68. Stewart, 151.

69. Jean Baudrillard, 'The System of Collecting', in *The Cultures of Collecting*, ed. John Elsner and Roger Cardinal (London: Reaktion, 1994), 24.

70. Zhang Liguo 章利国, '*Wenhua Chuancheng Shoucang You Xue – Lue Shuo Shouna Gai Shoucang Xue* 文化传承收藏有学 – 略说收纳该国收藏学 [Cultural Heritage and Collection Study: A Brief View of Collection in China]', *Meishu* 美术 11 (2018): 106–10

71. Within the literature on collecting, a distinction is often made between the collector and the hoarder, and this differentiation also includes a value judgement: one chooses to collect, while the other one has to, and this compulsion sullies the relationship between the object and its owner. I am not referencing this sort of differentiation or value judgement in my distinction between souvenir/accumulation and collection.

72. Christopher Y. Tilley, 'Objectification', in *Handbook of Material Culture*, ed. Christopher Y. Tilley (London: SAGE, 2006), 62.

73. Tilley, 'Objectification', 70.

74. Michael Rank, 'Chinese Posters of Revolution and Reform', *China Review* 16 (Summer 2000): 33.

75. Helen Wang, *Chairman Mao Badges: Symbols and Slogans of the Cultural Revolution* (London: British Museum Press, 2008), 51. Penny Brooke, interview with author, 02/04/2012, London.

76. Author's visit to Davin's home, 02-03/03/2014, Ilkley. Davin lived in China from 1963–1965 and 1975–1976.

Part II

Chapter 4

Individual Collections

The Global Journeys of Cultural Revolution Objects

People engage with objects in all sorts of different ways, and our engagements with objects both reflect our world views and help to shape them. One particular type of engagement is through the collection. Collecting can be seen as a particular type of engagement with material culture, and with the outside world through material culture, characterised by the selective and serial acquisition of objects. From the very start of the Cultural Revolution up to the present, small numbers of Britons have formed collections of Cultural Revolution objects. The question of *why* Britons formed these collections is necessarily specific to each individual. However, exploring *how* collections have been formed can open up the objects' shared routes of travel. Chapters 4 and 5 continue to tell the stories of individual and institutional engagements, but they also focus on the locations in which these objects have been and continue to be seen, arguing that the spaces in which we encounter objects shape the nature of that engagement.

In much Western theory, collections are understood as a form of private engagement, in which the collector remakes their world through the acquisition and classification of objects. This chapter argues, however, that drawing from the Chinese tradition of collecting can add a public aspect to our understanding of collecting, in which the collector is viewed as engaging with society, culture and history through the collection: collecting then can be seen as an inherently social activity. Moreover, as this chapter demonstrates, the concept of the collection as an inherently private and personal endeavour must be contrasted with the global systems of object distribution, value construction and knowledge production that inevitably shapes why, how and who collects. As such, this chapter continues to draw on the ideas introduced in the earlier chapters of this book of the different 'Chinas' imagined, nostalgised, idealised and engaged with.

Chapter 5 looks at the development of public collections of Cultural Revolution material culture in Britain. Many of these collections have their origins in private collections (or acquisitions) developed by British individuals who went to China in the 1970s, and so it is worth looking at the ways in which these individual collections have developed. This chapter follows the development of five different individual collections, and in doing so considers some of the routes of travel that objects have taken, both during the Mao years and since. Just as previous chapters have encountered individuals with a variety of subject positions towards China, ranging from the devotional to the apathetic, this chapter too encounters Trotskyists, anti-Stalinists, general leftists, as well as one individual without much sympathy for the Maoist experiment at all. In general, collecting is a time consuming and expensive process: it is hard to seriously engage with the material without at least some sympathy for the culture they represent. As this chapter demonstrates, however, this still leaves plenty of space for different ways of viewing China and different paths for engaging with objects.

UNDERSTANDING COLLECTING

Since the 1990s, Cultural Studies in the West has developed a persisting interest in collections and archives. This new academic literature has greatly heightened our awareness of the politics inherent in collecting practices, with nuanced understandings emerging that highlight the racial, gendered and cultural values that underpin what gets collected and by whom. Despite this nuance, however, a fairly coherent understanding of the psychology of the collector has emerged. Literature on collecting has largely positioned the desire to collect as an attempt to control and position the material world, vis-à-vis both the individual identity of the collector and society more broadly.[1] Collecting is frequently described as a primarily individual activity, in which the collector deals with social anxiety through the creation of a new world in which he (it is usually a he) can determine the identity of the objects that surround him.[2]

This redefinition of an object's identity, made relative to the owner, is typically predicated upon a denial of any use value the object may previously have had.[3] For a porcelain cup to be a 'collectible', therefore, it can no longer be used as a cup: it must be completely removed from its previous system of meaning and value and fitted into a new system of value defined by the collection.[4] This new uselessness is what defines the objects as collectable, and becomes its primary value, as it allows the object to become purely representational, and thus, bridge the space and time from its original context to that supplied by the collector.[5] Collecting, then, is seen as removing objects from circulation so as to bring, in Russell Belk's words, 'order to a controllable portion of the world', through the defined series of sets that make up any collection.[6]

This need to bring order to the world via control of objects is often interpreted in Freudian or pseudo-Freudian terms, which emphasise the collector's need for control.[7] Even those who do not frame it in such psychologised terms still tend to see it as a deeply anti-social activity. Hannah Arendt notes that the act of collecting not only encourages the collector to withdraw from the public sphere to the privacy of his own four walls, but that in doing so he 'takes along with him all kinds of treasures that once were public property to decorate them.'[8] Collecting, then, is typically seen as a withdrawal from the world, a process by which objects are removed from circulation and entered into a private world determined totally by the collector. Based on this understanding of collecting, it is a fundamentally private and even anti-social activity, driven by the ego of the collector.

And yet despite this suggestion that collecting is a private activity, in which collectors gathers objects around themselves, object acquisition can be, as the last chapter demonstrated, precisely a way of engaging with the outside world. Indeed, by looking outside of the European tradition of collecting, we find that the idea of collecting as a materialist attachment to worldly possessions is not universally shared. China also has a long tradition of collecting, and it has long been a pastime for elites and the imperial household; as a tradition, it offers a way to think about collecting beyond the private world building so emphasised in Western theory. Collecting in China did have individual functions: it was seen as a method of self-cultivation, spiritually, culturally and ethically.[9] But whatever the individual benefits accrued from collecting and the study of collected pieces, the ability to perform this cultivation was a significant part of the social construction of elite identity and networking, especially from the mid-sixteenth century on.[10] Collecting gave the owner cultural capital and the practice of collecting was utilised by individuals throughout society looking to access the literati lifestyle and the social networks that came with it.[11] Collecting within the Chinese tradition was, then, as much about outward-looking identity construction (both individual and cultural) and relationship building, as it was about inward-looking object acquisition.[12]

The Chinese Central Academy of Fine Arts scholar Zhang Liguo has argued that a Chinese theory of collecting remains undeveloped and has advocated for its development.[13] In his own tentative theorising, what is noteworthy is his emphasis on the social and cultural value of collecting, and the deep and intrinsic relationship between culture and collecting.[14] In other words, for Zhang, collecting is not the removal of material culture from society, or the privatisation of culture by an individual; rather, collecting is itself a cultural act, in which the individual connects with their culture both materially and spiritually through the object.[15]

The purpose of introducing the history of Chinese collecting is not to draw on the tired trope of Western individualism versus Chinese collectivism. Rather, quite the opposite, I suggest that these theories should be taken together: the attention in writings about the Chinese tradition to the social aspects of collecting can complement and add to the psychologised focus of much Western theory. Collecting may often be an individual activity, it may be about ordering and controlling material culture in ways relevant to the individual collector, but that does not necessarily mean it is purely a form of withdrawal from the world; it is also a way of engaging with both one's own and foreign cultures through its material culture. Just as in chapter 3, it was argued that individuals used Chinese objects as a way of engaging with a culture that remained opaque to them, it can be argued too that the collection can be not inward-looking world building, but rather outward-looking bridge building with other times and places.

Moreover, going beyond the simple binary of private versus public, the idea of collecting as a private and personal endeavour must be contrasted with the global networks of knowledge transmission and object distribution, which inevitably impacts on how objects are viewed. While specific decisions about what and how to collect are necessarily personal, our attitudes towards objects cannot be divorced from the larger socio-political environment that shapes how we see the world. Whether one views Cultural Revolution objects as little more than kitsch and propaganda, or as the output of an utopian system radically remaking society, are not just personal evaluations, but are also social ones, derived consciously or subconsciously from ongoing representations within political, economic and cultural systems that often have little to do with the specific objects. Thus, while it may be true that collectors derive their own classifications for these objects, the categories or sets determined necessarily relate to the social context in which the individual and object are entwined.

While each individual encountered in this chapter had different experiences of China, they all emerged out of the larger context of British imaginings of China outlined in the first two chapters of this book. This means, necessarily, that the understandings of Cultural Revolution culture were varied. As later sections of this chapter will demonstrate, for Peter Wain, based in Hong Kong, the Cultural Revolution represented primarily the destruction of Chinese art and culture. He saw the objects as little more than propaganda, but collected them as important socio-political records of a unique time in Chinese art history.[16] Conversely, Paul Crook, raised in China by CCP-supporting parents, gathered posters and Mao badges out of both an interest in the ideology they represented and in accordance with the social norms around him, in which urban Chinese youths bought, swapped and otherwise acquired these mass-produced objects. These collections, therefore, were spurred on by different ideologies and motivations, but neither can be divorced from the broader context of the extraordinary upheaval in China and the varying responses from the British left, popular culture and political establishment. It is argued then, that collecting, far from being a purely private activity, is one that is inseparable from the global transmission of objects and ideas.

CHILDHOOD COLLECTING IN CULTURAL REVOLUTION CHINA: PAUL CROOK

Paul Crook, the Beijing-raised son of Anglo-Canadian couple David and Isabel Crook, was thirteen when the Cultural Revolution began. His parents were long-term supporters of the Communist regime: they arrived in China before 1949 and stayed to teach English at the Beijing First Foreign Languages Institute.[17] The Crooks, like many of the regime's resident foreign supporters, eagerly welcomed the Cultural Revolution: they felt that the growing gap between working people and bureaucrats meant that Mao was correct to stop China from following in the footsteps of the Soviet Union.[18] Moreover, many foreigners felt that the Cultural Revolution would be an opportunity for them to escape the political and social isolation of foreign life in Beijing and would provide them with opportunities and outlets for their revolutionary enthusiasm and internationalism.[19] The Crook children, who attended ordinary Chinese schools and spoke fluent Chinese, were encouraged by their parents to take part in the Cultural Revolution as far as they, as foreigners, were able. One of the main ways the youngest child, Paul, engaged was through material culture.[20] He would purchase posters from New China Bookstores (新华书店 *Xinhua shudian*) and take them home to display them (see figure 4.1). He covered his bedroom walls this way, and would take down and store old posters when he had new ones.

He also built up a collection of over 400 Chairman Mao badges, largely through trading and swapping in the numerous badge markets that sprung up around Beijing. Urban schools were largely closed from June 1966 to 1968, and so Crook had plenty of spare time: badge markets were a place he went to spend time with friends, and badge collecting and trading was a type of entertainment. Despite the anti-capitalist ethos of the time, many individuals engaged in speculation, and Crook recalled enjoying trying to 'play' the market. He also took advantage of the fact that as a foreigner he could buy badges from the Friendship Store (友谊商店 *Youyi shangdian*), where certain badges, rare elsewhere, were often available. He would even buy them for his Chinese friends, but charge them – in badges of course – for this

Figure 4.1 A poster with the slogan 'Down with American Imperialism! Down with Soviet Revisionism!' (打到美帝！打到苏修！ *Dadao Meidi! Dadao Suxiu!*), owned by Paul Crook. The damage and repairs resulting from Crook's use of the poster are visible around the edges. *Source*: The Paul Crook Collection.

service. Crook recalled, however, that when his father found out about this most un-Communist activity, he quickly put a stop to it.

From 1968, Crook's personal situation changed. His parents were arrested for being on the wrong side of a Red Guard factional dispute on campus; his father would go on to spend five years in solitary confinement, while his mother spent three years locked up on the university campus.[21] While this undoubtedly caused substantial emotional distress, the fact that Crook and his two brothers continued to receive their parents' salaries, which they split between themselves, meant that their financial position remained stable. The cheap price of posters meant that Crook was able to purchase all of the posters that he wanted, as well as much of the limited supply of books and periodicals that were for sale.

While initially largely genuine in his support for the Cultural Revolution and the regime, his parents' disappearance and Crook's own growing maturity, combined with a more widely shared scepticism after Lin Biao's death,[22] meant that by the early 1970s, Crook was far more cynical about the regime, and in turn, about the ideology expressed through the posters. However, this cynicism provoked a different type of perspective that continued to fuel poster purchasing: in the manner of teenagers everywhere, Crook began to engage ironically. Their ugliness, rather than their beauty, became appealing, and Crook defined their appeal for him as 'kitsch'. Throughout the 1970s, Crook continued to purchase posters, but he was less interested in them for display: it had become a self-conscious collection, and as a collection, it took on a momentum of its own. Crook left China in 1973, first for Australia and then Britain, but on trips back to see his family, he would go on large poster-buying sprees. On one visit home, during the 'Criticise Lin Biao Criticise Confucius' (批林批孔 *piLin piKong*) campaign of 1973–1974, Crook recalled going to Xidan market in Beijing and buying every single available poster on that theme. He went on similarly large purchasing sprees in subsequent years, accumulating some 300 posters in total. He also purchased posters on various travels around China in the 1970s, taking advantage of the different posters that were available in different places.

Crook's poster collection and his attitude towards it developed in conjunction with both his own personal circumstances and broader social currents. It is noteworthy perhaps that he started his poster collection when he was thirteen, a common age for children to form collections. According to Crook, his collection was initially a reflection both of his genuine support for the regime, a result of his Communist upbringing, and his appreciation of the poster aesthetics: they were bright, colourful, cheerful and easy to understand. There was also a more experiential pleasure in trading badges with friends and at markets, and in making his bedroom his own through decoration. By the early 1970s, however, Crook, now a teenager, recalled being aware that these poster images, so closely associated with the regime, were not 'cool', but this provoked a new type of engagement with them. By the mid-1970s, when Crook was preparing to move his belongings to England, he became far more aware of them as a collection, and of purchases as ways of building the collection.

As a Chinese-speaking foreigner, Crook was able to take advantage of all of the different purchasing options then available. He bought from the large government-run chains, like New China Bookstores, as well as from the department stores directed at foreigners, such as the Friendship Stores. He engaged in trading at badge markets, and made small purchases of antiques at Liulichang antique market, which remained partly open to foreigners. He asked friends and family for stamps, developing a collection that numbered in the thousands. He even pilfered a few Little Red Books from the factory at which he was working in 1971, after Lin Biao's death provoked a recall of objects related to him: Little Red Books were targeted as the now-disgraced leader had provided a preface to most editions. Crook was, then, a resourceful and creative collector, who took advantage of his ability to – at least to a certain extent – move between the Chinese and foreigner communities by virtue of his language skills and Chinese school friends. He demonstrates that even though China lacked a developed market economy at this time, and consumer items were relatively scarce, there were still ample opportunities for collecting, if that was one's intention.

Crook's collection demonstrates that even at this time when the Chinese economy was suffering, the government made efforts to make politically acceptable material available at very low prices.[23] As Beverley Hooper, an Australian student who arrived in China in 1975, recalled there was something of a contradiction inherent in the available goods. She noted, 'Side by side with the extreme frugality was a large range of "non-essential" items produced purely for political purposes and sold at close to giveaway prices.'[24] Indeed, such was the extent of this sort of production that Mao himself intervened in 1969 to criticise the extensive production of Mao badges. He allegedly proclaimed, 'Give me back my airplanes', a reference to the huge amount of aluminium being used in badge production.[25] The Maoist aesthetic was visible on posters and printed texts, as well as everyday goods, such as kitchenware and textiles. If one eschewed elitist conceptions of collectable items, there were ample potential collectables.

The breadth of Crook's collection is indicative of the time he was in China. Few other foreigners actively traded in the badge markets for the simple reason that there were few foreigners in China in the late 1960s; by the 1970s, when the number of foreigners in China increased, badge markets had largely disappeared. Crook's collection is unique in the sense that it was developed at a time when few foreigners lived in China and incorporates a wide variety of the mass-produced material culture that was available at the time: posters, badges, stamps, books and a smaller number of paintings and scrolls.

CONTINUING FAMILY TRADITIONS: RICHARD KIRKBY

A rather different approach to purchasing objects was adopted by another Briton who lived in China during the Cultural Revolution, albeit later on than Crook. Richard Kirkby taught English in China from 1974 to 1979, based first in Nanjing, Jiangsu for three years and then in Jinan, Shandong for two years, both cities on China's eastern coast, and where few foreigners lived at that time. Kirkby had been an active part of the New Left as a student at the University of Bristol in the late 1960s, demonstrating against the Vietnam War and ongoing Western imperialism in Africa.[26] He had long been interested in socialism and had travelled in East Germany and Poland in the 1960s and early 1970s.[27] He studied city planning at London's Architectural

Association in the early 1970s, where he developed an interest in the process of urban development in China, which seemed to have had an industrial revolution without the urban squalor and slums of other countries.[28] Kirkby, like much of the British left by this time, was a strong anti-Stalinist, and while he was convinced by Trotsky's critique of the early course of the Chinese revolution, he also recalls that 'sitting in London and knowing nothing of the Cultural Revolution's horrors, Beijing's message undoubtedly had some primal appeal to the anti-Stalinist, "no-country" socialist.'[29]

Kirkby first visited China in 1973 on a Society for Anglo-Chinese Understanding (SACU) study tour of academics and students from the Architectural Association, but he had a connection to China long before this. His mother had been born in Sichuan in 1919, the child of Quaker medical missionaries, and he recalled his childhood home having a 'China drawer' that was full of embroidered silks, dolls and shadow puppets: the remnants of his mother's own childhood.[30] His paternal great uncle too had been a diplomat in China in the 1920s and was himself something of a 'curio collector'.[31]

As such, Kirkby was well placed to approach China materially. While in China, Kirkby acquired a range of objects, including paintings (originals and reproductions), Chairman Mao badges (often gifts from his students), stamps (also gifts), toys (see figure 4.2), Mao jackets, PLA plimsolls, antiques and Western objects like high-quality watches that Red Guards had confiscated at the start of the Cultural Revolution and that could be acquired by foreigners for low prices.[32] Kirkby also acquired some 100 small booklets called *xiaorenshu* (小人书), which contained images and small amounts of text (see figure 4.3). They were literacy tools intended for Chinese people, old and young, but were also useful for Kirkby, who was endeavouring to learn Chinese at this time, and was getting little support in his efforts from his university. Kirkby's main interest, however, was posters, and throughout his time in China he acquired over 300. He would cycle on weekends to the local New China Bookstore, and acquire, in a fairly systematic manner, the latest posters. He never displayed the posters once he got them home, but rather rolled them up and put them into storage.[33] When he returned from China, he brought them with him, and they were carefully stored in the United Kingdom. They were not, then souvenirs of his time in China, to be displayed and seen; rather they were a self-conscious collection, with steps taken to preserve the objects for the future.

Kirkby left China in 1979 under somewhat tense circumstances, but his engagement with China has been sustained. He published *Urbanization in China: Town and Country in a Developing Economy, 1949–2000 AD* in 1988, the first book on Chinese urbanization, and later developed a career dealing in antiques. He donated his poster collection first to the University

Figure 4.2 A children's toy (c.1978–79), comprising a pistol with rubber bullets and targets of the Gang of Four. The Gang of Four were held responsible for the Cultural Revolution after Mao's death. The toy was originally purchased by Richard Kirkby and is now in the collection of the Ashmolean Museum. *Source*: EA2010.289 Toy Gun with Targets, Image © Ashmolean Museum, University of Oxford.

of Westminster's Chinese Poster Collection, and later sold some of it to the Ashmolean Museum as the museum developed its own collection. Many of his *xiaorenshu* are now in the library of the School of Oriental and African Studies (SOAS). His collecting reflects quite a different experience to that of Paul Crook. Kirkby's posters are not the well-worn posters that decorated the young Crook's walls: rather these are well-preserved specimens, historical evidence of a particular time in China. Unlike Crook, who bought posters out of a genuine enjoyment of their aesthetic, for Kirkby, it was more related to their representative value, and perhaps as a continuation of his family's historical engagement with China. While Kirkby was clearly interested in trying to use China's material and visual environment to understand what was going on around him, the posters were less foundational to his experience and memories of China, when compared to some of the souvenirs encountered in chapter 3: indeed, he mentions the posters in his long and rich published personal account of his time in China only in passing.[34] And yet, they have had significant afterlives, in British public institutional collections, the topic of chapter 5.

Figure 4.3 A selection of *xiaorenshu* (small picture storybooks) including one about Norman Bethune (白求恩 Bai Qiu'en), a Canadian doctor celebrated by Mao. Owned by Richard Kirkby *Source*: The Richard Kirkby Collection.

COLLECTING THE LEFT IN BRITAIN: DAVID KING

What understandings of China as 'closed' during the Cultural Revolution ignore, and what recent research has made clear is that throughout the period, Beijing exported large amounts of material throughout the world: while the movement of people slowed down, the movement of *stuff* continued.[35] As detailed in chapters 1 and 2, objects and literature from Mao's China were available (particularly in London) if one was inclined to look for them, and many on the left were familiar with the imagery. The Little Red Book seems to have been the Maoist object most widely owned by foreigners, even if it was not necessarily always read.[36] While many bought a Little Red Book or a few posters, a few individuals developed more extensive collections at the time, even if they never travelled to China.

David King was one such collector. King was a left-wing graphic designer, author, and collector who passed away in 2016. He is best known for his collection of Soviet material, some of which is frequently displayed in London's Tate Modern, but he also had a substantial collection of Chinese objects.[37] His interest in Communist objects was multifaceted: as a graphic designer, he took great inspiration from the Russian constructivists of the 1920s, and in his work in the 1960s and 1970s, he was interested in the possibility of establishing a new visual form for the New Left.[38] He worked for the *Sunday Times Magazine* from 1965 to 1975, and alongside art editor Michael Rand, developed a signature visual aesthetic, at a time when even the colour supplement magazines were not particularly visually driven.[39] Through this, King discovered what became his life's work: a desire to recover visual alternatives to the Stalinist re-writing of history. During a 1970 research trip to the Soviet Union for a feature on the centenary of Vladimir Lenin's birth, he noticed the total absence of Leon Trotsky, and this led to an enduring project to search for visual evidence of those excluded from Stalinist narratives.[40] His research led to a 1971 cover story for the *Sunday Times Magazine*, entitled 'Trotsky: the Conscience of the Revolution', and the same year he co-authored a Penguin text on Trotsky that sold 25,000 copies.[41]

His interest in other Communist movements, including Chinese Communism, then, was related to this larger investigation of what went wrong in the Soviet Union and what other options might exist. King recalled, 'Suddenly in the late 1960s here, everybody was interested in Trotsky and one or two other figures, as major alternatives to Stalinism. There was a crisis, and people were looking for alternatives.'[42] For King, as with many on the left, Trotsky was a key figure, and while he never believed Maoism was going to be a model for cultural change in Britain, China remained a country worth observing because it seemed to be one of the few places attempting something different. The Cultural Revolution in particular was of interest, as it seemed to be the start of something genuinely new.[43]

Around the same time that King started collecting Soviet objects, he also started collecting Chinese ones. His first Chinese poster was a gift from photographer Donald McCullin, with whom King worked at the *Sunday Times*, and who rose to prominence for his coverage of the crisis in Biafra and the Vietnam War.[44] It was a poster entitled 'Long Live the Victory of the People's War' (人民战争胜利万岁 *renmin zhanzheng shengli wansui*) and depicted the triumvirate of worker, peasant and soldier, armed with guns, at the head of a large crowd of fighters, including ethnic minorities and women (see figure 4.4). Beneath the main image, there was a 1958 quotation from Mao denouncing imperialism.

Given the anti-Vietnam War and anti-imperialist feelings of the left, it is easy to see why such a poster would appeal to the young King. King owned around 200 posters, many of which he bought from bookshops in the 1960s and 1970s.[45] He also subscribed to Chinese periodicals and developed a collection of *China Pictorial* – the most visually driven Chinese export periodical – that included almost every issue from 1950 until the early 1980s. His interest in visual politics largely drove these acquisitions: he wondered how the aesthetic choices depicted in posters and periodicals might speak to the

Individual Collections

Figure 4.4 The first Chinese poster owned by David King, entitled 'Long Live the Victory of the People's War' (人民战争胜利万岁 *renmin zhanzheng shengli wansui*). *Source*: Photo © Tate.

politics of the era.[46] His interest in Chinese objects then was both ideological, as part of his search for alternative modernities and modalities to those available in the Soviet Union and the West, and visual, in his search for a new visual language for the left. For King, then, the specificity of China was less important than its role as an alternative to the Soviet Union and as a progressive force in the Cold War environment of the time.

The objects were clearly important to his personal life, and indeed his north London home was packed with objects: from the bookshelves of *China Pictorial* in the foyer, to the large framed Mao portrait on his staircase, there was a profusion of Soviet and Chinese material covering every surface.[47] These objects provided inspiration and content for his professional design work and research publications, but they were also the objects that surrounded him physically for much of his adult life.

King's objects fit the definition of a collection, as they gained value by virtue of their insertion into one or a number of overlapping series or sets (the left, socialism, Communist states, Chinese, Soviet etc.), but these were series with highly personal relevance for King. This highlights the reciprocal play of agency: these objects' identities were shaped by their insertion into the series or sets of values that define the collection, and in the collection their value was primarily relational. But they were also fundamental to

King's self-identity: they shaped him, his history, and his narrative of that history. His ownership re-contextualised the objects, but ownership of the objects also shaped him: we possess objects, but they also possess us. As Walter Benjamin wrote, 'ownership is the most intimate relationship that one can have to objects. Not that they come alive in him; it is he who lives in them'.[48]

In the early 2000s, King re-started collecting Cultural Revolution objects, concerned about both the destruction of many genuine objects and the widespread rise of fakes.[49] He purchased posters, sculptures and other objects from second-hand bookshops in Britain and the United States, such as London's Hanshan Tang books.[50] King also purchased objects from the auctions of Mao-era material that have occurred in the past ten years, primarily at the Bloomsbury Auction house. He was present at the 2009 auction that included objects from the Peter and Susan Wain collection, as well as at the 2012 sale, 'Red China, 1921–1976', where he acquired an early Mao badge and an early woodblock print portrait of Mao.[51]

He also visited China, where he acquired some 1,400 badges, along with substantial numbers of posters, journals and photographs.[52] These were acquired from the grown children of a couple who had been Red Guards during the Cultural Revolution. The children were looking to sell this collection as part of their effort to raise funds to purchase an apartment, which they were eventually able to do. King saw this purchase as an act of collecting for the future: he was collecting these objects as history, and as historical traces that might otherwise be lost. The family he bought them from, however, clearly saw them in a very different way: the family was poor, but they were able to capitalise on their remaining material resources from the Mao era in order to further their consumerist aspirations.

For King, then, one of the functions of his collection, and a function that became increasingly important in the 2000s, was as an archive. Indeed, given his dedication to recovering stories and images excluded by totalitarian narratives, his collection could perhaps be best understood as a 'counter-archive'. Charles Merewether describes the 'counter-archive' as 'a form of re-collection of that which has been silenced and buried.'[53] King's Soviet collection has long functioned in this way, as it has provided the basis out of which an alternative to the dominant narrative could emerge. Unlike his Soviet collection, King's Chinese collection remained largely silent: he did not publish on it or exhibit it, although other researchers have used his photographs.[54] His decision, however, to re-start building his Chinese collection in the 2000s suggests the same counter-archival impulse that long governed his Soviet collection. Large amounts of Cultural Revolution-era material was destroyed in China throughout the 1980s and 1990s, at least partly in conjunction with the dominant narrative that sees the period as the 'ten years of chaos'. Preserving the material then, was implicitly an argument that there were more complex narratives to be told about the era and the material culture it produced.

King developed his collection along very different routes from Paul Crook and Richard Kirkby. With the exception of his one trip to China, all of King's objects were purchased in the West. His collection emerged out of an interest in the Cultural Revolution that was, as other chapters have demonstrated, reasonably widespread in the West at the time. King was never aligned ideologically to China, but was interested in China as one of the only major countries attempting to put Marxist and socialist ideas into practice. Moreover, within the Cold War context, China's support for liberation movements around the world appealed to King's anti-colonial sympathies: indeed, he owned a number of anti-imperialist themed posters. Many of these were about international opposition to the Vietnam War, and often included English language text and images that would have been familiar to those on the left. He also owned posters that celebrated world unity: as a young Marxist, the visual depiction of the idea of the global Communist movement was enticing. In his later years, the development of the collection was inspired by more archival and historical motivations, out of the desire to preserve the traces of a movement often portrayed in totalising and wholly derogatory terms.

TAKING ADVANTAGE OF RISING INTEREST: PETER AND SUSAN WAIN

While King stated that he was never driven by financial motives, many others – both in China and in the West – have taken advantage of the growing interest in Mao-era objects, and their rising prices, to sell their collections. It seems likely that the rising prices and growing interest in such objects is mutually reinforcing. Mao badges, for example, started to reappear in Chinese markets in the late 1980s and early 1990s. In 1992, Wang Zhuangling wrote a short article that discussed the emerging market for badges and noted that they could fetch high prices overseas. The article was widely reproduced, and according to Bill Bishop, this further stimulated the market.[55] Bishop stated that by 1994, there were some 100,000 badge collectors in China, and over 2,000 who had acquired 10,000 badges or more.[56] Similarly, American collector and dealer Justin Schiller claimed that when he first visited mainland China in 1998, one could buy a first edition Little Red Book for a few hundred dollars, whereas prices now reach USD $10,000 for paper covers, with those in red vinyl worth double.[57]

Auctions have been a venue that some, like King, have used to develop their collections, and that others have used to monetise existing ones. Peter and Susan Wain are an example of collectors who successfully took advantage of the rising financial value of Mao-era objects. The Wains were Chinese antique specialists and Mao-era object collectors (with particular strengths in porcelain) who began their collection in the late 1960s and continued to collect after Mao's death. Peter Wain was a captain in the British army and served in Hong Kong as an education officer between 1968 and 1971.[58] Prior to this he had worked for Royal Doulton, the high-quality English porcelain company, and so was well placed to evaluate the contemporary Chinese porcelains on sale in Hong Kong in the Chinese-owned stores.[59] Wain purchased a number of high-quality porcelains at this time and continued to build up his collection of porcelains and other objects in subsequent years. He became a specialist on imperial-era Chinese and Japanese ceramics, involved in publishing and auctions.[60] This interest in porcelains of the highest quality was similarly visible in the Wain's Mao-era collection, which included many porcelains made at Jingdezhen, the famous site of the former imperial kilns.[61] The Wains continued to purchase objects during trips to China throughout the Reform Era, buying from markets, sometimes direct from factories, and wherever else they found interesting objects.

Until Peter's death in 2015, the Wains were some of Britain's better known private collectors of Mao objects due, in part, to a long relationship with the National Museum of Scotland (NMS), which held an exhibition of their collection in 2003–2004, and which acquired, with the help of the Art Fund, some 500 objects from the Wain collection in 2013, including posters, papercuts, paintings, magazines, Little Red Books, textiles, ceramics and glassware.[62] As the Wains aged, they donated and sold much of their collection to British museums, with the NMS purchasing the majority. However, they also took advantage of rising auction prices and sold a number of their objects at the 2009 Bloomsbury Auction House sale, entitled 'Mao and the Arts of New China, including the Collection of Peter and Susan Wain'.[63]

While international auction houses Christie's and Sotheby's have both included Mao-era objects in auctions from the early 2000s onwards, these have typically been single or small numbers of lots as parts of larger sales.[64] However, London's Bloomsbury Auctions has held a number of sales that focused extensively or even exclusively on Mao-era objects, with the first major sale coming in 2006, entitled 'Vintage Chinese Posters'.[65] The British Museum, British Library, V&A and the University of Westminster all had representatives at this sale and took advantage of the low prices of many lots. The 2009 Bloomsbury sale that featured the Wain collection got considerable press attention, described as the first Western auction devoted exclusively to Mao-era art.[66] Auction Central News stated that the sale was the largest group of Cultural Revolution artefacts ever to appear on the market anywhere in the world.[67] This sale was notable because it included more than just posters: there were also a number of high-quality porcelains, including some purchased by the NMS. Bloomsbury has periodically held other auctions since: Mao objects featured in a number of 2011 auctions and were the focus of sales in 2012 and 2013.[68] Throughout the period that Bloomsbury has been auctioning Mao-era objects in relatively large numbers, there has been a substantial increase in prices, particularly for certain types of objects, such as posters.

The increase in auction prices in Britain mirrors global trends, in particular in China, where collecting objects related to CCP history is now a well-developed field. As a result, prices both in China and elsewhere have risen, and while authentic badges are frequently still relatively cheap, many objects are now priced outside of some collectors' modest means. Rising prices have encouraged some collectors to sell, partially in an effort to monetise their collection, but also partially because they can no longer afford to continue to purchase new objects. In an interview in advance of the 2012 Bloomsbury sale, Rupert Powell, the deputy chairman of Bloomsbury Auctions, described the unnamed American vendor in precisely these terms. He stated that the collection had started quite casually some fifteen years ago, but had grown into an obsession for the vendor. However, as the market in China established itself, buying had become more difficult. Powell concluded, 'With collecting, the thrill of the chase is what drives you on and if you aren't buying anymore then it is time to sell'.[69] For others, ageing has been the impetus for donating or selling Mao-era objects, and a number of individuals who acquired objects in China in the 1960s and 1970s have already donated or sold their objects to museums, as seen with Richard Kirkby. As these individuals age, this process seems likely to continue.

INTERNET COLLECTIONS: CLINT TWIST

In recent years, a new market has emerged that is offering an alternative route for the transnational movement of Chinese objects: the internet. In Britain, an individual named Clint Twist has built up a collection of nearly 4,000 Mao badges using almost exclusively the internet.[70] Twist is an author and a habitual collector: throughout his life he has developed a number of collections based on what interested him aesthetically or intellectually, as well as what opportunities arose and what he could afford. As a child and teenager, he collected comic books, especially those from America. Living in London in the mid-1970s after university, he discovered Roman coins being sold on the Portobello Road in Notting Hill, and developed a collection. He stopped when he moved away from Notting Hill; the pleasure, for Twist, was always at least partially experiential: the pleasure of digging through an unsorted box of coins, trying to determine where and when each coin was from, whether they were real or fake, what they were worth.[71] It was the experience of getting to know different stall-holders, of developing a community of people with whom to share knowledge and objects. The pleasure, for Twist, was also related to knowledge acquisition, an underemphasised driver of private collecting. This educational element of collecting can work in different ways: for Richard Kirkby, acquiring and studying the *xiaorenshu* was a way of learning Chinese. For Twist, there was a less direct reason. Collecting particular objects gave him a focal point for research: he would purchase books and visit libraries in an effort to learn more about the historical and cultural context of the objects he owned. An aesthetic interest largely drove his acquisition habits, but this was then developed through the subsequent acquisition of knowledge. For Twist, therefore, the objects themselves contained embodied knowledge, but they also served as an entry point into new fields of enquiry. Twist's career was educationally focused; he worked in museums before taking up writing non-fiction books, often aimed at young people. He was interested, therefore, in knowledge acquisition and dissemination, and his collections have been a driver, as well as a way of structuring his research interests.

Twist's first purchase of Mao badges came in 2004 and was largely opportunistic. He had visited an antique store in Nottingham where he came across a bowl of Mao badges, on sale for one pound each. He found them aesthetically attractive, and so bought eight. As described in the book's Introduction, this was not his first encounter with Maoist material culture: he had got a Little Red Book from the Chinese Embassy in London in the late 1960s. Though too young to be actively involved in the social movements of the late 1960s, he had been interested in the British counterculture and had read underground magazines like *Oz* and *International Times* (*IT*). He read about the Cultural Revolution in these magazines and in the mainstream media, and while not really understanding much about it, had desired Mao's famous book, which he knew was available from the Chinese embassy. He did not, however, particularly search out information on China at this time.

When he saw the badges in 2004 then, he knew what they represented, and they had, for him, an instantaneous left-wing connotation, but they did not speak to a previous youthful interest in China in the way they would have for some others encountered in this book. Two things enabled Twist's chance encounter with the badges in the Nottingham antique store to turn into a true collection. The first was Twist's discovery of Helen Wang's *Chairman Mao badges: symbols and slogans of the Cultural Revolution* a few years later.[72] Twist had purchased the initial badges because they were cheap and attractive, but he lacked knowledge about the historical and cultural contexts in which they were important. Twist's discovery of Wang's book, a catalogue of the British Museum's Chairman Mao badge collection, provided the starting point for his exploration of Cultural Revolution cultural production, which, in turn, made him more interested in his existing badges (which, at that point, were just one of a number of collected things) and drove his desire to acquire more.

The second enabler has been the internet, and it seems unlikely that Twist would have been able to form a substantial collection of Mao badges without it. While antique and second-hand stores, as well as auctions, are sites for acquisitions, they remain a limited market. Instead, Twist has relied on the internet, which has enabled him to quickly and relatively cheaply develop a substantial collection. Melissa Schrift mentioned in her 2001 book that the internet was a new site for the buying and selling of Mao badges, and the market has expanded considerably since.[73] Sites like eBay carry, at any given time, numerous listings for Mao badges (often called pins), posters, stamps, Chinese clothing, porcelains, sculptures and wooden carvings; some are real, some are replicas (sometimes acknowledged, often not). They are sold by individuals as well as by dealers. Badges remain one of the most affordable Cultural Revolution objects on the market; there has been far greater appreciation in prices for stamps, posters and porcelains.[74]

Twist started purchasing badges over eBay in 2011 and has now built up a collection numbering almost 4,000, all of which, aside from the initial eight, have been purchased online. Many of these purchases have come from already formed collections: his most substantial purchase was of 800 badges, bought from an American who had resided in Hong Kong from 1974 to 1994. Because the badge market is not as well established as that of stamps or posters, there remains a wide variation of prices on sites like eBay. Badge dealers tend, unsurprisingly, to be well acquainted with the prices the market can bear. Individuals selling their own old badges or those of their family members, however, may be relatively ignorant of the relevant market prices, and so overestimate or underestimate the price likely to be achieved in auction. Twist purchased a set of ninety-five badges from a woman in London who had put them on eBay with a reserve price of only five pounds. Twist approached her privately to enquire about purchasing them directly, but she turned down his offer of ninety pounds, preferring to wait for the auction. Twist, however, made the only bid and so acquired them for only six pounds. Another time, Twist bought a single badge on eBay for the fixed price of two pounds ninety-five pence. The vendor, however, decided on reflection that it was not worth that much, and so sent Twist the badge, along with a pound coin!

Online websites like eBay can therefore be an efficient and cost-effective way to build up collections, even if it comes with difficulties in authentication. Purchasing online makes identifying fakes much more difficult, and Twist believes he has acquired some 200 fakes, on top of his authentic badges. These he displays in his home, stuck to the wall with blue tack, while his authentic items are carefully organised and stored in drawers. Fakes began to be produced in the early 1990s, at around the same time that interest in Maoist objects began to revive and prices started to rise.[75] American Bill Bishop collected around 3,000 badges while resident in China in the early 1990s, but he stopped purchasing them in 1993, because he felt that fakes were becoming too widespread.[76] Many Mao-era objects on sale today in Chinese markets are

104 Chapter 4

fakes, and the high quality of some fakes can make it difficult to tell the difference between the two. For many Western tourists, just looking for a souvenir of their time in China, a fake may well be sufficient, but for genuine collectors, fakes are a constant danger when it comes to new acquisitions.

Twist has an aesthetic interest in the badges, but he is also interested in them for what they can tell us about Cultural Revolution China, and for Twist their main value is as a counter-factual rejoinder to established narratives. Twist argued:

> I collect them because there is this contradiction—to use the Maoist terminology—between the uniformity of Chinese society, uniformity of thought, uniformity of dress, the Little Red book, and the incredible diversity [of badges]—and there's a message there—it says something about Chinese society. A creativity. Why do people want to make different ones? I'm sure the government would

Figure 4.5   A Chairman Mao badge (c.1968) in Clint Twist's collection, depicting the Hongqi CA770 saloon car. The text reads 'Revolutionary Committees Are Good' (革命委员会好 geming weiyuanhui hao). The badge is associated with the Jilin Standard Auto Parts Factory (吉林汽车标准件厂 Jilin qiche biaozhunjian chang). Source: The Clint Twist Collection.

Individual Collections 105

Figure 4.5 (Continued)

have been happier if there had just been one, and everyone wore the same thing. But they didn't, and it wasn't just Red Guard factionalism. [. . .] It's a subconscious manifestation of the refusal of the conformity that's being imposed from the top down. I think that's what makes them interesting: that they're ever so slightly subversive.[77]

For Twist, the diversity of badges can be seen as proof of the continued agency of Chinese individuals and groups, even during this period which is often interpreted in terms of authoritarian totalities (see figure 4.5).

As a private collector, Twist is interested in knowledge acquisition for his own purposes, but he is also interested in sharing this with the wider public. Retired, and so with extensive free time, he is keen to widen access to knowledge about badges and the main way he has done this so far has been to start a website and a Twitter feed in which he displays his own badges.[78] While there are obviously limited aesthetic options given the small size of the badges, Twist's website demonstrates the surprisingly rich and complex imagery badge makers drew on.

CONCLUSION

Collecting in Western academic literature has primarily been described as a private encounter, an intimate relationship between a person and their objects. It is of course this, and this chapter has encountered five different collectors, all of whom have engaged with China, and thus with their Chinese objects, in different ways. And yet, the focus on the private side of collecting should not distract from the public lives these objects have also had. Each of the collectors encountered in this chapter have displayed their objects publicly in some manner: Paul Crook's posters were used as part of the University of Westminster's exhibitions and featured on their websites; Richard Kirkby's posters have been displayed by the Ashmolean Museum; David King's photographs have been reprinted in books and his posters displayed by the Tate Modern; Peter and Susan Wains objects have been on both temporary and long-term display at the NMS, and finally Clint Twist's badges were displayed at the Grantham library, as described in the Book's introduction, and are seen online on his website and social media. In some cases, these public lives have taken place whilst the objects are still owned by the collectors, in others, it has taken place after being gifted or sold to a public institution. Nevertheless, it highlights that 'private' does not necessarily mean 'hidden'; individual ownership does not mean that that the object is completely removed from public view. Moreover, by contextualising the collection within the global movement of people and objects, this chapter has argued that even the most private relationships are still shaped by forces – political, economic and cultural – larger than the individual. It also highlights that entry into a personal collection is not necessarily the final stage of an object's lifecycle: many of the Cultural Revolution objects that were either exported to Britain or brought back from China by visitors eventually left private possession and entered public institutional collections.

NOTES

1. A good summary of this literature can be found in Russell Belk, 'Collectors and Collecting', in *Handbook of Material Culture*, ed. Christopher Y. Tilley et al. (London: SAGE, 2006), 534–45.
2. Jean Baudrillard, 'The System of Collecting', in *The Cultures of Collecting*, ed. John Elsner and Roger Cardinal (London: Reaktion, 1994), 24.
3. Walter Durost first advanced this view as early as 1932. Mieke Bal, 'Telling Objects: A Narrative Perspective on Collecting', in *The Cultures of Collecting*, ed. John Elsner and Roger Cardinal (London: Reaktion, 1994), 111.

4. There was considerable outrage in 2014 when collector Liu Yiqian drank tea out of his newly purchased Chenghua chicken cup, worth over $36million. The outrage was voiced in terms of the potential to damage the historical object, but we may wonder if it was also, at least in part, because it blurred the lines between the used and collected object.

5. Hannah Arendt, 'Introduction: Walter Benjamin: 1892-1940', in *Illuminations: Essays and Reflections*, ed. Walter Benjamin, trans. Harry Zohn (New York: Schocken Books, 2007), 42; Philipp Blom, *To Have and to Hold: An Intimate History of Collectors and Collecting* (London: Penguin, 2003), 164.

6. Belk, 'Collectors and Collecting', 540.

7. See, for example, Jacques Derrida, *Archive Fever: A Freudian Impression*, trans. Eric Prenowitz (Chicago; London: The University of Chicago Press, 1996); Werner Muensterberger, *Collecting: An Unruly Passion: Psychological Perspectives* (Princeton, NJ; Chichester: Princeton University Press, 1994); Jean Baudrillard, *The System of Objects* (London: Verso, 1996).

8. Arendt, 'Introduction: Walter Benjamin: 1892-1940', 43.

9. Kathlyn Maurean Liscomb, 'Social Status and Art Collecting: The Collections of Shen Zhou and Wang Zhen', *The Art Bulletin* 78, no. 1 (March 1996): 132.

10. Craig Clunas, *Superfluous Things: Material Culture and Social Status in Early Modern China* (Cambridge: Polity Press, 1991).

11. Scarlett Jang, 'The Culture of Art Collecting in Imperial China', in *A Companion to Chinese Art*, ed. Martin J Powers and Katherine R. Tsiang (Chichester: Wiley Blackwell, 2016), 52–53; Liscomb, 'Social Status and Art Collecting: The Collections of Shen Zhou and Wang Zhen'.

12. Jang, 'The Culture of Art Collecting in Imperial China'.

13. Zhang Liguo 章利国, 'S*houcang lilun xianzhuang he Zhongguo shoucangxue de yiyi ji yanjiu fanwei* 收藏理论现状和中国收藏学的意义及研究范围 [The present situation of collecting theory and the significance and research scope of Chinese collecting science]', *Rongbaozhai* 荣宝斋 08 (2010): 250.

14. Zhang Liguo 章利国, '*Wenhua Chuancheng Shoucang You Xue - Lue Shuo Shouna Gai Shoucang Xue* 文化传承收藏有学 - 略说收纳该国收藏学 [Cultural Heritage and Collection Study: A Brief View of Collection in China]', *Meishu* 美术 11 (2018): 107.

15. Zhang Liguo 章利国, 'Wenhua Chuancheng Shoucang You Xue [Cultural Heritage and Collection Study]', 107.

16. Peter Wain, 'Mao Zedong and Art', in *Mao: Art for the Masses: Revolutionary Art of the Mao Zedong Era, 1950-1976* (Edinburgh: National Museums of Scotland, 2003), 6.

17. On the Crooks, see David Crook and Isabel Crook, 'An Anglo-Canadian Couple's 30 Years in New China', in *Living in China: Twenty Authors from Abroad* (Beijing: New World Press, 1979), 40–62; Isabel Crook and David Crook, *Revolution in a Chinese Village, Ten Mile Inn* (London: Routledge & Kegan Paul, 1959); David Crook, 'Hampstead Heath to Tian An Men: The Autobiography of David Crook', 2014, http://davidcrook.net/simple/main.html (accessed 03/08/2020); Zhengling Li, Junwei Ning, and Israel Epstein, *David and Isabel Crook in China* (Beijing: Foreign Language Teaching and Research Press, 1995).

18. Crook, 'Hampstead Heath to Tian an Men', Chapter 12.

19. Anne-Marie Brady, *Making the Foreign Serve China: Managing Foreigners in the People's Republic* (Lanham, MD; Oxford: Rowman & Littlefield, 2003), 150.

20. Paul Crook, interview with author, 02/04/2013, London. The following description of Crook's purchasing activity comes from my interview with him.

21. For details of David Crook's experiences in confinement, see his autobiography. Crook, 'Hampstead Heath to Tian an Men'.

22. Defence Minister Lin Biao was a key Cultural Revolution leader and the designated successor of Mao Zedong. He died, however, in a plane crash in 1971 after an alleged coup attempt, in an event that was a great blow to the radical government leaders.

23. Karl Gerth argues that throughout the Mao years, and including the Cultural Revolution, government policies actually worked against the stated socialist goals and instead recreated and expanded capitalist practices and consumerism. Karl Gerth, *Unending Capitalism: How Consumerism Negated China's Communist Revolution* (Cambridge: Cambridge University Press, 2020).

24. Beverley Hooper, *Inside Peking: A Personal Report* (London: Macdonald and Jane's, 1979), 79.

25. Mao quoted in Melissa Schrift, *Biography of a Chairman Mao Badge: The Creation and Mass Consumption of a Personality Cult* (New Brunswick, NJ: Rutgers University Press, 2001), 72.

26. Richard Kirkby, *Intruder in Mao's Realm: A Foreigner in China during the Cultural Revolution* (Hong Kong: Earnshaw Books, 2016), 6–7.

27. Kirkby, *Intruder in Mao's Realm*, 8–9.

28. Richard Kirkby, 'Sex in Mao's China: How a Foreign Barbarian Blushed', South China Morning Post, 24 November 2016, https://www.scmp.com/magazines/post-magazine/long-reads/article/2048586/sex-maos-china-how-foreign-barbarian-blushed [accessed 03/08/2020].

29. Kirkby, *Intruder in Mao's Realm: A Foreigner in China during the Cultural Revolution* Foreword.

30. Kirkby, *Intruder in Mao's Realm*, 4.

31. Kirkby, *Intruder in Mao's Realm*, 5.

32. Richard Kirkby, interview with author, 01/12/2013, London.

33. Richard Kirkby, interview with author, 01/12/2013, London.

34. Kirkby, *Intruder in Mao's Realm*.

35. On the movement of objects abroad, see Alexander C. Cook, ed., *Mao's Little Red Book: A Global History* (Cambridge: Cambridge University Press, 2014).

36. In my interviews, as well more anecdotally, the Little Red Book was the most common object people mention having.

37. David King, interview with author. I spent a number of days at King's collection in July 2012 and December 2012–January 2013, during which I studied his objects, and interviewed King. King's Chinese and Soviet collection is now housed in the Tate Archive and Library, under reference number TGA 20172.

38. Christopher Wilson, 'Reputations: David King', *Eye*, Summer 2003, http://www.eyemagazine.com/feature/article/repuations-david-king [accessed 03/08/2020].
39. King quoted in Wilson.
40. David King, *Red Star Over Russia: A Visual History of the Soviet Union from the Revolution to the Death of Stalin* (New York: Abrams, 2009), 14. See also David King, *Russian Revolutionary Posters* (London: Tate Publishing, 2015); David King, *The Commissar Vanishes: The Falsification of Photographs and Art*, New Edition (London: Tate Publishing, 2014); David King, *Trotsky: A Photographic Biography* (Oxford; New York: Wiley-Blackwell, 1986).
41. James Woudhuysen, 'David King: Graphic Designer, Ranged Left', *Blueprint* 2, no. 11 (1984): 34–38.
42. David Walsh, 'Uncovering the Truth about Trotsky and the Russian Revolution "Continues to Run My Life": A Conversation with the Remarkable David King', *World Socialist Web Site*, 4 December 2008, http://www.wsws.org/en/articles/2008/12/king-d04.html [accessed 03/08/2020].
43. David King, personal communication, 15/04/2015.
44. David King, interview with author, 18/07/2012, London.
45. David King, interview with author 17/07/2012.
46. King, personal communication, 15/04/2015.
47. For a glimpse inside King's home, see this photo essay from Tate. 'Inside the Home of Collector David King – Picture Essay', *Tate* [accessed 2/062020], https://www.tate.org.uk/whats-on/tate-modern/exhibition/red-star-over-russia/inside-home-collector-david-king [accessed 03/08/2020].
48. Walter Benjamin, 'Unpacking My Library: A Talk about Book Collecting', in *Illuminations: Essays and Reflections*, trans. Harry Zohn (New York: Schocken Books, 2007), 67.
49. King, personal communication, 15/04/2015.
50. King, personal communication, 15/04/2015.
51. King interview with author, 12/12/2012. Bloomsbury Auctions, *Red China: 1921-1976* (London: Bloomsbury Auctions, 2012).
52. King, personal communication, 15/04/2015.
53. Charles Merewether, 'Introduction: Art and the Archive', in *The Archive*, ed. Charles Merewether (London: Whitechapel, 2006), 16.
54. Delia Davin's biography of Mao, for example, used photographs from the David King Collection. Delia Davin, *Mao Zedong* (Stroud: Sutton, 1997).
55. Bill Bishop, 'Badges of Chairman Mao Zedong', 1996, http://museums.cnd.org/CR/old/maobadge/ [accessed 03/08/2020].
56. Bishop, 'Badges of Chairman Mao Zedong'.
57. Justin G. Schiller, '1964: The Little Red Book', *The New Antiquarian*, 30 October 2014, http://www.abaa.org/blog/post/1964-the-little-red-book [accessed 03/08/2020].
58. Colin Gleadell, 'Sale of Revolutionary Chinese Art at Bloomsbury Auctions', *The Telegraph*, 27 October 2009, http://www.telegraph.co.uk/culture/art/artsales/6447181/Sale-of-revolutionary-Chinese-art-at-Bloomsbury-Auctions.html [accessed 03/08/2020].

110   *Chapter 4*

59. Gleadell, 'Sale of Revolutionary Chinese Art at Bloomsbury Auctions'.

60. Peter Wain, *Miller's Chinese & Japanese Antiques Buyer's Guide* (Tenterden: Miller's, 1999), 6.

61. See the catalogue for the 2003–2004 exhibition for more details. Peter Wain, *Mao: Art for the Masses: Revolutionary Art of the Mao Zedong Era, 1950-1976* (Edinburgh: National Museums of Scotland, 2003).

62. 'The Art Fund in 2013/14: Annual Report' (London, UK: The Art Fund, 2013), 63, https://www.artfund.org/assets/about-us/annual-report/art-fund-review-digital-double-2013.pdf.

63. Bloomsbury Auctions, *Mao and the Arts of New China, Including the Collection of Peter and Susan Wain* (London: Bloomsbury Auctions, 2009).

64. Mao-era stamps had featured in Christie's Hong Kong sales in the 1990s; the first Mao-era objects in auctions in the West did not appear until the early 2000s, and in larger numbers from 2006. Original or early editions of Little Red Books were the most common objects, although from around 2006, more diversity appeared, including porcelain, textiles, documents including letters, and posters.

65. Bloomsbury Auctions, *Vintage Chinese Posters* (London: Bloomsbury Auctions, 2006).

66. Gleadell, 'Sale of Revolutionary Chinese Art at Bloomsbury Auctions'.

67. anon, 'Mao-Velous Chinese Propaganda Art at Bloomsbury's London, Nov. 5', Auction Central News, 3 November 2009, https://www.liveauctioneers.com/news/auctions/upcoming-auctions/mao-velous-chinese-propaganda-at-bloomsburys-nov-5/ [accessed 03/08/2020]. It is worth noting that this is likely not true. There are large and frequent auctions of these objects in China.

68. Bloomsbury Auctions, *Asia: Books, Prints & Posters* (London: Bloomsbury Auctions, 2011); Bloomsbury Auctions, *Red China: 1921-1976*; Bloomsbury Auctions, *Chinese Propaganda Posters* (London: Bloomsbury Auctions, 2013).

69. Powell quoted in Emily Allen, 'Great Haul of China: Collector Auctions £1m Haul of Artefacts from Chairman Mao's Regime Snapped up over a 15-Year Period', Mail Online, 27 September 2012, http://www.dailymail.co.uk/news/article-2209351/Great-haul-China-Collector-auctions-1m-haul-artefacts-Chairman-Mao-s-regime-snapped-15-year-period.html [accessed 03/08/2020].

70. Clint Twist, interview with author, 15/04/2015, Grantham. All information about Twist comes from author's personal communication with him, in person (December 2014) and over email (April 2015 & September 2015) and Twitter, and from his talk to the China-Britain Youth Association, entitled 'Mao Badges: Art, symbolism and Collection of Chairman Mao memorabilia from the Cultural Revolution to the present-day'. (24 November 2015), text provided by Twist.

71. Clint Twist, interview with author, 03/12/2014, Grantham.

72. Helen Wang, *Chairman Mao Badges: Symbols and Slogans of the Cultural Revolution* (London: British Museum Press, 2008).

73. Schrift, *Biography of a Chairman Mao Badge*, 190. In China, there is a large online market for the trading of Communist objects, including social media sites such as WeChat and auction sites such as Confucius Old Books Net (孔夫子旧书网 *kongfuzi jiushu wang*) and 7788 Collection (7788 收藏 7788 *shoucang*).

74. He Zhenggu 何政谷, '*Tan Hongse Shoucangpin Zhong Ciji de Meili* 谈红色收藏品中瓷器的魅力 [On the Charm of Porcelain Red Collectibles]', *Wenwu Jianding Yu Jianshang* 文物鉴定与鉴赏 10 (2011): 34–35; Laurie Chen, 'Beijing Red Letter Day: Rare Stamp from Cultural Revolution Era Sells for $2 Million at Auction', *South China Morning Post*, 23 November 2018, https://www.scmp.com/news/china/society/article/2174725/beijing-red-letter-day-rare-stamp-cultural-revolution-era-sells-2.
75. Bishop, 'Badges of Chairman Mao Zedong'.
76. Bishop, 'Badges of Chairman Mao Zedong'.
77. Twist, interview with author, 03/12/2014, Grantham.
78. See www.maozhang.net and on Twitter: @maobadge

Chapter 5

Public Collections

Collection and Display of Cultural Revolution Objects in British Public Institutions

BRITISH COLLECTIONS IN A COMPARATIVE CONTEXT

Britain is unusual amongst other Western nations in having several public museums with collections of Mao-era political art and artefacts. A number of British public museums have developed substantial collections of Mao-era and Cultural Revolution objects, but this has not been the case in most countries. In the United States, for example, there are a number of privately owned collections of Maoist material, as well as some collections held by universities, and material held in archives.[1] But the Smithsonian Institution's two museums of Asian art (the Freer Gallery of Art and the Arthur M. Sackler Gallery), while owning some twentieth-century paintings, calligraphy and seals, do not own the sort of politically influenced art under discussion in this book in any substantial number.[2] Similarly, while San Francisco's Asian Art Museum has a collection of modern ink paintings, very few of them date from the Cultural Revolution decade, and even fewer are representative of or even acknowledge the political context of that era in any way.[3]

The same is true in much of the Western world.[4] When objects that date chronologically from the Mao era appear in collections of Chinese art they tend to be objects demonstrative of the literati tradition, and largely exclude the sort of political content that most of the objects included in this book contain. Given, then, how unusual these British collections are, it is worth considering the process by which more political and often mass-produced Mao-era and Cultural Revolution objects have been collected and displayed by British public institutions.

114   *Chapter 5*

This chapter focuses on the British Museum, the Victoria & Albert (V&A) Museum, the Ashmolean Museum, the National Museum of Scotland (NMS) and the University of Westminster, but a number of other British institutions have also developed small collections of Mao-era objects in recent years.⁵ The British Library in London has a collection of around 125 Chinese posters, acquired in 2006–2008 and 2015, primarily from Hanshan Tang books in London.⁶ Chinese revolutionary model opera posters were displayed as part of the Library's 2013 exhibition 'Propaganda: Power and Persuasion', where they were reportedly very positively received.⁷ The London-based Muban Foundation was established by Christer von der Berg and Verena Bolinder-Müller in 1997 in order to collect Chinese woodblock prints and other printed material, out of concern for the gradual decline of woodblock printmaking in China.⁸ It has held a number of exhibitions of its collection in locations around the United Kingdom, and while it is perhaps best known for its collection of post-Mao era prints, it also includes many from the Mao-era and the preceding revolutionary era.⁹ The Oriental Museum in Durham has, under curator Craig Barclay, built a small collection that includes Mao-era posters, papercuts, printed cards and other ephemera.¹⁰ While they have not displayed any of their own objects, the museum did host the University of Westminster's exhibition 'The Political Body: Posters from the People's Republic of China in the 1960s and 1970s' in 2004 and hosted a Muban exhibition on twentieth-century woodblock prints in 2021. A few other museums also have small numbers of objects: the Horniman Museum in London has what they describe as a Red Guard headband with Uighur and Mandarin script, which was collected by curator Ken Teague in Xinjiang province in 2000, as well as some 1970s papercuts depicting ancient Chinese architecture.¹¹ The Museum of East Asian Art in Bath has a single Mao-era object. It is described as an ivory sculpture of a group of Red Guards with a howitzer, fording a stream, and has been on display. The museum's founder Brian McElney acquired the object in Hong Kong in the 1980s and donated it to the museum in 1996.¹² A number of museums have, therefore, acquired a few objects in recent years, but Mao-era objects continue to be relatively rare in British museums, even those with substantial Chinese collections.

While many Cultural Revolution objects have been acquired by British institutions, until recently, very few have been on long-term display. When research for this book first began in 2011, it was rare to see Mao-era objects on long-term (or even short-term) display at British public institutions, despite the existence of these objects within the museum's collections. This general paucity of Mao-era material on permanent display in British museums means that this chapter must start by acknowledging that the most basic answer to the question of how British museums have represented Maoist China is to note that they have not. The image constructed of China in these and other museums with Chinese collections until very recently and in many places still continues to be overwhelmingly that of an imperial China. And yet, Mao-era collections have emerged at a number of Britain's most august public institutions and they are increasingly on display. Looking at the different institutions' collections and displays demonstrates the different narratives that can and have started to emerge. Moreover, this chapter argues while these objects represent China, they can also be interpreted as representing the legacy of British engagements with Mao's China, as many of the objects in British public institutional collections were originally owned by British individuals who lived in or visited China during the Cultural Revolution. Highlighting these personal histories contributes to this book's larger argument, which is that engagement with material and visual culture can be seen as an important facet of British engagement with the Cultural Revolution, and these contemporary museum collections serve as both a legacy and continuation of these engagements.

THE BRITISH MUSEUM AND THE V&A: COLLECTING THE TWENTIETH CENTURY

Excluding the Contemporary

While institutions like the British Museum are typically associated with historical objects, many of these now historical objects were contemporary when they were first collected. Curator Anne Farrer noted that the Hans Sloane collection, which laid the foundations for the British Museum after Sloane's 1753 death, was made up primarily of contemporary or recently produced objects that only became historical objects retrospectively.[13] Throughout the nineteenth century, the British Museum collected both historical and contemporary objects, but gradually, a historical preference came to take hold.

The establishment of what became the V&A, following the Great Exhibition of 1851, was initially a response to concerns that mechanisation was diminishing British industrial design.[14] It had, therefore, primarily educational aims concerning contemporary art and design; for founder Henry Cole, as Anthony Burton has written, 'the museum was not a repository for historic relics, but a way of changing people's taste.'[15] And yet, despite this, an antiquarian interest very quickly set in, and by the time Sir Cecil Harcourt Smith became V&A director in 1909, it was, as Smith discovered, a general rule not to acquire anything less than fifty years old.[16] And yet, due to the existence of the V&A, many at the British Museum felt that they could focus solely on the historical.[17]

Throughout much of the twentieth century, both museums predominantly focused on historical acquisitions. This trend was reinforced by what Frances Carey has called 'an inherent conservatism which came to equate modernism with the ephemeral fashions of a dubious avant-garde in Europe and the adulteration and decline of indigenous cultures the world over.'[18] Carey argues that the Westernising influences visible on many different cultures' twentieth-century objects have left curators in many European museums wary of incorporating them within the temporal span of the geographic region in question. In doing so, these museums often seek 'to impose an artificial standard of "authenticity" on their [non-European cultures'] material culture which denies them the right of change and assimilation.'[19]

In the case of Chinese objects, both the British Museum and the V&A benefited from the development of Chinese ceramics as a field of study and collection in the early twentieth century.[20] Tastes changed over time, but what remained through the first half of the twentieth century was what art historian Stacey Pierson has called the 'imperial fetish' amongst collectors of Chinese art and ceramics in Britain, which embodied the twentieth-century ideal of a disappeared imperial and 'traditional' China.[21] The combination of the reigning taste in imperial objects, both museums' general suspicion of the contemporary, a political and aesthetic apathy towards the Communist regime and an awareness of the political sensitivity of the period meant that they almost entirely restricted their Chinese collections to the imperial period for most of the twentieth century.

Collecting the Twentieth Century at the British Museum

This began to change in the late 1970s and early 1980s. David Wilson became the director of the British Museum in 1977, and he placed great emphasis on the collection of twentieth-century material.[22] In what was then the Department of Oriental Antiquities, this initially resulted primarily in the acquisition of pre-1949 and post-1978 prints. The former were often acquired from diplomats who had been based in China before 1949.[23] The latter were primarily acquired by curator Anne Farrer, who purchased contemporary woodcut prints made at Chinese academies in the late 1980s and 1990s.[24] This built on the museum's pre-existing collection of Chinese prints, and while the British Museum now has a substantial collection of twentieth-century Chinese prints and paintings, relatively few are from the Mao era, and most are not explicitly political. Indeed, curator Mary Ginsberg has argued that 'A specific objective when collecting twentieth-century paintings was to find works showing cultural continuity or innovation within the existing traditions of literati or *xieyi* painting. In other words, not political painting—not propaganda.'[25] While paintings and posters demonstrative of cultural continuities did continue to be produced in the Mao era, they were more common before and after, and this, combined with Anne Farrer's interest in contemporary printmaking, meant that politicised Mao-era works were not a priority.

However, Mao-era objects have still entered the collection, initially primarily through donations and more recently through targeted acquisitions. Employees of the museum or other British institutions have been frequent contributors, as have former diplomats and scholars. In the 1990s, curator Dame Jessica Rawson donated a number of Mao-era and Reform-era posters, while Shelagh Vainker, a British Museum and later Ashmolean Museum curator, donated a Mao bust and a porcelain plaque of Mao and Lin Biao.[26] Gordon Barrass, who worked at the British consulate in Beijing from 1970 to 1972, donated twenty-seven posters from the Cultural Revolution in 2002, alongside his collection of nineteenth- and twentieth-century calligraphy, some of which dated from the Mao era.[27] In 2005, Andrew Bolton, a V&A and later Metropolitan Museum of Art curator donated 1990s Mao memorabilia as well as genuine Mao-era objects: a papercut, a poster and a number of porcelain sculptures (see figure 5.1).[28] In 2013, American collector and scholar Alfreda Murck donated her collection of 373 twentieth-century teapots, including many from the Mao era.[29]

Figure 5.1 Papercut of the five key Marxists: Karl Marx, Frederick Engels, Vladimir Lenin, Joseph Stalin and Mao Zedong, donated to the British Museum by Andrew Bolton. *Source*: © The Trustees of the British Museum.

Important purchases include a series of ration coupons purchased in 1993 from dealer Colin Narbeth in 1993, seventy-four Mao-era posters purchased from a 2006 Bloomsbury Auction sale, as well as a 1965 National Day Celebration Scroll, acquired in 2017 from Hanshan Tang books.[30]

Just as acquisitions in the Asia Department have largely come from donations, the same is also true in the Department of Coins and Medals, which has Britain's only substantial public collection of Mao badges. The first two badges entered the collection in 1978, as a gift from J. Carr. Throughout the 1980s and early 1990s, donations came from staff members such as Jessica Rawson and Coins and Medals Curator Joe Cribb.[31] Other donations were external, such as from academic Christopher Dyer, who had been gifted the badges by a Chinese student in the mid-1980s, who knew that Dyer had a copy of the Little Red Book and was interested in the Cultural Revolution.[32] After Helen Wang, a curator in the Department of Coins and Medals, wrote an article in which she mentioned the British Museum's collection of just over 100 badges, Sheng Guanxi, a Chinese academic and numismatist, offered Wang around 200 duplicates from his private collection.[33] Other donations came from individuals who were students or teachers in China in the 1960s–1980s: Penny Brooke, a student in China in the 1970s and later Great Britain-China Centre deputy director; Michael Rank, a student in China in the mid-1970s and later a journalist; and Christina Mungan, an English teacher in Hangzhou in the 1980s.[34] More recently, curator Mary Ginsberg has donated a number of Chinese military medals from the 1950s that she acquired in Bishkek, Kyrgyzstan.[35]

Therefore, while museum policy from the early 1980s encouraged the acquisition of twentieth-century art, this has only recently led to the incorporation of Mao-era or the Cultural Revolution objects in substantial numbers. These acquisitions did not, until very recently then, reflect any specific appreciation of Cultural Revolution material culture, but rather, as Ginsberg has noted, 'although political art was not specifically sought, it naturally features large in the output of countries whose cultural policy has specifically promoted propaganda'.[36]

COLLECTING THE TWENTIETH CENTURY AT THE V&A

Just as the British Museum adopted a policy of twentieth-century collecting in the late 1970s and early 1980s, so too did the V&A. Roy Strong, the youngest V&A director upon his appointment in 1974, felt that the V&A risked losing relevance if it ignored the more recent past, commenting in a 1974 letter: 'I want to get the twentieth century into that place and make it alive and a comment on our times.'³⁷ In the early 1980s, the Far Eastern Department had three young curators (Craig Clunas, Rose Kerr and Verity Wilson), all of whom had studied in China in the 1970s, and who shared a commitment to twentieth-century collecting.³⁸ This marked a substantial change from before: Rose Kerr recalled that when she joined the department in 1978, nothing from the Mao era was collected, or even considered.³⁹

A 1995 article by Verity Wilson reflected the substantial change in attitudes in the department, as she commented that a 1966 porcelain dish depicting Cai Yongxiang saving a train (see figure 5.2 for a similar object, made of lacquer) was 'as central in its way to the V&A's wider purposes as are the more obviously "important" objects.'⁴⁰ And yet she also noted the difficulties of collecting this sort of material, due to 'the relative dearth of scholarship on twentieth century Chinese design and the practical difficulties which until very recently inhibited collecting in China itself.'⁴¹ While purchasing trips were made to China in the 1980s, the acquisitions were almost all contemporary objects. With the Cultural

Figure 5.2 A lacquer dish depicting Cai Yongxiang saving a train, similar to the porcelain dish described by Verity Wilson, in the V&A Museum Collection. *Source*: © Victoria and Albert Museum, London.

Revolution just recently finished, it represented a still very raw memory for many people, and in any case Kerr recalled that there were few Mao-era objects available for sale in mainland China in the early-to-mid-1980s.[42]

Some of the earliest Mao-era acquisitions came from Hong Kong porcelain collector Simon Kwan (see figure 5.3). Kwan felt that the time had not yet come to evaluate the history of the Mao era, but that modern ceramics were desperately underappreciated, writing:

> In twenty or thirty years time museums all over the world will realise that there is a big time gap in their collection of Chinese ceramics. Most people believe that the heritage of Chinese ceramics is dead after [Qing dynasty Emperor] Qianlong. But it is not so.[43]

In 1989–1990, Kwan donated part of his collection of twentieth-century (including Mao-era) ceramics to the V&A, explaining 'I understand that the Victoria & Albert Museum is the only museum interested in this field.'[44]

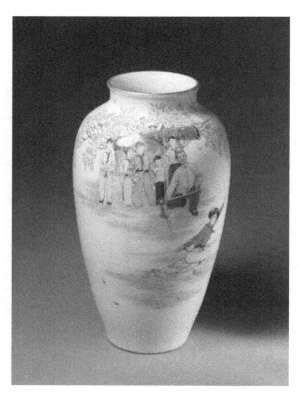

Figure 5.3   A porcelain vase painted in overglaze enamels and gilt, made in Jingdezhen (c.1975–1979). Donated by Simon Kwan to the V&A Museum. *Source*: © Victoria and Albert Museum, London.

The collection developed further in the 1990s, both through purchases and donations, and many of the acquisitions came from individuals who also contributed to other museums. Gordon Barrass, better known for his sale and donations of calligraphy to the British Museum, donated Mao-era textiles to the V&A; Peter Wain, best known for his relationship with the NMS, donated textiles and a ceramic.[45] Andrew Bolton, mentioned in the context of his British Museum donations, contributed substantially to the V&A's collection. Bolton visited China in 1997 in order to gather material related to Britain's handover of Hong Kong to China; while there, he also acquired a number of badges.[46] He later donated a number of objects, including an alarm clock from the late 1960s, and a porcelain set from 1972 depicting children playing tennis.

Many of the donations made since 2000 have come from people with personal experience of Mao's China, including museum professionals. Curator Rose Kerr, who retired in 2003, donated a number of badges from her time in China in the 1970s, and Beth McKillop, who joined the V&A from the British Library in 2004, and who was also a student in China in the mid-1970s, donated a number of posters in 2009 and 2010, while her husband Andy donated a Mao suit.[47]

While former students from 1970s China and museum curators have provided many donations, other examples, such as those of Dr Anthony Reynolds and Lady Anne Heseltine, can demonstrate the broader legacies of British engagements with revolutionary and Mao-era China at the V&A. In 2001, Dr. Anthony Reynolds donated twelve posters that his wife had acquired in China in 1974.[48] From 1941 until 1952, Reynolds was part of the Friends Ambulance Unit (FAU), a volunteer ambulance unit staffed primarily by conscientious objectors who wanted to contribute to the war effort in a peaceful capacity. The FAU was involved in the 'China Convoy', which helped move supplies from Burma to China; it also helped with reconstruction efforts after the Japanese surrender in 1945.[49] Members of the FAU China Convoy have made periodic trips back to China, including in 1974. The group visited Yan'an – an important site for the Communist Revolution, but also for the FAU, as they had broken across the Guomindang (Nationalist Party) blockade to take supplies to the city during the war – and it was here that Johanne, Reynold's wife, who had herself worked for the Quaker Service Council in Chengdu from 1940 to 1946, acquired the posters that were later gifted to the V&A.[50] The Reynolds donation, therefore, is a testament to a prior British engagement with China, which was born out of sympathy for the plight of the Chinese as British allies in the Second World War.

In 2008, Lady Anne Heseltine donated nine posters that she had acquired in Beijing in 1973 (see figure 5.4).[51] Heseltine has long been involved with numerous British cultural institutions. She is also the spouse of Conservative

Figure 5.4 A 1971 poster, donated by Lady Anne Heseltine to the V&A Museum. The slogan reads, 'Be always prepared to wipe out the invading enemies' (常备不懈务歼入侵之敌 *Chang bei buxie jian ruqin zhi di*). *Source*: © Victoria and Albert Museum, London.

politician and businessman Lord Michael Heseltine. Britain and China had agreed to full diplomatic relations in 1972, and this led to a flurry of official visits and delegations, particularly from the Department of Trade and Industry.[52] Heseltine, in his role as Minister for Aerospace and Shipping, joined one such delegation in March 1973.[53] The posters were likely acquired on the afternoon of 27 March, which was set aside as time for the wives of the delegates to go shopping.[54] These posters, then, speak to a period in which government interest in China was increasing, in large part because of fears that Britain might fall behind other Western nations in the rush to take advantage of what was seen as China's untapped market.[55] Taking the Reynolds and Heseltine donations together demonstrates some of the very different routes through which objects have come to their shared end point in a national collection, as well as the diversity of engagements with China.

The V&A representatives were at the aforementioned 2006 Bloomsbury Auction, but only acquired a small number of posters. Rather, like the British Museum, much of the V&A's collection of Cultural Revolution material has resulted from donations. Instead, a major priority for its Asia Department has been to collect representatives of contemporary art and design, as seen in their 2008 exhibition 'China Design Now'.[56]

In summary, for much of the twentieth century, Britain's two most important public collections of Chinese objects almost entirely excluded post-imperial China from their collections. Since the 1980s, both the British Museum and the V&A have collected Mao-era objects as part of broader policies to incorporate the twentieth century into their already established Chinese collections. This did not represent a specific appreciation of Mao-era visual culture, but was rather part of a larger attempt to bring the collections up to date. Within this, however, as Rose Kerr has noted, 'Cultural Revolution items were self-evidently significant' as the representatives of one of the most unique periods in China's recent history.[57] As tracing the development of the collections has shown, there is often overlap in the individuals who have contributed to collections of numerous museums, and these individuals represent many of the diverse strands of engagement with Mao-era and Cultural Revolution China discussed elsewhere in this book.

Displaying the Mao Era: The British Museum and V&A

At both the British Museum and V&A, the absence of the Mao era in displays can be at least partly explained by the time period in which the permanent galleries were established: both the T.T. Tsui Gallery at the V&A and the Joseph Hotung Gallery at the British Museum were opened in the early 1990s, when the twentieth-century collections were still in their infancy. However, while the British Museum did not put post-imperial objects on permanent display until 2017, the V&A was much more proactive early on about rotating the objects on display and incorporating the twentieth century, including Mao-era objects, into the main China gallery (the T.T. Tsui Gallery), the Twentieth Century Design Gallery and the Ceramics Study Gallery. At the British Museum, the 2017 re-design of the Joseph Hotung Gallery aimed to bring the story of China up to the present. Curator Jessica Harrison-Hall commented on the necessity of this, stating 'China is a living culture . . . It's not some ancient culture. It's alive and it's here today, and it's an incredibly creative place. How could we do a new gallery about China without bringing it right up to the present day?'[58] The new gallery includes a twentieth century case that features objects on a six-month rotating display, including Mao-era objects. This indicates that the British Museum is moving towards a more encompassing and modern understanding of 'China', and one that does not just skip over the Mao era, as many other museums have done.

While the British Museum and V&A both now have Mao-era objects on long-term display, it remains true that institutions also carry their own histories with them, and this drives both acquisitions and the presentation of objects in exhibitions. The difference between the V&A as a design museum and the British Museum as a history museum is exemplified perhaps by how the V&A's 1999 exhibition 'Mao: From Icon to Irony' and the British Museum's 2008 'Icons of Revolution: Mao badges then and now' differed.

The V&A exhibition considered the different ways in which Mao's image had been used over time and spanned the 1940s until the 1990s. The exhibition included examples of contemporary art and fashion which drew on the Mao image, capturing, as the title suggests, the Chairman's transition from icon to image ripe for ironical re-appropriation. The exhibition, then, was less about Mao as a historical figure, and more about what the different visual depictions of Mao have represented in a changing China. The 'Icons of Revolution' exhibition at the British Museum, by contrast, focused primarily on the Mao era itself (and the preceding decades), investigating the emergence of the Mao badge as a material form in a specific political context.[59] It did mention the post-Mao revivals of Maoist imagery, but only peripherally. That the two museums deal differently with similar objects and similar themes, in these examples, the idea of 'icon', is not surprising, as it is a reflection of the different orientations of the institutions. However, it suggests that it is productive for different institutions in Britain to have collections of Mao-era objects because this enables different narratives to emerge from them.

The V&A has more frequently put Mao-era objects on long-term display, but has only held one temporary exhibition that showcased them.[60] The British Museum has, in recent years, more frequently included Mao-era objects in its temporary exhibitions, such as in the 2010 exhibition 'The Printed Image in China: from the 8th to the 21st centuries', which situated the Mao era as part of the broader sweep of Chinese print history.[61] More notable was the 2013 exhibition 'The Art of Influence: Asian propaganda', which looked at Chinese materials within both the geographical context of Asia (primarily China, Japan, North Korea, Vietnam, and India) and through the concept of 'propaganda'. The exhibition's introductory panel acknowledged the pejorative meaning of the term propaganda in English, but argued that it should not be reduced to just 'sinister manipulation'.[62] The catalogue, by curator Mary Ginsberg, argued instead that 'the main goal of propaganda—and propaganda art—is to create involvement. [. . .] Propaganda aims to inspire action and belief in a common cause'.[63] The exhibition argued that propaganda has played a significant role in wars and nation-building, and therefore deserved to be studied and displayed, despite the role governments and other political actors played in its creation. The exhibition chose works that demonstrated the artistic diversity of propaganda, as well as foregrounding the cultural and artistic continuities that helped make these works palatable to their audiences. A 1969 Mao badge, for example, used both traditional Chinese symbolism (plum blossoms, which symbolise resilience and perseverance) and Communist symbolism (the important revolutionary sites Jinggang Mountains, Yan'an and Tian'anmen) (see figure 5.5).

The decision to collect Mao-era objects was primarily about temporal expansion of what was considered 'China' and much of its display has

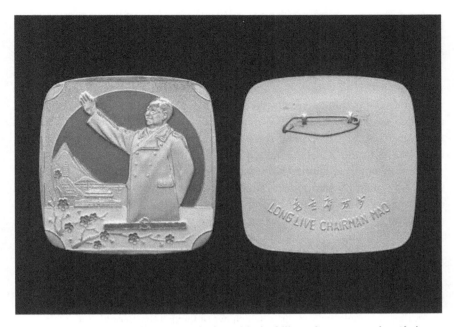

Figure 5.5 A c.1969 Chairman Mao badge with the bilingual text 'Long Live Chairman Mao' (毛主席万岁, *Mao Zhuxi Wansui*) on the reverse in Lin Biao's calligraphy. Donated by Simmons and Simmons to the British Museum. *Source*: © The Trustees of the British Museum.

similarly placed Mao-era objects within a longer timespan: this is a reminder that while many may think of blue and white Ming porcelain when they think of Chinese art, all artistic traditions are fluid and changing, and the political objects from the Mao era speak as much to China's history as any other object.

COLLECTING AFTER 2000: THE ASHMOLEAN MUSEUM AND THE NATIONAL MUSEUM OF SCOTLAND

Expanding into New Mediums: The Ashmolean's Mao-Era Collection

Unlike the British Museum and the V&A, the Ashmolean has long collected twentieth-century Chinese objects, but, until recently, this has been almost exclusively ink paintings. Since the late 1950s, the Ashmolean has focused on acquiring modern, often contemporary, works in the literati tradition, typically landscapes of ink and colour on paper.[64] This was chosen as the focus of the collection because of difficulties of 'authentication, expense and availability associated with early paintings'.[65] Much of the early collection was purchased from commercial establishments such as Collet's Chinese Gallery and featured works by Chinese artists working in Hong Kong, Taiwan, Singapore and the diaspora, as well as mainland China, although the availability of works from the mainland decreased after 1966.[66] The museum's collection of modern ink paintings has been added to by a number of large donations: the Jose Mauricio and Angelita Trinidad Reyes collection numbers over 500 items, and the Michael and Khoan Sullivan collection of over 400 paintings was bequeathed in 2013.[67]

The non-political nature of the works collected appears to be both a question of availability and a conscious decision by early curators. Ashmolean curator Peter Swann wrote the introduction for the catalogue of a 1964 exhibition of contemporary *guohua* paintings at Collet's Chinese Gallery, in which he described the state of contemporary Chinese art:

> Contemporary Chinese painting is following two broad and seemingly mutually exclusive lines. One is inspired by western art styles and materials and as yet has produced little to recommend it. The other is along the traditional lines using familiar materials in a manner which we immediately recognise as Chinese painting. This trend shows vitality, flashes of originality and gives proof of a living force in Chinese painting. It receives encouragement from official circles and seems relatively free from the demands of propaganda.[68]

Swann, therefore, largely wrote off the developments in Chinese oil painting and works done in a socialist realist style ('western art styles and materials'), but celebrated some of the works done in a traditional style and without political content ('free from the demands of propaganda'). Swann's preference for ink painting meant that art in other styles were almost entirely excluded from the Ashmolean's collection, and indeed, the majority of works that were acquired lacked any visible political content. The overall image of 'Chinese painting' that the Ashmolean collection constructed, then, was one that continued along the traditional lines of literati painting, in the sense of both form and content.

That the museum's focus on modern ink paintings necessitated excluding much of the broader category of Chinese art was implicitly acknowledged with the 2006 decision to widen the range of the modern collection to include the graphic arts.[69] In 2006 and 2007 artist and curator He Weimin collected over one hundred woodblock prints dating from the 1940s to the present, which were displayed in the exhibition 'Chinese Prints 1950–2006', held in October 2007 and February 2008.[70] More explicitly political objects similarly began to be acquired around this time. The museum purchased a collection of ninety posters from the 1970s from academic Richard Kirkby in early

2006, after Kirkby approached the museum.⁷¹ Other objects were donated, including 159 papercuts gifted by journalist and academic John Gittings, a large number of which dated from the Cultural Revolution.⁷² Former *Daily Telegraph* journalist Nigel Wade donated a collection of material from the late 1970s, including a porcelain figure, bamboo fan, posters, matchboxes, and architectural tile fragments (see figure 5.7).⁷³ These objects were acquired in order to broaden the narrative the museum could construct, as, according to Vainker and He, 'the three different media [paintings, prints, posters] together present a comprehensive view of art in China in the second half of the twentieth century.'⁷⁴ Therefore, whereas for the V&A and the British Museum, Mao-era or Cultural Revolution objects were acquired as part of a decision to expand the collection temporally, the Ashmolean had long collected twentieth-century works. Acquiring posters and other Mao-era objects was an expansion in terms of medium; it was also the recognition and incorporation of a more explicitly political type of imagery.

Filling Gaps: The National Museum of Scotland

Like the Ashmolean, Edinburgh's National Museum of Scotland's (NMS) collection of Mao-era objects has also been built in recent years. The museum acquired its first Mao-era object in 2000, but the collection grew substantially between 2009 and 2015, under curator Kevin McLoughlin. McLoughlin noted that the museum's China collection was, like many British collections of Chinese objects, biased towards Qing material, and moreover, he identified a gap between the Republican (1912–1949) and Reform Eras (post-1978). He decided therefore to specifically pursue objects from the Mao era.⁷⁵ The NMS is a universal history museum along the lines – if not the scope – of the British Museum. It collects from a social historical perspective, and given the importance of the Mao era to the twentieth century, McLoughlin argued that Mao-era objects could represent Chinese culture and history in meaningful ways, just as imperial objects could.⁷⁶ The relatively affordable nature of Mao-era objects, along with their continued relevance in contemporary China provided further justification. These objects also constitute a highly distinct visual culture, and as a result, continue to evoke strong reactions, both in China and the West, with feelings ranging from nostalgia and fascination to aversion. Mao's towering presence in twentieth-century visual culture (and indeed history and politics) meant that, for McLoughlin, excluding Maoist material would leave an inexplicable gap.

The Mao-era objects in the NMS collection are primarily from the collection of Peter and Susan Wain. The Wains, who were antique dealers and China specialists, built up their collection of Mao-era objects over many years of visits to China.⁷⁷ The first object to enter the NMS collection was a 1971 commemorative panel, celebrating the opening of the Yangtze river bridge at Nanjing, which was donated in 2000 through the National Art Collections Fund (now known as the Art Fund) (see figure 5.8).[78] In 2007, the Wains' gifted a number of silk panels and other objects, and in 2009, the NMS purchased fifteen ceramics at a Bloomsbury Auction which featured part of the Wain collection, including a spectacular under-glaze blue vase (see figure 5.6).[79] In 2013, NMS acquired most of the Wains' remaining collection, in a purchase supported by the Art Fund, and which included, amongst other objects, approximately 170 primarily Cultural Revolution-era posters.[80] The NMS collection is now particularly strong in the Cultural Revolution era, but also contains a number of objects from the 1950s and from the Reform period. It contains posters, textiles, and lacquers, but is perhaps most distinctive in Britain for its Cultural Revolution-era ceramics, including many from Jingdezhen.

Figure 5.6 A large porcelain vase with Chairman Mao painted in under-glaze blue.
Made at the Jiangxi Company of Ceramic Industry (Jingdezhen) in 1968. Now in the National Museums Scotland Collection. *Source*: Image © National Museums Scotland.

Ruptures or Continuities? Temporary Exhibitions at the Ashmolean and NMS

Both the Ashmolean Museum and the NMS have long collected twentieth-century Chinese objects but began to build their collections of Mao-era material culture after 2000. For the Ashmolean this was an expansion of medium and politics, to include the mass-produced politicised offerings discussed in this book; for the NMS this was primarily a temporal expansion, to fill the gaps between the Republican and contemporary periods. While they have collected at roughly the same time, the two museums have displayed their Mao-era objects in very different ways.

The Ashmolean is unique in having the only gallery dedicated to Chinese paintings in the United Kingdom, the Khoan and Michael Sullivan Gallery for Chinese Painting, which displays temporary exhibitions. However, the exhibitions tend to be of the Museum's non-politicised ink paintings, both historical and contemporary. There is also an Eastern Art Paintings Gallery, which hosts temporary exhibitions, including Chinese objects. Their permanent galleries only go as far as the end of the Qing dynasty in 1911, and this, combined with the rather 'traditional' nature of the paintings on display in the Sullivan gallery means that the image of China presented at the Ashmolean remains a largely 'traditional' one.

Conversely, the NMS has regularly had Mao-era objects on display since 2011. From 2011-2014, the 'Looking East' gallery included a display case on the Cultural Revolution, which acknowledged that 'the Cultural Revolution had a catastrophic effect on Chinese society', but also noted the high quality of artworks such as the ceramics made at Jingdezhen. The gallery closed for redevelopment, but in 2019, the 'Exploring East Asia' gallery was opened, featuring a case on contemporary China, which includes the Mao era. According to curator Qin Cao, the aim of the new display was to emphasise the variety of the Mao-era collection, and so included a number of different media: textiles, lacquer and ceramics.[81]

And yet, the Ashmolean has been more active in using their politicised objects in temporary displays, and have taken quite a different approach to the NMS in their display. They displayed the artists' prints acquired by He Weimin in 2007 and 2008 and, in 2011–2012, put on two linked exhibitions which looked at cultural production from the 1960s and 1970s, entitled 'Art in China in the 1960s and 1970s', featuring ink paintings and woodblock prints and 'Cultural Revolution: State Graphics in China in the 1960s and 1970s', featuring posters and other ephemera.[82] In 2019, the 'Cultural Revolution' exhibition was also displayed at the Williams Morris Gallery in London.[83] In 2020, they also had planned a small exhibition entitled 'Art in China 1949-1979', which was affected by the museum closure in light of the COVID-19 pandemic.

130   Chapter 5

Their temporary exhibitions have frequently worked to integrate art and graphics from the 1960s and 1970s into the larger history of Chinese painting. The 2011 graphics exhibition featured, alongside the more expected images of leaders and political messages, poster versions of revolutionary landscapes, which demonstrated continuities with traditional compositions and techniques. They also displayed objects that demonstrated that even during the Cultural Revolution, aesthetics were not solely dominated by political messages. Rather, objects like matchboxes also carried images promoting public health and safety, literacy, as well as landscapes, historical and literary subjects (see figure 5.7).[84]

The NMS took quite a different approach in their one temporary exhibition of Mao-era objects, 'Mao: Art for the Masses: revolutionary art of the Mao Zedong era, 1950-1976'. This 2003-2004 show was curated by and featured objects from the collection of Peter Wain, a long-term friend of the museum.[85] It included ceramics, posters and badges and was an unusual exhibition of Cultural Revolution objects in the United Kingdom, firstly for being based on a private collection and secondly for the large number of high-quality

Figure 5.7 A matchbox depicting the Nanjing Yangzi River bridge, one of the engineering successes of the Cultural Revolution. Presented by Nigel Wade to the Ashmolean Museum. Source: EA2010.120.2 Matchbox depicting Nanjing Bridge, Image © Ashmolean Museum, University of Oxford.

ceramics on display. And yet, whereas the Ashmolean chose to emphasise the traditional continuities, the NMS chose to emphasise the ruptures.

As viewers entered the exhibition space, they were confronted with forty-eight identical porcelain Chairman Mao busts, their iridescent smear glaze giving off an eerie luminosity.[86] The resounding sameness of these busts, which Wain found still in their original boxes at a police station in the Himalayas decades after Mao's death, spoke to an idea of aesthetic uniformity embodied in the exhibition's title.[87] In many ways, the emphasis on the ruptures of the Mao era and especially the Cultural Revolution is the norm in Western exhibitions, which tend to emphasise the violence, upheaval and 'redness' of the period. In the Wain exhibition, this was clearly tied to Wain's views on Chinese history and politics, as throughout the catalogue, he emphasised the degradation of traditional arts, the ill-treatment of senior masters and the lack of respect for their art, which, he argued, reached its height during the Cultural Revolution, and which he saw as a singularly disastrous period for Chinese artists.[88]

And yet, while there were examples of 'art for the masses' in the exhibition (the busts, twenty posters and fifty-three badges), there were also examples of what one reviewer called 'the finest traditional craftsmanship'.[89] One of the most spectacular objects was the large lacquer plaque, inlaid with mother of pearl, commemorating the opening of the Nanjing Yangtze River Bridge (see figure 5.8). It was designed by senior artists, executed by a senior master and is estimated to have taken over 6,000 man-hours to produce.[90] It was commissioned by General Xu Shiyou as a gift for Lin Biao, although it was never collected. This, then, was an object commissioned by elites, intended for elites, and produced by elites.

The trauma of the Cultural Revolution for many artists should not be ignored or forgotten, but the emphasis on ruptures ignored the artistic continuities that were also on display. As academic Harriet Evans observed in her review, while the objects on display seemed on the surface to reinforce stereotypes about socialist realism, the ornate details and the delicacy of the objects showed a more complex picture, of art that combined the traditional and the modern, the symbolic and the realistic, the simple and the ornate.[91]

It might be suggested that this more complex picture of artistic production is what the Ashmolean tried to achieve in their 2011–2012 exhibition. Curiously, however, this seems to have been largely lost on reviewers. A review in *Culture24*, for example, stated:

> The visual world of China during the 1960s and 1970s was as uniform as those worn by the Red Guard, with styles and subject matter officially sanctioned by the Party. Simple graphics and bold colours were the order of the day, taken from the 'socialist-realism' style-guide of the Soviet Union.[92]

Figure 5.8 Detail of a lacquer panel inlaid with mother of pearl, entitled 'Official Opening of the Nanjing Yangzi River Bridge', 1971. Gift of Mr and Mrs Peter Wain and David Hyatt King, to the National Museums Scotland. *Source*: Image © National Museums Scotland.

It seems that many reviewers' pre-conceived ideas about the nature of political manipulation under Mao meant they were resistant to the more complex depictions of the period on display in the exhibition.

Both the Ashmolean and the NMS have a number of Mao-era objects that might be considered elite: the modern ink paintings at the Ashmolean, and the porcelain at the NMS. The Ashmolean's 2011–2012 exhibitions used them to highlight continuities of traditional techniques and forms even in mass-produced objects, whereas the NMS emphasised the ruptures. Peter and Susan Wain clearly appreciated the high skill and craftsmanship of their Mao-era objects: they spent many decades building up their collection. But the overriding picture presented by the catalogue is of a small number of master works being swept away by the enormous 'output of mass-produced Mao kitsch'.[93] This narrative does a disservice to the objects, portraying them as little more than cheaply produced and crudely executed government-directed propaganda. The Ashmolean and NMS have both held exhibitions that focused on the Mao era, but which were dominated by Cultural Revolution objects, emphasising the slippage between the Cultural Revolution and the

Mao era as a whole that allows the Cultural Revolution to come to stand for the Mao era as a whole in the popular imagination.

THE UNIVERSITY OF WESTMINSTER CHINA VISUAL ARTS PROJECT

The final institution included here is not a museum, but rather a university: the University of Westminster, which has long had the United Kingdom's largest public collection of Mao and Reform-era posters, as well as other objects. It was founded at around the same time that the British Museum and V&A began contemporary collecting, but the Westminster collection demonstrates a much more direct origin out of the British engagements with Cultural Revolution China that has been discussed throughout this book.

Building the Collection

The China Visual Arts Project (hereafter Westminster Collection) was founded in the late 1970s by academic and journalist John Gittings at what was then the Polytechnic of Central London (now the University of Westminster). Gittings built up a personal collection of Chinese objects, both as a resident in Hong Kong in the late 1960s and on two trips to mainland China with the Society for Anglo-Chinese Understanding (SACU) in 1971 and 1976.[94] He also bought posters in Chinese bookstores in London, including Chinatown's Guanghwa bookstore.[95]

Other early contributors included British students who started going to China for language and other study in the 1970s, as well as friends and colleagues of Gittings. One of the most prominent early donors was Paul Crook, who, as discussed in chapter 4, built up a substantial collection of posters and other objects while living with his family in Beijing during the Cultural Revolution. Crook donated a large number of his posters to the Collection in the late 1970s, where they remained until he took them back in 2013 in order to carry out personal research.[96] The Crook donation gave the Collection a strength in images from the early Cultural Revolution that many, particularly Western collections lack, due to the low number of foreigners in China at this time.

Other donations came into the Collection from a wide variety of sources. The Collection's long-term curator, Harriet Evans, who was a student in China from 1975 to 1977, donated a number of posters and other objects over the years, both that she had bought in the 1970s, and later, that she purchased in Beijing markets in the late 1990s.[97] Anna Merton, who worked with John Gittings on the original catalogue in the late 1970s and early

1980s, had spent 1974 in Beijing, and she too donated a number of posters and other objects including photographic slides.[98] The posters of Richard Kirkby, the academic encountered in chapter 4, were temporarily housed at Westminster, before they were sold to the Ashmolean Museum in 2006.[99] Gordon Barrass, a British diplomat in China from 1970 to 1972, who has also gifted objects to the V&A and the British Museum, and is best known for his collection of modern Chinese calligraphy, donated nineteen posters, many of which cover the 'Criticise Lin Biao, Criticise Confucius' (批林批孔 *piLin piKong*) campaign of 1973-1974, and feature examples of writing and calligraphy.[100] Ellen Laing, a prominent scholar of Chinese art, donated posters in the 2000s,[101] and there have been a number of smaller donations over the years. A substantial number of posters were also bought in the 2006 Bloomsbury Auction, which allowed the curators Harriet Evans and Katie Hill to develop the Collection in 1950s and early 1960s images of women and children (see figure 5.9).[102] By 2015, the collection had over 800 posters, as well as books, toys and games, photographic slides, and other ephemera.

The collection has changed its function over time. Gittings' original name for it was the China Visual Arts Project, and it was established with largely educational intentions: to accompany language learning at the PCL, one of the earliest British institutions to teach modern Chinese language.[103] Its aim was at least partly comparative: the late 1970s and early 1980s was a period of huge change within China as the country embarked upon 'Reform and Opening', and this was captured too in aesthetic changes visible on posters. Posters from the early Reform era tend to feature scenes of science, technology and urban life, with cooler greens and purples replacing red as the dominant colour (see figure 5.10). This comparative purpose is captured in the cataloguing structure, which includes a category dedicated to the 'Four Modernizations', while no other political campaign received its own section.[104] The Four Modernisations was a campaign launched by Deng Xiaoping in 1978 to encourage modernisation in agriculture, industry, national defence, and science and technology, and it became a common trope through which China was discussed in the West at this time. The inclusion of the Four Modernisations as a category is a reflection of both a specific visual style, and also as a way of viewing China at the Collection's moment of inception. And yet, the rapid changes in language and aesthetics also limited the utility of the pre-Reform-era posters for language teaching purposes, and so despite the original intentions, the posters were not extensively used for teaching.[105]

In 2015, the Collection was transferred to the University Archives. It was re-catalogued, photographed, and made available for use in teaching, under the guidance of Senior Archivist Anna McNally. In 2019, the original name of the Collection was restored, due to McNally's desire to include a broader

Figure 5.9 A 1953 poster celebrating women's rights. Yang Xianrang 杨先让, 'We have the right to vote and be voted for' (我们有选举权和被选举权 *women you xuanjuquan he bei xuanjuquan*). **The University of Westminster Archive.** *Source*: Reproduced with the permission of the University of Westminster Archive.

understanding of the scope of the collection beyond just posters, as well as to honour the original intentions behind the collection.[106]

The transfer also, however, signified a change in the objects' status. McNally argues that it should be seen as an archive, rather than as a special collection (or 'unique and distinctive collection' to use, as McNally notes, the term preferred by Research Libraries UK).[107] She argues that while the materials within do fit the definition of a 'unique and distinctive collection', they are more usefully viewed in the context of the definition of an archive: a gathering of materials used in the conduct of the University's affairs, or which have 'grown out of its [the University's] functional activity.'[108] Viewing it this way encourages us to see it not just in terms of what it can represent about the visual culture of China, but also 'what it says about us [the University of Westminster] as an institution'.[109] For McNally, its identity as an archive of University activity rather than as a special collection of Chinese

Figure 5.10 A typical poster promoting the Four Modernizations. Chang Zhaonian and Chang Ming 场兆年, 场明, 'Produce more without waste, to achieve the Four Modernizations every person must contribute more to the motherland' (增产节约，实现四化人人为祖国多做贡献 *Zengchan jieyue, shixian sihua ren ren wei zuguo duo zuo gongxian*). The University of Westminster Archive. *Source*: Reproduced with the permission of the University of Westminster Archive.

material, means that it ought not to be further added to, except in terms of documenting its use.[110] Unlike, therefore, the other institutional collections, which continue to grow and change over time, the Westminster Collection is unlikely to substantially change its shape in the future.

Changing Functions: From Teaching Aid to Display, and Back Again

While the original function of the collection was in teaching, it has also been used in research and display. Gittings organised two exhibitions of posters and papercuts in 1979 and 1980.[111] A sign of how quickly attitudes in China had changed towards the Mao era can be seen in the response from diplomats from the Chinese embassy in London, who, invited to the 1979 exhibition, 'found it hard to hide their incredulity at, and even distaste for, the organiser's interest' in this art, just three years after Mao's death.[112]

Lack of funding resulted in little work being done on the Collection throughout much of the 1980s and 1990s, but at the end of the 1990s, a propitious meeting between curator Harriet Evans and academic Jeffrey Wasserstrom, then at Indiana University, resulted in a travelling exhibition, conference and book, entitled *Picturing Power in the People's Republic of China: Posters of the Cultural Revolution*, edited by Harriet Evans and Stephanie Donald. This marked the beginning of a new period of activity for the posters, which were now seen primarily as a collection, rather than as a teaching aid. This marked the start of a period of heightened activity as well as a name change: it came to be known as the University of Westminster Chinese Poster Collection. While the timing of its increased activity was largely circumstantial, it meant that the Collection's curators were been able both to take advantage of and contribute to the upswing of interest in Mao-era material and visual culture that has taken place since the late 1990s.

Throughout much of the first decade of the 2000s, art historian Katie Hill held the position of curator and oversaw the construction and launch of the first and second websites, as well as curating the 2004 Arts and Humanities Research Council (AHRC) funded travelling exhibition 'The Political Body: Posters from the People's Republic of China in the 1960s and 1970s', which examined the relationship between gender and representation of the body in Chinese art between the mid-1960s and the 1980s.[113] There were also small exhibitions at the Lakeside Theatre, University of Essex, and at a hotel in Folkestone during Hill's time at Westminster.

An incident that occurred during the Folkestone exhibition, however, underlines that the rejuvenation of the collection at Westminster in the 2000s took place within a context defined by broader social ideological antipathy to the Chinese government and the cultural outputs of the Mao years. While in general the posters were apparently very well received by the local community, one replica of a poster that depicted Chinese ethnic minorities in unity with the larger nation had a comment written on it denouncing the Chinese government and its policies in Tibet (see figure 5.11). The graffiti more likely reflected disagreement with contemporary Chinese policies and a general hostility to the Chinese government, rather than anything specific to the period in which the poster was produced, but it does reflect some of the broader attitudes towards China that exist within Britain.

This is not the only time Westminster's posters have been damaged. In 2010 Harriet Evans and Stephanie Donald co-curated an exhibition at the University of Sydney, Australia, entitled 'China and Revolution: History, Memory and Parody in Contemporary Art.'[114] The exhibition explored the relationship between art from the Cultural Revolution and contemporary works by artists who grew up during the Cultural Revolution.[115] The framing company glued the posters to cardboard backing, rather than putting them directly in frames as had been expected.[116] The posters could not be removed from the cardboard, and so were permanently damaged. The framer's actions

Figure 5.11 An image of the original poster in the University of Westminster Collection, a replica of which was written on at the Folkestone Exhibition. 'Long live the unity of every nationality in this country!' (全国各族人民大团结万岁! *Quan guo ge zu renmin da tuanjie wansui!*), 1975. *Source*: Reproduced with the permission of the University of Westminster Archive.

implicitly reflected a general disregard of the posters as valuable works of art, likely because they were mass produced and government made. The actions corresponded with the view that these are not objects that deserved to be treated with respect, either as art or as sensitive historical artefacts. This incident, therefore, reflects one of the common ways objects from Mao's China continue to be viewed: as cheap and crude propaganda, with little intrinsic value.

Westminster exhibitions have consistently sought to alter such views, and one of the ways they have done so is to demonstrate the continued relevance of the imagery in contemporary China. The 2010 exhibition mentioned above showed the impact the Cultural Revolution had on a number of artists; a 2011 London exhibition 'Poster Power: Images from Mao's China, Then and Now' put posters in dialogue with objects from everyday life in contemporary China that drew on Maoist imagery.[117] In the preface to the catalogue Harriet Evans argued that the continued presence of Cultural Revolution-style imagery in contemporary China was indicative of the complex legacy of the posters of the period. The exhibition included recently produced Chinese playing cards, stamps, postcards, advertisements, and contemporary art objects, all of which drew on Cultural Revolution imagery and aesthetics in some way. A postcard advertisement for a Beijing bar, for example, featured a muscular worker, portrayed in a socialist realist style, but standing in front of a disco ball, and pointing to the word 'party' (舞会, *wuhui*).

Since 1999, posters have also been displayed online, both on standalone websites, and via sites like Twitter.[118] They have also been used in a variety of outreach projects, such as teaching in primary and secondary schools in London.[119] They have also been used in some public events as part of the University's Difference Festivals in 2018 and 2019.[120] Since the transfer of the posters to the University archive in 2015, objects have been used in teaching history, language, and archival studies, and efforts remain on-going to make the objects available digitally and physically for teaching and study.

While the Westminster Collection is based in a university rather than a museum, it shares many of the same legacies as the museums: the collection was built primarily through donations from people who spent time in China in the Mao era and early Reform era, as well as through targeted acquisitions. It has been used in temporary displays, but due to its location in an educational institution, has also been used more widely in teaching and outreach work. The objects have been celebrated and studied, but also denigrated and damaged, reflecting the various attitudes that people retain towards the Mao era.

CONCLUSION

Thinking about the process through which British public institutions have acquired Mao-era and Cultural Revolution objects tells us something about the process through which these objects have become 'museum worthy'. When the V&A and the British Museum first began collecting the twentieth century in the early 1980s, the more overtly politicised products of the Mao era, and the Cultural Revolution in particular, were largely excluded. This was in part because few objects from the Cultural Revolution were available at this point, but was more significantly because the mass-produced offerings that were available were often not considered appropriate museum material. However, over time, this attitude began to change, contributed to, in part, by a broader change in art history that began to pay serious attention to the cultural production of the Mao years. V&A curator Rose Kerr recalled, 'I think prior to 1992 I didn't regard anything I owned as being "museum worthy", but perspective changes as the years go by,' and she has since donated a number of objects she purchased as a student in the 1970s.[121]

For the V&A and the British Museum, both dedicated to collecting the broad sweep of Chinese history, once the decision was made to include the twentieth century, it was only a matter of time before the Cultural Revolution would enter the museum. The Cultural Revolution was an undeniably important period in China's recent history, however, it might be assessed in political terms, and moreover it produced a distinctive (if more diverse than is often acknowledged) and eye-catching visual culture that is well suited to museums' search for 'representative' examples. The Ashmolean and NMS have long collected twentieth-century Chinese objects, but the political content of the Mao era was something of a lacuna, that has been filled primarily since 2000. The University of Westminster collection specifically targeted Mao era and early Reform-era objects, but it too has experienced ebbs and flows in institutional interest, funding and activity.

The formation of these collections highlight a number of factors about institutional collecting more broadly. The first is the ad hoc nature of museum collecting. As former British Museum Director David Wilson noted, 'Policy, accident and serendipity all play their part in the process of collecting.'[122] Chance occurrences, donations or minor purchases can take on a life of their own. For example, the British Museum has the nation's largest public collection of Mao badges, but it has not purchased a single one of its objects. The collection did not develop due to a specific curatorial policy, and therefore trying to fit the collection into a coherent narrative is necessarily a post-hoc construction.

Secondly, it is important to note the influence of museum curators, who typically have a fairly wide scope to purchase objects within their research interests, as long as they can be justified by price and with reference to existing collections or museum policy.[123] Much of the NMS collection, for example, was acquired while Kevin McLoughlin was at the museum, while Mary Ginsberg has been influential in building and promoting the British Museum's Mao-era collection.

While this chapter may have made it seem that it was inevitable that these objects would end up in British national museums, it is worth remembering that in many countries and many museums in Britain, this has not been the case. Institutional openness to the twentieth century has been one of the driving factors, but as this chapter has pointed out, particularly with the case of the British Museum, the V&A, the Ashmolean and the Westminster Collection, donations or sales from individuals who lived in or visited China in the 1970s have also been key. The public collections have grown as individuals who bought objects during the Cultural Revolution have aged. While these objects may not have initially had much financial value, their economic and historical value has grown and will continue to grow in coming years. Donating or selling these objects to public collections thus constitutes something of a legacy for these individuals.

Once these objects have been incorporated into institutional collections, they have dual meanings: while the objects are Chinese and can be used to represent a particular moment in Chinese history, they can also be seen as the material traces of British engagements with Mao's China. When, in 2009 and 2010, V&A Deputy Director Beth McKillop, who had been a student in China in the mid-1970s, offered a number of posters to the V&A's Asia Department, curator Zhang Hongxing accepted them less because they were important historical documents for China, and more because they were a legacy of a particular British experience of Mao's China.[124] Similarly, Anna McNally views the Westminster Collection as much as an archive of University activities as a special collection of Chinese visual arts.

Maoism did not have the same political, ideological or cultural influence in Britain that it did in other countries; however, the formation of public collections based in large part on the private souvenirs or collections of British individuals is a testament to the fact that many in Britain were interested in, inspired by, and drawn to the events in Mao's China, even if it was on a less political level than that witnessed elsewhere. The development of public institutional collections has served as a legacy of this engagement, even if that was not initially their intention. Paying attention to the individual stories behind these museum collections, as this chapter has done, is a way of constituting an understanding of the diverse experiences Britons had of Mao-era China that go beyond simple questions of political influence.

The objects that have been displayed in British museums range from mass-produced posters to elite ceramics; they vary in style from socialist realist projections of the Mao cult to more neutral images of landscapes or daily life. When taken together, they have demonstrated the multiplicity of themes and styles of Cultural Revolution cultural production, and when taken separately, they have demonstrated some of the different narratives that can emerge from these objects. Museums always have more objects than they are able to display, in either temporary or permanent exhibitions, so it is perhaps not surprising that these Mao-era objects have not been seen more often. It is clear, however, that museums in Britain are gradually moving beyond their 'imperial fetish', to tell a broader and more modern story of China.

NOTES

1. Many private collectors in the United States are also dealers. For example, collector Dwight McWethy runs The East is Red online shop (www.theeastisred.com), and Justin Schiller, who has a substantial collection of Little Red Books and other objects, runs Battledore Ltd (https://www.childlit.com/). David J. Davies, another private collector, exhibited his collection in three locations in Oregon and Washington in 2002. See the online exhibit: 'Ordinary Life in Extraordinary Times', *Burke Museum*, 2002 https://www.burkemuseum.org/static/ordinarylife/ [accessed 10/07/2020]. A selection of universities with Mao-era art include: the Center for Chinese Studies at the University of Michigan, which has a collection of Chinese Papercuts (http://

quod.lib.umich.edu/c/ccs1ic); the East Asian Library at the University of California Berkeley has the Ann Tompkins (Tang Fandi) and Lincoln Cushing Chinese Poster Collection (www.docspopuli.org/ChinaPosters.html); the University of California San Diego has a Chinese Cultural Revolution Posters Collection donated by Professor Paul Pickowicz (http://library.ucsd.edu/dc/collection/bb67250839). The Hoover Institution Archives at Stanford University has a Chinese Cultural Revolution Collection that includes Red Guard newspapers, graphics and sound recordings of revolutionary model operas and songs (https://www.hoover.org/library-archives/collections/china).

2. New York's Metropolitan Museum of Art and the Museum of Fine Arts in Boston both have works that respond to Mao and the Mao era in some way, such as Andy Warhol 'Mao Tse-tung' prints (1972–1973) or Gerhard Richter's 'Mao' (1968), but they do not own Chinese political art of that era.

3. They do, however, have one Cultural Revolution vase, which depicts a military scene (Object ID:2013.47). It was a gift and is not on display.

4. The Museum of Arts and Crafts (*Musée des arts et métiers*) in Paris does, however, own a number of Cultural Revolution posters, which have been exhibited.

5. The David King Collection, discussed in Chapter 4, is now housed in the Tate Archives, including both his Soviet and Chinese objects.

6. Amy Jane Barnes, 'Chinese Propaganda Posters at the British Library', *Visual Resources* 36, no. 2 (2020): 2–4.

7. Barnes, 'Chinese Propaganda Posters at the British Library', 3.

8. Ellen Johnston Laing, *Art and Aesthetics in Chinese Popular Prints: Selections from the Muban Foundation Collection* (Ann Arbor: University of Michigan Press, 2002), 2.

9. See https://www.mubanexhibitions.org/ for a list of exhibitions.

10. Craig Barclay, personal communication, 25/06/2015.

11. See object 2004.1224 & object 1975.166i.

12. Nicole Chiang, personal communication, 30/06/2015; Object ID 1363.

13. Anne Farrer, 'Twentieth-Century Chinese Prints at the British Museum: The Formation and Development of the Collection', in *Collecting Chinese Art: Interpretation and Display*, ed. Stacey Pierson (London: Percival David Foundation of Chinese Art, 2000), 105.

14. John Ayers, *Far Eastern Ceramics in the Victoria and Albert Museum* (London: Sotheby Parke Bernet, Published in Association with the V&A Museum, 1980), 2.

15. Anthony Burton, *Vision & Accident: The Story of the Victoria and Albert Museum* (London: V&A Publications, 1999), 30; Roy Strong, 'The Victoria and Albert Museum - 1978', *The Burlington Magazine*, May 1978, 276.

16. Burton, *Vision & Accident: The Story of the Victoria and Albert Museum*, 168.

17. Frances Carey, *Collecting the 20th Century* (London: Published for the Trustees of the British Museum by British Museum Press, 1991), 8.

18. Carey, *Collecting the 20th Century*, 8.

19. Carey, *Collecting the 20th Century,* 9.

20. A number of substantial collections were split between the British Museum and the V&A. Stacey Pierson, *Collectors, Collections and Museums: The Field of*

Chinese Ceramics in Britain, 1560-1960 (Bern; Oxford: Peter Lang, 2007), 145–46; Roderick Whitfield, 'Landmarks in the Collection and Study of Chinese Art in Great Britain', in *Europe Studies China: Papers from an International Conference on The History of European Sinology*, ed. Ming Wilson and John Cayley (London: Han-Shan Tang Books, 1995), 205–6.

21. Craig Clunas, 'China in Britain: The Imperial Collections', in *Belief in China : Art and Politics; Deities and Mortality*, ed. Robert Benewick and Stephanie Donald (Brighton: Green Centre for Non-Western Art and Culture, 1996), 12–15; Pierson, *Collectors, Collections and Museums*, 137.

22. David M. Wilson, *The British Museum: A History* (London: British Museum Press, 2002), 306–10.

23. Collections include wartime woodcuts from Peter Thompson, early twentieth-century popular prints from Jean-Pierre Dubosc, 1940s prints from Geoffrey Roome. Roderick Whitfield, personal communication, 26/05/2015; Mary Ginsberg, 'Revolutionary Art at the British Museum', *Transactions of the Oriental Ceramic Society*, 2007 2006; Anne Farrer, 'Twentieth-Century Chinese Prints at the British Museum: The Formation and Development of the Collection', in *Collecting Chinese Art: Interpretation and Display*, ed. Stacey Pierson (London: Percival David Foundation of Chinese Art, 2000), 108–9.

24. Roderick Whitfield, personal communication, 25/06/2015; Clarissa von Spee, 'Introduction: Printing the Pictorial in China - Historical and Cultural Contexts', in *The Printed Image in China: From the 8th to the 21st Centuries*, ed. Clarissa von Spee (London: British Museum, 2010), 25; Wilson, *The British Museum*, 310.

25. Ginsberg, 'Revolutionary Art at the British Museum', 34–35.

26. Jessica Rawson's objects have reference numbers 1993, 0522, 0.1-6, while Shelagh Vainker's are 1993.0302.1-2.

27. Graham C. Greene, 'Foreword', in *The Art of Calligraphy in Modern China*, by Gordon S. Barrass (London: British Museum, 2002), 7.

28. Some of Bolton's objects include, 2005, 0128, 0.1-2; 2005, 0127, 1-6.

29. Alfreda Murck's teapots have the reference numbers: 2013, 3007.1-373.

30. Posters purchased at the Bloomsbury Auction have the reference numbers 2006, 0501, 0.1-75. The National Day scroll has acqusition number: 2017,3008.1

31. Helen Wang, *Chairman Mao Badges: Symbols and Slogans of the Cultural Revolution* (London: British Museum Press, 2008), 51.

32. Christopher Dyer, personal communication, 06/02/2012.

33. Wang, *Chairman Mao Badges*, iv.

34. Penny Brooke, interview with author, 02/04/2012, London;

Acquisition numbers for these objects are: Brooke 2007, 4005.1-37, Rank's badges were donated after his death by his wife Esther, with the numbers 2019, 4117.1-163; while alive he donated a variety of paper ephemera, under 2014, 4004.1-12; 2015, 4094.1-2; 2015, 4055.1; 2015, 4147.1; Mungan 2014, 4041.1-94.

35. Object numbers: 2012, 4127.1-3.

36. Ginsberg, 'Revolutionary Art at the British Museum', 39.

37. Roy Strong, *The Roy Strong Diaries, 1967-1987* (London: Phoenix, 1997), 140.

38. Rose Kerr, personal communication, 20/06/2015.

39. Rose Kerr, personal communication, 20/06/2015. The Far Eastern Department made a policy decision in 1983 to devote the majority of its annual acquisition funds to the purchase of twentieth-century objects. V&A Archive, File 90/1098; Acquisitions Gifts Proposed: Modern Chinese Ceramics Simon Kwan. Letter: Rose Kerr to Simon Kwan, 06/06/1990.

40. Verity Wilson, 'Celebrating Twenty-Five Years in the Far Eastern Collection of the Victoria and Albert Museum', *Orientations* 26, no. 10 (November 1995): 62.

41. Wilson, 'Celebrating Twenty-Five Years in the Far Eastern Collection of the Victoria and Albert Museum', 62.

42. Rose Kerr, personal communication, 20/06/2015.

43. V&A Archive, 90/1098, Letter: Simon Kwan to Rose Kerr, 31/05/1990.

44. V&A Archive, 357; 11: 89/1320 Letter from Kwan to Kerr, 11/08/1989.

45. These donations have the acquisition numbers: Gordon Barrass: FE.28-1999-FE.34-1999; Peter Wain: FE.35-1999-FE.42-1999.

46. Amy Jane Barnes, *Museum Representations of Maoist China: From Cultural Revolution to Commie Kitsch* (Farnham: Ashgate, 2014), 158.

47. Kerr's badges have the object numbers FE.4-6-2001. The object numbers of Beth McKillop's recent donations include FE.26-27-2009, FE.56-62-2009, FE.26-30-2010, while that of Andy McKillop's Mao suit is FE.3-2005.

48. V&A Archive, Far Eastern Department, File 2001/382, Acquisition: Gift, Chinese revolution posters (12), the gift of Antony Reynolds. Acquisition RF: Justification, written by Rose Kerr, 09/05/2001.

49. Anthony Reynolds, 'Revisiting the Convoy Route', *China in Focus* 2 (1997): 16; Tony Reynolds, 'China Days', *China in Focus* 9 (Winter 2000): 17; Tony Reynolds, 'Tony Reynolds', *Cotteridge Quaker Meeting*, no date, http://www.cotteridge.quaker.eu.org/new_page_11.htm#contents [accessed 10/08/2020].

50. V&A Archive FE 2001/382, Letter from Anthony Reynolds to Rose Kerr, 13/06/2001.

51. V&A Archive, Asian Department, File 2008/293, Acquisition: Gift. Chinese propaganda posters (9), 1969-1975, the gift of Lady Heseltine. Letter from Gill Saunders to Lady Heseltine, 02/11/2007.

52. Reinhard Eisel, 'Britain's China Policy from 1949 to 2005: From an Idealistic Approach to Return to a Focus on the Economic Factor', *EU-China European Studies Centres Programme; CAP Working Paper*, May 2007, 10, http://www.cap.lmu.de/download/2007/2007_eu-china_eisel.pdf [accessed 10/08/2020].

53. The National Archives, FCO 21/1115, Visit of Peter Walker, Secretary of State for Trade and Industry, and Michael Heseltine, Minister for Aerospace and Shipping, to China, 24–31 March 1973.

54. The National Archives, FCO 57/450, Visit of Peter Walker, Secretary of State for Trade and Industry, and Michael Heseltine, Minister for Aerospace and Shipping, to China: 24–31 March 1973, Outline Programme.

55. Tom Buchanan, *East Wind: China and the British Left, 1925-1976* (Oxford: Oxford University Press, 2012), 207; Eisel, 'Britain's China Policy', 9–10.

56. Hongxing Zhang, Lauren Parker and Beth McKillop, *China Design Now* (London: V&A Publishing, 2008). Beth McKillop, interview with author, 13/07/2015, London.

57. Kerr quoted in Barnes, *Museum Representations of Maoist China*, 134.

58. Harrison Hall quoted in Wei Sun, 'British Museum Reopens China Gallery', *Global Times*, 17 December 2017, http://www.globaltimes.cn/content/1080654.shtml [accessed 03/08/2020].

59. Helen Wang, 'Icons of Revolution. Mao Badges Then and Now' (British Museum, 2008), https://www.academia.edu/1098957/Icons_of_Revolution._Mao_badges_then_and_now_exhibition_text_ [accessed 10/08/2020].

60. A number of Chinese posters were, however, displayed in 2002 and 2003 as part of the exhibition 'Propaganda Posters from the Schreyer Collection'. The Schreyer Collection includes posters from a number of countries including: Britain, the United States, Germany, France, Japan, the Soviet Union and other countries. These posters are part of the Prints and Drawing Department, whereas most of the V&A's Chinese posters in the Asia Department.

61. Clarissa von Spee, *The Printed Image in China: From the 8th to the 21st Centuries* (London: British Museum, 2010).

62. 'The Art of Influence: Asian Propaganda', British Museum, exhibition visited July 2013.

63. Mary Ginsberg, *The Art of Influence: Asian Propaganda* (London: British Museum Press, 2013), 14.

64. Shelagh Vainker, *Chinese Paintings in the Ashmolean Museum Oxford* (Oxford: Ashmolean Museum, 2000), 17; Shelagh Vainker, 'The New Galleries of Chinese Art', *Arts of Asia* 41, no. 3 (2011): 111–12.

65. Vainker, *Chinese Paintings in the Ashmolean Museum Oxford*, 17.

66. Vainker,*Chinese Paintings in the Ashmolean Museum Oxford,* 18; Vainker, 'The New Galleries of Chinese Art', 112.

67. The Sullivan bequest also contains a few items with political content, such as posters. 'Sullivan Collection of Modern Chinese Art Bequeathed to the Ashmolean', *University of Oxford News & Events*, 13 December 2013, https://www.ox.ac.uk/news/2013-12-13-sullivan-collection-chinese-art-bequeathed-ashmolean [accessed 04/08/2020]; Shelagh Vainker, *Modern Chinese Paintings: The Reyes Collection in the Ashmolean Museum, Oxford* (Oxford: Ashmolean Museum, 1996), 5.

68. Peter C Swann, 'Introduction', in *Chinese Paintings of Today: An Exhibition of Works Collected and Presented by Collet's Chinese Gallery*, ed. Mary Shen and Sheila Dorrell (London: Collet's Chinese Gallery, 1964), 1.

69. Shelagh Vainker, 'The New Galleries of Chinese Art', *Arts of Asia* 41, no. 3 (2011): 112.

70. Weimin He and Shelagh Vainker, *Chinese Prints 1950-2006 in the Ashmolean Museum: 1950-2006* (Oxford: Ashmolean Museum, 2007).

71. Ashmolean Museum University of Oxford, 'Annual Report of the Visitors of The Ashmolean Museum, August 2006-July 2007' (Oxford: The Ashmolean Museum, 2008), 41. Richard Kirkby, interview with author, 01/12/2015, London.

72. Ashmolean Museum University of Oxford, 'Annual Report of the Visitors of The Ashmolean Museum August 2007-July 2008' (Oxford: The Ashmolean Museum, 2009), 40.

73. Ashmolean Museum University of Oxford, 'Annual Report of the Visitors of The Ashmolean Museum August 2008-July 2010' (Oxford: The Ashmolean Museum, 2010), 61.

74. He and Vainker, *Chinese Prints 1950-2006 in the Ashmolean Museum*, ix.

75. Kevin McLoughlin, personal communication, 28/05/2013; 23/01/2014.

76. McLoughlin, personal communication, 28/05/2013.

77. Peter and Susan Wain, personal communication, 18/10/2013. See chapter 4 for more on the Wains.

78. 'NMS Chinese Collection Donations and Acquisitions of Material Originating in Peter Wain's Collection' dated 27/03/2013, provided by Kevin McLoughlin.

79. Bloomsbury Auctions, *Mao and the Arts of New China, Including the Collection of Peter and Susan Wain* (London: Bloomsbury Auctions, 2009).

80. 'The Art Fund in 2013/14: Annual Report' (London, UK: The Art Fund, 2013), https://www.artfund.org/assets/about-us/annual-report/art-fund-review-digital-double-2013.pdf.

81. Cao Qin, personal communication, 03/06/2020.

82. This exhibition ran twice: first from March- 3 July 2011, secondly from 11 July to November 2011. While the categories were the same in each exhibition, the actual objects on display differed.

83. 'Exhibitions: Cultural Revolution: State Graphics in China from the 1960s to the 1970s', Williams Morris Gallery, 2019, https://www.wmgallery.org.uk/whats-on/exhibitions-43/cultural-revolution/past/2019 [accessed 04/08/2020].

84. 'Revolutionary Images on Everyday Objects: Cultural Revolution: State Graphics in China in the 1960s and 1970s (I)', Ashmolean Museum, 2011, http://jameelcentre.ashmolean.org/collection/6980/9372/9375 [accessed 04/08/2020].

85. Zhang Hongxing, interview with author, 09/06/2015, London.

86. Kate Day, 'Mao: Art for the Masses at Royal Museum, Edinburgh', *Culture 24*, 26 May 2003, http://www.culture24.org.uk/art/craft/ceramics/art16869 [accessed 04/08/2020].

87. Catherine Elsworth, 'Collecting the Cultural Revolution', *The Guardian*, 11 January 2003.

88. Peter Wain, 'Mao Zedong and Art', in *Mao: Art for the Masses: Revolutionary Art of the Mao Zedong Era, 1950-1976* (Edinburgh: National Museums of Scotland, 2003), 4.

89. Alison Hardie, 'Art for the Masses: Revolutionary Art of the Mao Zedong Era, 1950-1976', *IIAS Newsletter*, March 2002, 39.

90. Peter Wain, *Mao: Art for the Masses: Revolutionary Art of the Mao Zedong Era, 1950-1976* (Edinburgh: National Museums of Scotland, 2003), 46.

91. Harriet Evans, 'Mao: Art for the Masses', *Orientations* 34, no. 9 (November 2003): 64.

92. Nick Owen, 'Workers of the World, Unite! The Cultural Revolution Comes to the Ashmolean Museum', *Culture24* (blog), 26 September 2011, http://www.culture24.org.uk/art/painting%20%26%20drawing/art364858 [accessed 03/08/2020].

93. Peter Wain, 'Mao Zedong and Art', 6.

94. John Gittings, 'Excess and Enthusiasm', in *Picturing Power in the People's Republic of China: Posters of the Cultural Revolution*, ed. Stephanie Donald and Harriet Evans (Lanham: Rowman & Littlefield Publishers, 1999), 29. Gittings interview with author, 15/10/2013, Oxfordshire. For more on Gittings, see chapter 3.

95. The administrative files for the Collection are now housed in the University of Westminster Archive, under the title China Visual Arts Project Archive, CPC/9, Administration. When this research was carried out they were housed in the stand-alone University of Westminster Chinese Poster Collection Archive, and will be referred to as the Poster Collection Archive here. Gwanghwa Company Invoice No. 000067, 22/04/1982. Invoice made out to John Gittings, Chinese Visual Aids Project, Polytechnic of Central London. 33 posters were purchased for £12.95

96. Westminster Archive, The Paul Crook Collection. 23/04/2013. A document in the archive lists the 195 posters that were returned to Crook in April 2013.

97. Westminster Archive, Beijing Curio City Receipts. A photocopy of a number of receipts remain from purchases Evans made of books and posters in July 1999.

98. Harriet Evans, interview with author, 03/04/2013, London.

99. Westminster Archive, The archive contains numerous letters and emails between Richard Kirkby and Harriet Evans. Slides of Kirkby's posters still in the collection attest their posters' previous presence at Westminster.

100. Westminster Archive, Gordon Barrass Collection, no date. Katie Hill catalogued Barrass' nineteen posters, likely in 2008.

101. Evans, interview with author, 03/04/2014, London.

102. Westminster Archive, Bloomsbury Auction House receipt, 06/09/2006. A receipt from Bloomsbury Auction House states that forty-five lots were purchased, but as many lots contained numerous posters, it is not clear from this document the exact number of posters acquired.

103. Former diplomat and key figure in promoting Sino-British friendship Derek Bryan was instrumental in establishing the modern Chinese language programme, first at Holborn College of Law, Languages, and Commerce, and then at the Polytechnic of Central London, after Holborn was incorporated into it.

104. The catalogue has seventeen categories. Most of them are thematic, such as: agriculture, international relations, politics, women, leaders, and so on. The Four Modernizations category, therefore, is conceptually quite different.

105. Harriet Evans recalled working with a colleague in the early 1990s to match slides of the posters with key terms being studied by students in an effort to use the poster images for teaching, but acknowledged this was a relatively short-lived experiment. Evans, interview with author, 03/04/2013, London.

106. Anna McNally, personal communication, 21/07/2020.

107. Anna McNally, 'Not Just Curious Objects: The China Visual Arts Project Archive', *Journal of Design History* 31, no. 4 (2018), 391.

108. McNally, Not Just Curious Objects', 391.
109. McNally, Not Just Curious Objects', 392.
110. Anna McNally, personal communication, 21/07/2020.
111. The Westminster Archive contains the publicity information for two exhibitions: 'Chinese Popular Art and Political Culture' in 1979 at the PCL and 'Chinese Posters' in 1980 at the London College of Printing.
112. Gittings, 'Excess and Enthusiasm', 29.
113. Katie Hill, *The Political Body: Posters from the People's Republic of China in the 1960s and 1970s* (London: University of Westminster Chinese Poster Collection, 2004).
114. The exhibition was also shown at the RMIT Gallery at RMIT University in Melbourne, Australia in early 2011.
115. Harriet Evans and Stephanie Hemelryk Donald, *China and Revolution: History, Parody and Memory in Contemporary Art* (Sydney: The University of Sydney, 2010).
116. Harriet Evans, interview with author, 03/04/2013, London.
117. Harriet Evans, *Poster Power: Images from Mao's China, Then and Now* (London: University of Westminster, 2011).
118. The Contemporary China Centre Blog tweets about posters under the handle @CCCblogUoW.
119. Harriet Evans and the author were involved in a number of outreach projects with local schools in 2014.
120. Anna McNally, personal communication, 21/07/2020.
121. Rose Kerr, personal communication, 20/06/2015.
122. David M. Wilson, *The British Museum: Purpose and Politics* (London: British Museum Publications, 1989), 24.
123. Mary Ginsberg, personal communication, 15/05/2015.
124. Zhang Hongxing, interview with author, 09/06/2015, London.

Conclusion

Legacies of Engagements with Cultural Revolution Objects

This book has detailed the plurality of engagements that British individuals and institutions have had with Cultural Revolution objects, as well as the broader idea of the Cultural Revolution. It has been argued that Britons of a variety of political persuasions have used Cultural Revolution art, propaganda and material culture more broadly as part of their way of understanding this confusing period of Chinese history, in ways that speak to, but cannot be reduced to, political perspectives and ideology. But it should be acknowledged that both at the time and since, the Cultural Revolution has been largely seen in much of the Western world as a disaster: a period of political manipulation, extreme violence and lost life chances. This is true of both academia and larger social perspectives and has been solidified by the Chinese Communist Party's own 1981 evaluation of the period, which deemed it 'the most severe setback and the heaviest losses suffered by the Party, the state and the people since the founding of the People's Republic'.[1] This perspective has dominated too in China, where it is frequently referred to as the 'ten years of chaos' and a 'cultural desert', and remains a largely taboo topic in public discourse.

Beyond this, the term 'Cultural Revolution' has become a shorthand in Western media for periods of chaos, violence or just social change. The references often have little to do with the actuality of the Cultural Revolution in China. The widespread calls for social justice, institutional change and historical re-evaluations that shook the British and American establishments in 2020 and 2021 were, for example, likened by some in the media and political sphere to the Cultural Revolution. US President Donald Trump, for example, argued in a speech on 4 July 2020 that 'cancel culture' was a 'left-wing *cultural revolution* [. . .] designed to overthrow the American revolution'.[2] British Prime Minister Boris Johnson has also used the analogy, albeit before he became prime minister, when he compared criticism of a scientist's clothing choices to 'a scene from Mao's cultural revolution when weeping intellectuals were forced to confess their crimes against the people'.[3] More recently, academic John Gray wrote in the *Daily Mail* that 'It is not far-fetched to compare the methods of this "woke movement" to those of Chairman Mao's Red Guards, who terrorised the Chinese people half a century ago', and concludes 'In some ways, today's Twitter Maoism is worse than the original Chinese version'.[4] The idea that criticism on Twitter is equivalent to being the victim of a Red Guard struggle session is extremely problematic, and the comparisons lack any real intellectual or historical legitimacy. But they do demonstrate the continued rhetorical power that accusations of Cultural Revolution behaviour maintain in Anglo-American society even today: for all the other perspectives suggested throughout this book, the dominant mainstream view of the Cultural Revolution remains a purely and entirely negative one. As chapter 1 observed, these associations continue to have power within segments of popular culture too, with the Mao Suit still used in film to represent either robotic conformity or power-hungry evil. It is clear that the overwhelming representation of the Cultural Revolution, in both China and the West is negative. And yet, this book concludes by arguing that interest in the material culture of the Cultural Revolution continues to exist and that contemporary understandings of Mao's China and the Cultural Revolution remain channelled in part through its material and visual culture. As part of this, objects have continued their transnational movement, including in new ways, such as through digital environments.

RED LEGACIES

In China, Cultural Revolution objects and aesthetics continue to be widely visible. The aesthetics are found in contemporary Chinese art, design and advertising, often being used ironically or critically.[5] The objects themselves also remain present and are collected in large numbers as part of the larger field of 'Red Relic Collecting'(*hongse wenwu shoucang* 红色文物收藏) or 'Red Collecting' (*hongse shoucang* 红色收藏).[6] This field is not limited to the Cultural Revolution, nor given the continued sensitivity of the Cultural Revolution in China, is it conceived in such terms. Instead, the field is much more broadly conceptualised as including a wide variety of objects made since the founding of the CCP in 1921; nevertheless, given that billions of Mao badges and propaganda posters were produced during the Cultural Revolution, it is not surprising that objects from this era dominate numerically. While some collectors acquire these objects for economic purposes, most analysis of the field has positioned it in terms of nostalgia for the supposed purity of the Mao era and a rejection of the radically altered direction of contemporary China.[7] Red Collecting is one aspect of the Mao era's 'red legacies' in China itself, and the continued presence of objects, aesthetics and cultural products from the era is often explained as being indicative of the fact that individual and collective memories of the Cultural Revolution are far more complex than the 'ten years of chaos' trope would allow.[8] Rather, memories of the period, its politics and its cultural production are varied, ranging from nostalgia to revulsion.

Dozens of Red Collectors have their own private museums or exhibition halls across China, but these tend to be small and poorly publicised.[9] They also tend to lack didactic information, preferring instead an abundance of visual material over textual explanations which could cause problems for them. There are a few more public sites, such as the huge Jianchuan Museum Cluster (建川博物馆 *Jianchuan bowuguan*) in Anren, Sichuan, owned by former government official and real estate magnate Fan Jianchuan, and which has a number of museums dedicated to the Mao years.[10] There is also the Shanghai Propaganda Poster Art Centre (上海宣传画艺术中心 *Shanghai xuanchuanhua yishu zhongxin*), which displays private collector Yang Peiming's posters and is very popular with foreign visitors.[11] Public museums in China, by contrast, almost entirely exclude Cultural Revolution objects as well as discussion of the history of the period. The Chinese National Museum (中国国家博物馆 *Zhongguo guojia bowuguan)*, in Beijing's Tiananmen Square, is the museum most closely associated with the rise and rule of the CCP.[12] While it displays history paintings in a central gallery, including those from the Mao era, its permanent display of modern Chinese history, entitled 'The Road to Rejuvenation', which covers the period 1839 to the present, largely excludes the events between 1949 and 1978, except for a few foreign policy successes.[13] There is, therefore, a total silencing of all voices – critical or laudatory – with regards to the Cultural Revolution in China's National Museum, and academic Kirk Denton notes that this is the norm in most Chinese history museums.[14] In the Chinese private and commercial sphere, therefore, Cultural Revolution aesthetics continue to be commonly seen; however, the complicated historical and political legacy of the period means that it has been and continues to be largely excluded from public museums.

In Britain, however, the situation is largely reversed. Despite the history of engagement with Cultural Revolution objects and aesthetics outlined in the first three chapters of this book, they are today only occasionally drawn on by British artists, designers and advertisers, in part, no doubt, because of the negative associations with the period outlined at the start of this Conclusion. Instead, the primary location where the public can see Cultural Revolution objects are now museums and other public institutions, as detailed in chapter 5. British public and private collections are tiny compared to Chinese private collections, both in terms of scope and frequency. Writing in 2008, collector Qin Jie estimated there were 100,000 serious or hobbyist Mao badge collectors in China, and the number and size of collections have continued to grow since.[15] As such, there is no doubt that China itself remains the most important archive for these objects. And yet, given the continued sensitivity that surrounds these objects in the Chinese public sphere, which prohibits much serious academic research and discussion of the time period, British and other global collections are also important archives, and ones which can facilitate research, and the publicisation of research, into the cultural production of the Cultural Revolution. The co-curator of two important North American exhibitions on the Cultural Revolution, Zheng Shengtian, quoted an unnamed Chinese scholar as writing 'The Cultural Revolution occurred in China, but the study of the Cultural Revolution occurred outside of China.'[16] For Zheng, an artist who suffered substantially during the Cultural Revolution, collections and exhibitions on the Cultural Revolution in the West are important, precisely because he sees them as currently the only way to recover the 'lost chapter' of Chinese art history.[17] The difficulties of researching Mao-era art history in China itself means, for Zheng, that Western collections and exhibitions have a crucial role to play both in artefact preservation, and in knowledge production about this still highly sensitive period. Western collections, then, are archives in both of Jacques Derrida's senses of the term: as storehouses, but also as the foundation from which history is or could be written.[18]

A similar perspective on the importance of collections has also been advanced by Hong Kong-based collector Simon Kwan, one of the major donors of Mao-era porcelains to the V&A Museum. He wrote, in a 1989 letter to V&A curator Rose Kerr, 'I think that these pieces should be kept by a museum and be preserved as a record of the works of our time. Let our children appraise them. It might be good or it might be bad.'[19] For Kwan, then, in 1989, the time had not yet come to properly evaluate the cultural products of the Mao years. Indeed, the sensitivity that continues to surround the Cultural Revolution would suggest that in China, the time has still not yet come. But for Kwan, what was important was that twentieth-century porcelains were in museums, where they could be preserved until an atmosphere emerged in which they could be dealt with in a more disinterested manner. Moreover, for Kwan, preserving Mao-era objects was crucial to constructing a lineage of Chinese artistic production that continued up to the present. Regardless of individual and institutional perspectives on the political and cultural events of the Mao era, its objects are important social, cultural and historical artefacts, and the fact there are a number of British collections of them will leave these institutions well placed to contribute to debates about Mao-era Chinese history and art history as perspectives continue to change and develop in the future.

Indeed, British and North American collections and exhibitions of Mao-era and Cultural Revolution art and cultural production have already contributed to contemporary academic understandings of the period. While there were some early efforts to take seriously the cultural production of the Mao era, it long remained, in art historian Ellen Laing's words 'dismissed wholesale as pure propaganda or routine socialist realism'.[20] In the past twenty years within academia, a much more nuanced understanding of the cultural production of the period, as well as the relationship between culture, politics and broader society has developed. The new works demonstrate that the Cultural Revolution and its system of cultural production was not an aberration, but rather was in many ways a continuation of existing cultural debates that ran throughout the twentieth century, even if they took most extreme expression at this time.[21] This literature has also moved away from an approach that saw the people of China as a unified mass, driven purely from above, towards an attempt to find agency in both cultural production and audience responses.[22] This recent literature has demonstrated that cultural production and even exhibitionary culture during the Mao era was not just a reflection of politics, but in fact played a central role in the attempt to construct a new socialist culture for China.[23]

Many of the early key texts that substantially added to our understanding of the period's art production came out of exhibitions and collections in Europe and North America. Publications about the collections of the University of Westminster in the United Kingdom and the IISH-Landsberger Collection in the Netherlands and connected to exhibitions at the University of British Columbia in Canada and the Asia Society in New York, were, and remain, key sources that have contributed to this recent expansion of understanding.[24] Perhaps this is not surprising: much of the re-evaluation has been about arguing that there was greater diversity in cultural production than is typically acknowledged. Collections and exhibitions encourage us to look for differences between objects; as Susan Stewart has written, 'To group objects in a series because they are "the same" is to simultaneously signify their difference. In the collection, the more the objects are similar, the more imperative it is that we make gestures to distinguish them.'[25] These studies, frequently edited volumes, have combined attention to the specificity and diversity of the objects themselves with contextual oral historical and archival research in China, resulting in the transnational production of knowledge. Overall, study of cultural production and the role that it played (and continues to play) in the lives of ordinary people has resulted in the emergence of more nuanced understandings of the period. This shift is not about downplaying the suffering and violence of the period, but rather about moving beyond an understanding of the period as '"the people-as-one" under the gaze of a supreme "Other"', as Michael Dutton has called it, and instead recognising the period for all of its 'heterogenous excess'.²⁶ This attention has shifted not only our understanding of the period's cultural production, but also the importance of culture in the broader political and social changes. One outcome of this is that contemporary understandings of Mao's China and the Cultural Revolution are increasingly channelled through its material and visual culture.

THE FUTURE OF CULTURAL REVOLUTION OBJECTS

Alongside the changing academic attitude towards Cultural Revolution cultural production, there has also been a change in its economic value. Since the early 1990s, there has been a significant appreciation in the market prices of Mao-era objects, initially in China, but also abroad, particularly for objects like stamps, posters and porcelains. What began as cheap, mass-produced objects have become recognised in China as 'cultural relics' in their own right,²⁷ and this legitimacy is paralleled in Britain in their appearance in auctions and museum exhibitions. There will be a limit to the price inflation these objects can reach in China: the majority of serious collectors were born in the Mao era, and thus, the objects speak to their youths. The younger generation, born in the Reform Era, have not, as of yet at least, entered the field of Red Collecting in the same numbers, and so as the older generation ages and passes away, it is unclear whether the market will be sustained. This is particularly true in the context of Xi Jinping's China, which has seen a tightening of official control over historical narratives, including towards sensitive periods of Party history such as the Cultural Revolution.²⁸ Many Red Collectors state that they are collecting for the nation and intend to donate their objects to the nation when they die.²⁹ Those objects from the pre-1949 revolutionary period in Chinese history may indeed be welcomed by public collections, but those from the Cultural Revolution are unlikely to be. As such, the future of Cultural Revolution objects in China, from a medium-to-long-term perspective, is somewhat uncertain.

In Britain, public collections of Mao-era objects are likely to continue to grow in coming decades, primarily through donations, as people who purchased, collected or otherwise acquired these objects age. These objects are meaningful to these individuals due to their links with their own life stories: it is logical to assume their children will not have the same attachments to them. As such, individuals in Britain will face the same question as Chinese collectors: what to do with their Cultural Revolution objects? As previous chapters of this book have made clear, donations from these individuals have already been the primary route of travel through which objects have entered museum collections, and this process is likely to accelerate over the next ten to twenty years. It is not, however, necessarily the case that museums will always accept donations, given the costs associated with preservation and storage, and so smaller institutions, including university library and archives may become increasingly important sites for these objects.[30]

As well as increasingly appearing in British museums, Cultural Revolution objects are also increasingly visible online, and the internet has provided an outlet for a range of interests, ranging from academic, to commercial, to other more sensational or journalistic forms. The online lives of Mao-era objects needs to be seen as part of China's 'red legacy', in which authentic objects mix with, influence, and are appropriated by post-revolutionary culture.[31] The internet has enabled the global physical movement of Maoist material culture through their sale in auctions and on dealer websites. It has also enabled the dispersion of Maoist imagery, both in the sense of images of original Mao-era objects, and more contemporary images that re-appropriate the aesthetic.[32] The internet has increased the visibility of these objects outside China, and has facilitated circulation of both objects themselves (through online auction sites as well as online 'stores'), and of images of the objects, which are now visible on a wide variety of websites.

Just as incorporation into museum collections has changed how we view these objects, so too does digitisation. Media theorist Marshall MacLuhan suggested that outmoded technologies do not disappear, but rather become art forms. For example, once widespread printing rendered fine handwriting unnecessary as a crucial practical skill, it became a ceremonial art in the form of calligraphy.[33] When a medium is no longer functionally necessary, it can be experienced in a new way: as pleasure.[34] Once rendered effectively functionless because they have been surpassed technologically, we can experience them in a way not dissimilar to how we experience collected objects: aestheticised and re-contextualised to suit our own needs. According to Paul Levinson, this process has been accelerated by the internet, and he has argued: 'As medium after medium moves from its traditional stand-alone position to become content on the Internet, we can expect a commensurate increase in the public's appreciation of these older media as art.'[35]

Sinologist Stefan Landsberger has argued that from the 1980s onwards, the Chinese government has predominantly used electronic media rather than propaganda posters to propagate behavioural norms.[36] While some contemporary posters continue to draw on Mao-era themes or aesthetic styles, they are still visually very different from those of the Mao era. Does the out-of-datedness of the Mao-era posters, combined with the strikingly different visual aesthetics and visual atmosphere of contemporary China, allow us to shift from 'use' to aesthetic appreciation of these now historical objects? Perhaps, then, the material medium's irrelevance actually constitutes its value: it is the distance of these original posters from their intended environment, their seemingly anachronistic status, their very *materiality*, that renders them valuable.

The same danger that objects face in China also applies to objects in Britain and to their digital lives: how will they be viewed by the younger generation? The aesthetics are familiar to much of the older generation in the West, even if they were never interested in Maoism or Mao's China. But for those born later, these objects lack relevance both to their own lives and to the China they encounter today, and it is hard to foresee serious engagement outside of an academic capacity. Similarly, while museum and university collections in the United Kingdom are likely to continue to grow for the next few years, this will not last forever: it seems possible that we are now in the 'golden age' of Cultural Revolution object collecting, both in China and elsewhere.

CONCLUSION

While the future of these objects remains somewhat uncertain, this book has argued that Cultural Revolution material culture have had much more complex lives in Britain than might be expected. It argued that while Britain has been largely excluded from the emerging academic field of global Maoisms due to its relatively small 'Maoist' movement in the 1960s and 1970s, British individuals and institutions across the political spectrum had deep and sustained engagements with Mao's China. One of the key channels for these engagements was the material culture – art, propaganda, and other objects – that China both exported around the world and that Britons brought back with them from China. It has emphasised the centrality of China, and ideas about China, to the larger historical period of the 'global sixties', in which China was both a Cold War enemy and a source of hope, inspiration and leadership. These Chinese objects were casual purchases, souvenirs and collectibles for British individuals throughout time, and they have been gradually incorporated into some of Britain's most prestigious public institutions. Here they have a dual function: both as archives of a controversial period in China's history and as archives of British engagements with that China and the British imagination of it. Through exploring the lives of these Chinese objects, this book has opened up previously underacknowledged routes of travel that these objects have taken, as well as the diverse meanings they have had for various individuals and institutions. In doing so, this book has offered a new approach to Sino-British relations that seeks to go beyond elite politics and considers instead the realm of objects in constructing ideas, structuring experiences, and shaping memories of Mao's China in Britain.

NOTES

1. Communist Party of China, 'Resolution on Certain Questions in the History of Our Party since the Founding of the People's Republic of China', *Marxists.org*, 27 June 1981, http://www.marxists.org/subject/china/documents/cpc/history/01.htm [accessed 04/08/2020]; Article 19.

2. Thomas Burnham, 'The Analogy between the Cultural Revolution and "Cancel Culture": A Historical Perspective', *Positions Politics* (blog), 21 January 2021, https://positionspolitics.org/thomas-burnham-the-analogy-between-the-cultural-revolution-and-cancel-culture-a-historical-perspective/ italics in the original. For further examples of this sort of rhetoric in US media, see Roger Helle, 'America's Coming Cultural Revolution', *The Patriot Post*, 22 July 2020, https://patriotpost.us/articles/72316-americas-coming-cultural-revolution-2020-07-22; Andrew Sullivan, 'You Say You Want a Revolution?', *Intelligencer*, 26 June 2020, https://nymag.com/intelligencer/2020/06/andrew-sullivan-you-say-you-want-a-revolution.html.

3. Ella Alexander, 'Dr Matt Taylor: Boris Johnson compares attacks on scientist to 'a scene from Mao's cultural revolution', *The Independent*, 17 November 2014, https://www.independent.co.uk/news/people/boris-johnson-compares-dr-matt-taylor-s-accusers-islamist-maniacs-and-attacks-him-scene-mao-s-cultural-revolution-9865200.html [accessed 04/08/2020].

4. John Gray, 'It's Not an Exaggeration to Compare Methods of New "woke Movement" to Mao's Red Guards', *Daily Mail Online*, 18 July 2020, https://www.dailymail.co.uk/debate/article-8537583/JOHN-GRAY-not-exaggeration-compare-methods-new-woke-movement-Maos-Red-Guards.html [accessed 04/08/2020].

5. Ruth Y. Y. Hung, 'Red Nostalgia: Commemorating Mao in Our Time', *Literature Compass* 12, no. 8 (2015): 371–84.

6. Emily Williams, 'Collecting the Red Era in Contemporary China', *Made in China* 2, no. 3 (2017): 78–83.

7. See, for example, Jennifer Hubbert, '(Re)Collecting Mao: Memory and Fetish in Contemporary China', *American Ethnologist* 33, no. 2 (2006): 145–61; Michael Dutton, 'From Culture Industry to Mao Industry: A Greek Tragedy', *Boundary 2* 32, no. 2 (2005): 151–67.

8. Barbara Mittler, *A Continuous Revolution: Making Sense of Cultural Revolution Culture* (Cambridge, MA: Harvard University Press, 2012).

9. One of the main national Red Collecting Associations has published a guide to some of the display halls, see: *Zhongguo Shoucangjia Xiehui* 中国收藏家协会 [China Association of Collectors], '*Quanguo Hongse Bowuguan, Zhanlanguan, Jiating Shoucangguan, Diyiji* 全国红色博物馆，展览馆，家庭收藏馆，第一集 [All China Red Museum, Exhibition Hall and Home Collection Hall, Volume 1]', *Zhongguo Hongse Shoucang* 中国红色收藏 6 (2017).

10. Denise Y. Ho and Jie Li, 'From Landlord Manor to Red Memorabilia: Reincarnations of a Chinese Museum Town', *Modern China*, 5 July 2015, 1–35; Michael Rowlands, Stephan Feuchtwang, and Lisheng Zhang, 'Rupture and Repair: A Museum of the Red Age Confronts Historical Nihilism', in *Ruptures*, ed. Martin Holbraad, Bruce Kapferer, and Julia F. Sauma (London: UCL Press, 2019), 52–69.

11. Yang's posters have also been exhibited abroad, including in Edinburgh in 2014. Natascha Gentz and Peiming Yang, eds., *Poster Art of Modern China, Exhibition Catalogue, the University of Edinburgh*, 2014.

12. Marzia Varutti, *Museums in China: The Politics of Representation after Mao* (Woodbridge, Suffolk: The Boydell Press, 2014), 113.

13. Observations based on numerous personal visits since 2011.

14. On the exclusion of the Cultural Revolution from a number of other modern history museums, see Kirk A. Denton, *Exhibiting the Past: Historical Memory and the Politics of Museums in Postsocialist China* (Honolulu: University of Hawai'i Press, 2014), 91, 174, 185, 197.

15. Qin Jie 秦杰, *Hongse Shoucang* 红色收藏 *[Red Collections]* (Nanchang, Jiangxi: Jiangxi Renmin Chubanshe, 2007), 10.

16. Shengtian Zheng, 'Searching for the "Lost Chapter" in the History of Contemporary Chinese Art', in *Art of the Great Proletarian Cultural Revolution, 1966-76*, ed. Scott Watson and Shengtian Zheng (Vancouver: Morris and Helen Belkin Art Gallery, 2002), 14.

17. Zheng, 'Searching for the "Lost Chapter" in the History of Contemporary Chinese Art', 15.

18. Derrida noted the dual associations of the term. The archive refers both to the domiciliation of objects and artefacts, but it is from this gathering together that the power to determine history arises. Jacques Derrida, *Archive Fever: A Freudian Impression*, trans. Eric Prenowitz (Chicago & London: The University of Chicago Press, 1996).

19. V&A Archive; Box 357, Main File 11, extension 89/1320, 7-8 pieces of post 1949 Chinese Ceramics' from Simon Kwan. Letter from Simon Kwan to Rose Kerr, 11 August 1989.

20. Ellen Johnston Laing, *The Winking Owl: Art in the People's Republic of China* (Berkeley, CA; London: University of California Press, 1988), ix.

21. Xiaobing Tang, *Visual Culture in Contemporary China: Paradigms and Shifts* (Cambridge: Cambridge University Press, 2015); Paul Clark, *The Chinese Cultural Revolution: A History* (Cambridge: Cambridge University Press, 2008).

22. Mittler, *A Continuous Revolution*; Harriet Evans, 'Ambiguities of Address: Cultural Revolution Posters and Their Post-Mao Appeal', in *Red Legacies in China: Cultural Afterlives of the Communist Revolution*, ed. Jie Li and Enhua Zhang (Cambridge, MA; London: Harvard University Press, 2016), 87–114; Geng Yan, *Mao's Images: Artists and China's 1949 Transition* (Wiesbaden: J.B. Metzler, 2018).

23. Laikwan Pang, *The Art of Cloning: Creative Production during China's Cultural Revolution* (London & New York: Verso, 2017); Tang, *Visual Culture in Contemporary China*; Denise Y. Ho, *Curating Revolution: Politics on Display in Mao's China* (Cambridge: Cambridge University Press, 2018).

24. Harriet Evans and Stephanie Donald, eds., *Picturing Power in the People's Republic of China: Posters of the Cultural Revolution* (Lanham, MD; Oxford: Rowman & Littlefield, 1999); Richard King, ed., *Art in Turmoil: The Chinese Cultural Revolution, 1966-76* (Vancouver: UBC Press, 2010); Melissa Chiu and Shengtian

Zheng, eds., *Art and China's Revolution* (New Haven, Conn; London: Asia Society, New York in association with Yale University Press, 2008). Dutch sinologist Stefan Landsberger has perhaps done more than anyone to develop understandings of posters of the period, through a prolific publication record and his important website, www.chineseposters.net. See Stefan Landsberger, *Chinese Propaganda Posters : From Revolution to Modernization* (Amsterdam: Pepin, 1995); Stefan Landsberger, Duo Duo, and Anchee Min, *Chinese Propaganda Posters : From the Collection of Michael Wolf* (Köln: Taschen, 2008); Stefan Landsberger and Marien van der Heijden, *Chinese Posters: The IISH-Landsberger Collections* (Munich: Prestel, 2009); Stefan R. Landsberger et al., *Chinese Propaganda Posters* (Köln; London: Taschen, 2011).

25. Susan Stewart, *On Longing: Narratives of the Miniature, the Gigantic, the Souvenir, the Collection* (Durham, NC: Duke University Press, 1993), 155.

26. Michael Dutton, ed., *Streetlife China* (Cambridge: Cambridge University Press, 1998), 241.

27. Zhonghua Renmin Gongheguo Wenhuabu 中华人民共和国文化部 [Ministry of Culture of the People's Republic of China], 'Wenwu Cangpin Dingji Biaozhun 文物藏品定级标准 [Rating Standards for Cultural Relic Collections]' (Zhonghua Renmin Gongheguo Wenhuabu 中华人民共和国文化部 [Ministry of Culture of the People's Republic of China], 5 April 2001), http://www.lawinfochina.com/display.aspx?lib=law&id=1829&CGid=. Of the fourteen descriptions of 'typical first-class cultural relics', six make explicit reference to the CCP and the Communist movement or modern Chinese history more broadly.

28. The new CCP party history, published in 2021, for example, greatly reduced the space given to discussing the Cultural Revolution, and instead of describing it as a catastrophe for which Mao was responsible, hedges its criticisms of the period to primarily issues of implementation. 'Zhongguo Gongchandang Jianshi' Bianxie Zu 《中国共产党简史》编写组 ['A Brief History of the Chinese Communist Party' Writing Group], *Zhongguo Gongchandang Jianshi* 中国共产党简史 *[A Brief History of the Chinese Communist Party]* (Beijing: Renmin Chubanshe, Zhonggong Dangshi Chubanshe, 2021).

29. Emily Williams, 'Red Collections in Contemporary China: Towards a New Research Agenda', *British Journal of Chinese Studies* 11 (2021): 71–90.

30. This process is already underway: SOAS library has already acquired some of Richard Kirkby's *xiaorenshu*, the University of Sheffield has incorporated the SACU library, and slight further afield, Xi'an Jiaotong-Liverpool University in Suzhou China has developed a CCP History Collection based on David Goodman's collection of objects from the 1970s and after.

31. There has been extensive discussion of the Mao era's 'red legacy' in contemporary China. See, for example, Geremie Barmé, *Shades of Mao: The Posthumous Cult of the Great Leader* (Armonk, NY: M.E. Sharpe, 1996), Geremie Barmé, *In the Red: On Contemporary Chinese Culture* (New York: Columbia University Press, 1999); Dutton, *Streetlife China*; Jie Li and Enhua Zhang, eds., *Red Legacies in China: Cultural Afterlives of the Communist Revolution* (Cambridge, Massachusetts; London: Harvard University Press, 2016).

32. Natalie Siu Lam Wong, 'On the (Re)Emergence of Cultural Revolution Imagery in China, Hong Kong and Singapore in the 21st Century' (University of Westminster, 2010), Unpublished Thesis.

33. Paul Levinson, *Digital McLuhan: A Guide to the Information Millennium* (London; New York: Routledge, 1999), 152.

34. Levinson, *Digital McLuhan,* 13.

35. Levinson, *Digital McLuhan,* 14.

36. It should be noted, however, that government posters continue to be widely visible on road sides or in the underground in contemporary China. Landsberger, *Chinese Propaganda Posters,* 14.

Bibliography

Ahmed, Sara. *The Cultural Politics of Emotion*. Edinburgh: University of Edinburgh Press, 2004.
Alexander, Ella. 'Dr Matt Taylor: Boris Johnson Compares Attacks on Scientist to 'a Scene from Mao's Cultural Revolution'. *The Independent*, 17 November 2014, https://www.independent.co.uk/news/people/boris-johnson-compares-dr-matt-taylor-s-accusers-islamist-maniacs-and-attacks-him-scene-mao-
Alexander, Robert Jackson. *Maoism in the Developed World*. Westport: Praeger, 2001.
Ali, Tariq. *Street Fighting Years: An Autobiography of the Sixties*. 2nd Edition. London: Verso, 2005.
Allen, Emily. 'Great Haul of China: Collector Auctions £1m Haul of Artefacts from Chairman Mao's Regime Snapped up over a 15-Year Period'. *Mail Online*, 27 September 2012. http://www.dailymail.co.uk/news/article-2209351/Great-haul-China-Collector-auctions-1m-haul-artefacts-Chairman-Mao-s-regime-snapped-15-year-period.html.
Andreas, Joel. *Rise of the Red Engineers: The Cultural Revolution and the Origins of China's New Class*. Stanford, CA: Stanford University Press, 2009.
Arendt, Hannah. 'Introduction: Walter Benjamin: 1892-1940'. In *Illuminations: Essays and Reflections*, edited by Walter Benjamin, 1–58, translated by Harry Zohn. New York: Schocken Books, 2007.
Ashmolean Museum. 'Revolutionary Images on Everyday Objects: Cultural Revolution: State Graphics in China in the 1960s and 1970s (I)', 2011. http://jameelcentre.ashmolean.org/collection/6980/9372/9375.
Ashmolean Museum University of Oxford. 'Annual Report of the Visitors of The Ashmolean Museum, August 2006-July 2007'. Oxford: The Ashmolean Museum, 2008.
———. 'Annual Report of the Visitors of The Ashmolean Museum August 2007-July 2008'. Oxford: The Ashmolean Museum, 2009.

———. 'Annual Report of the Visitors of The Ashmolean Museum August 2008-July 2010'. Oxford: The Ashmolean Museum, 2010.
Auction Central News. 'Mao-Velous Chinese Propaganda Art at Bloomsbury's London, Nov. 5'. 3 November 2009. https://www.liveauctioneers.com/news/auctions/upcoming-auctions/mao-velous-chinese-propaganda-at-bloomsburys-nov-5/.
Ayers, John. *Far Eastern Ceramics in the Victoria and Albert Museum*. London: Sotheby Parke Bernet, Published in Association with the V&A Museum, 1980.
Baker, Mike. 'The Political Report'. *Red Front: For Working-Class Power for a Socialist Britain!*, October 1967: 3-5.
Bal, Mieke. 'Telling Objects: A Narrative Perspective on Collecting'. In *The Cultures of Collecting*, edited by John Elsner and Roger Cardinal, 97–115. London: Reaktion, 1994.
Barberis, Peter, John McHugh, and Mike Tyldesley. *Encyclopedia of British and Irish Political Organizations: Parties, Groups and Movements of the 20th Century*. London: Pinter, 2000.
Barbrook, Richard. *Imaginary Futures: From Thinking Machines to the Global Village*. London; Ann Arbor: Pluto Press, 2007.
Barmé, Geremie. *In the Red: On Contemporary Chinese Culture*. New York: Columbia University Press, 1999.
———. *Shades of Mao: The Posthumous Cult of the Great Leader*. Armonk, NY: M.E. Sharpe, 1996.
Barnes, Amy Jane. 'Chinese Propaganda Posters at the British Library'. *Visual Resources* 36, no. 2 (2020): 124–47.
———. *Museum Representations of Maoist China: From Cultural Revolution to Commie Kitsch*. Farnham: Ashgate, 2014.
Baudrillard, Jean. 'The System of Collecting'. In *The Cultures of Collecting*, edited by John Elsner and Roger Cardinal, 7–24. London: Reaktion, 1994.
———. *The System of Objects*. London: Verso, 1996.
BBC News. 'Maoist Cult Leader Aravindan Balakrishnan Jailed for 23 Years', 29 January 2016. https://www.bbc.com/news/uk-england-35443423.
Belk, Russell. 'Collectors and Collecting'. In *Handbook of Material Culture*, edited by Christopher Y. Tilley, Webb Keane, Susanne Küchler, Michael Rowlands, and Patricia Spyer, 534–45. London: SAGE, 2006.
Benjamin, Walter. 'Unpacking My Library: A Talk about Book Collecting'. In *Illuminations: Essays and Reflections*, translated by Harry Zohn, 59–67. New York: Schocken Books, 2007.
Bishop, Bill. 'Badges of Chairman Mao Zedong', 1996. http://museums.cnd.org/CR/old/maobadge/.
Blackman, Cally. 'Clothing the Cosmic Counterculture: Fashion and Psychedelia'. In *Summer of Love: Psychedelic Art, Social Crisis and Counterculture in the 1960s*, edited by Christoph Grunenberg and Jonathan Harris, 201–22. Liverpool: Liverpool University Press, 2005.
Bland, William. 'Report of the Central Committee of the MLOB on the Situation in the People's Republic of China'. *Red Front: Special Edition*, January 1968.

Blom, Philipp. *To Have and to Hold: An Intimate History of Collectors and Collecting*. London: Penguin, 2003.
Bloodworth, Dennis. 'How Mao Rides the Dragon'. *The Observer*, 11 September 1966.
Bloomsbury Auctions. *Asia: Books, Prints & Posters*. London: Bloomsbury Auctions, 2011.
———. *Chinese Propaganda Posters*. London: Bloomsbury Auctions, 2013.
———. *Mao and the Arts of New China, Including the Collection of Peter and Susan Wain*. London: Bloomsbury Auctions, 2009.
———. *Red China: 1921-1976*. London: Bloomsbury Auctions, 2012.
———. *Vintage Chinese Posters*. London: Bloomsbury Auctions, 2006.
Brady, Anne-Marie. *Making the Foreign Serve China: Managing Foreigners in the People's Republic*. Lanham, MD; Oxford: Rowman & Littlefield, 2003.
Brantlinger, Patrick. *Crusoe's Footprints: Cultural Studies in Britain and America*. London: Routledge, 1990.
Brett, Guy. 'China's Spare-Time Artists'. *Studio International*, January-February 1975.
———. 'Chinese Painters Celebrate the New Way of Life'. *The Times*, 11 September 1974.
———. *Exploding Galaxies: The Art of David Medalla*. London: Kala Press, 1995.
———. 'In Millet, the Peasant Is a Heavy Figure, Bowed down by Toil, Earth-Bound. These Chinese Picture Themselves Lightly, They Step Lightly'. *Arts Guardian*, February 1976.
———. 'Internationalism among Artists in the 60s and 70s'. In *The Other Story : Afro-Asian Artists in Post-War Britain*, edited by Rasheed Araeen, 111–15. London: Southbank Centre, 1989.
———. *Peasant Paintings from Hu County, Shensi Province, China*. London: Arts Council of Great Britain, 1976.
———. 'Peasant Paintings from Huxian, Shensi Province, China'. *Art Monthly* 1 (October 1976).
———. 'Spare Time Art Workers'. *China Now*, 49, 1975: 9, 12-13.
———. 'Talking with Huhsien Painters'. *China Now*, 69, December 1976: 8-10
———. 'The Changing Face of Chinese Art'. *The Times*, 21 May 1974: 11.
———. *Through Our Own Eyes: Popular Art and Modern History*. London: GMP, 1986.
———. '"We Give You What We Saw"'. *China Now*, Winter 1977, 2–6.
Bu, Weihua. *Zalan Jiu Shijie: Wenhua Dageming de Dongluan Yu Haojie, 1966–1968 [Smashing the Old World: Turmoil and Calamity of the Cultural Revolution, 1966-1968]*. Hong Kong: Chinese University Press, 2008.
Buchanan, Tom. *East Wind: China and the British Left, 1925-1976*. Oxford: Oxford University Press, 2012.
Buchli, Victor. 'Introduction'. In *The Material Culture Reader*, edited by Victor Buchli, 1-13. London: Routledge, 2020.
Burnham, Thomas. 'The Analogy between the Cultural Revolution and "Cancel Culture": A Historical Perspective'. *Positions Politics* (blog), 21 January 2021.

https://positionspolitics.org/thomas-burnham-the-analogy-between-the-cultural-revolution-and-cancel-culture-a-historical-perspective/.
Burton, Anthony. *Vision & Accident: The Story of the Victoria and Albert Museum.* London: V&A Publications, 1999.
Byungiu, Shin, and Gon Namkung. 'Films and Cultural Hegemony: American Hegemony "Outside" and "Inside" the "007" Movie Series'. *Asian Perspective* 32, no. 2 (2008): 115–43.
Callahan, William A. *Sensible Politics: Visualizing International Relations.* Oxford: Oxford University Press, 2020.
Carey, Frances. *Collecting the 20th Century.* London: Published for the Trustees of the British Museum by British Museum Press, 1991.
Caute, David. *The Year of the Barricades : A Journey through 1968.* New York: Harper & Row, 1988.
Chen, Jian. 'China and the Bandung Conference: Changing Perceptions and Representations'. In *Bandung Revisited: The Legacy of the 1955 Asian-African Conference for International Order*, edited by Amitav Acharya and See Seng Tan, 132–59. Singapore: National University of Singapore Press, 2008.
———. *Mao's China and the Cold War.* Chapel Hill: The University of North Carolina Press, 2001.
Chen, Laurie. 'Beijing Red Letter Day: Rare Stamp from Cultural Revolution Era Sells for $2 Million at Auction'. *South China Morning Post,* 23 November 2018. https://www.scmp.com/news/china/society/article/2174725/beijing-red-letter-day-rare-stamp-cultural-revolution-era-sells-2.
Cheung, Yin-ki. 'Iconography of Socialist Revolution: Construction of an Optimistic Imagery in Maoist China, 1949-1976'. *G-SEC WORKING PAPER No.20*, 2007.
China Pictorial. 'Peasants' Paintings'. 1966 36-39.
China Reconstructs. 'Peasant Paintings of Huhsien'. 1974: 17-20.
Chiu, Melissa, and Shengtian Zheng, eds. *Art and China's Revolution.* New Haven, CT; London: Asia Society, New York in association with Yale University Press, 2008.
Christiansen, Samantha, and Zachary A. Scarlett. *The Third World in the Global 1960s.* New York & Oxford: Berghahn Books, 2012.
Christie, Herta. 'Astonishing Diversity'. *China Now*, 47, December 1974, 9.
Clark, Paul. *The Chinese Cultural Revolution: A History.* Cambridge: Cambridge University Press, 2008.
Clore, Vivien. 'When the State Decrees Thou Shalt Not Fall in Love'. *Daily Mail,* 29 November 1966.
Clunas, Craig. 'China in Britain: The Imperial Collections'. In *Belief in China : Art and Politics; Deities and Mortality*, edited by Robert Benewick and Stephanie Donald, 10–17. Brighton: Green Centre for Non-Western Art and Culture, 1996.
———. 'Souvenirs of Beijing: Authority and Subjectivity in Art Historical Memory'. In *Picturing Power in the People's Republic of China: Posters of the Cultural Revolution*, edited by Stephanie Donald and Harriet Evans, 47–62. Lanham: Rowman & Littlefield Publishers, 1999.
———. *Superfluous Things: Material Culture and Social Status in Early Modern China.* Cambridge: Polity Press, 1991.

Collier, John, and Elsie Collier. *China's Socialist Revolution*. London: Stage 1, 1973.
Communist Party of China. 'Resolution on Certain Questions in the History of Our Party since the Founding of the People's Republic of China'. *Marxists.org*, 27 June 1981. http://www.marxists.org/subject/china/documents/cpc/history/01.htm.
Cook, Alexander C. *Mao's Little Red Book: A Global History*. Cambridge: Cambridge University Press, 2014.
Cope, Dave. 'Radical Bookshop History Project'. *Left on the shelf*. Accessed 3 June 2014. http://www.leftontheshelfbooks.co.uk/images/doc/Radical-Bookshops-Listing.pdf.
Cork, Richard. *Art for Whom?* London: Arts Council of Great Britain, 1978.
———. 'Painting the Village Red'. *Evening Standard*, 9 December 1976.
Cradock, Percy. *Experiences of China*. New ed. London: John Murray, 1999.
Croft, Michael. *Red Carpet to China*. New York: St. Martin's Press, 1958.
Croizier, Ralph. 'Hu Xian Peasant Painting: From Revolutionary Icon to Market Commodity'. In *Art in Turmoil : The Chinese Cultural Revolution, 1966-76*, edited by Richard King, 136–63. Vancouver: UBC Press, 2010.
Crook, David. 'Hampstead Heath to Tian an Men: The Autobiography of David Crook', 2014. http://davidcrook.net/simple/main.html.
Crook, David, and Isabel Crook. 'An Anglo-Canadian Couple's 30 Years in New China'. In *Living in China: by Twenty Authors from Abroad*, 40–62. Beijing : New World Press, 1979.
Crook, Isabel, and David Crook. *Revolution in a Chinese Village, Ten Mile Inn*. London: Routledge & Kegan Paul, 1959.
Dallas, Ian. 'red guard pointers' *International Times*, Issue 11, 21 April 1967, 4. http://www.internationaltimes.it/archive/page.php?i=IT_1967-04-21_B-IT-Volume-1_Iss-11_005&view=text.
Davin, Delia. *Mao Zedong*. Stroud: Sutton, 1997.
Davis, Madeleine. 'The Marxism of the British New Left'. *Journal of Political Ideologies* 11, no. 3 (October 2006): 335–58.
Day, Kate. 'Mao: Art for the Masses at Royal Museum, Edinburgh'. *Culture 24*, 26 May 2003. http://www.culture24.org.uk/art/craft/ceramics/art16869.
Denton, Kirk A. *Exhibiting the Past: Historical Memory and the Politics of Museums in Postsocialist China*. Honolulu: University of Hawai'i Press, 2014.
Derrida, Jacques. *Archive Fever: A Freudian Impression*. Translated by Eric Prenowitz. Chicago & London: The University of Chicago Press, 1996.
Dobrogoszcz, Tomasz. 'The British Look Abroad: Monty Python and the Foreign'. In *Nobody Expects the Spanish Inquisition: Cultural Contexts in Monty Python*, edited by Tomasz Dobrogoszcz, 83–93. Lanham, MD: Rowman & Littlefield, 2014.
Doggett, Peter. *There's a Riot Going on: Revolutionaries, Rock Stars and the Rise and Fall of '60s Counter-Culture*. Edinburgh: Canongate Books, 2008.
Dong, Guoqiang, and Andrew G Walder. *A Decade of Upheaval: The Cultural Revolution in Rural China*. Princeton, NJ: Princeton University Press, 2021.
Dugger, John. *Microcosm*. London: Sigi Krauss Gallery, 1971.

Dutton, Michael. 'Cultural Revolution as Method'. *The China Quarterly* 227 (2016): 718–33.

———. 'From Culture Industry to Mao Industry: A Greek Tragedy'. *Boundary 2* 32, no. 2 (2005): 151–67.

———, ed. *Streetlife China*. Cambridge: Cambridge University Press, 1998.

Eisel, Reinhard. 'Britain's China Policy from 1949 to 2005: From an Idealistic Approach to Return to a Focus on the Economic Factor'. *EU-China European Studies Centres Programme; CAP Working Paper*, May 2007. http://www.cap.lmu.de/download/2007/2007_eu-china_eisel.pdf.

Elbaum, Max. *Revolution in the Air: Sixties Radicals Turn to Lenin, Mao and Che*. London & New York: Verso, 2002.

Elsworth, Catherine. 'Collecting the Cultural Revolution'. *The Guardian*. 11 January 2003, 115.

Esherick, Joseph, Paul Pickowicz, and Andrew G. Walder, eds. *The Chinese Cultural Revolution as History*. Stanford, CA: Stanford University Press, 2006.

Evans, Harriet. 'Ambiguities of Address: Cultural Revolution Posters and Their Post-Mao Appeal'. In *Red Legacies in China: Cultural Afterlives of the Communist Revolution*, edited by Jie Li and Enhua Zhang, 87–114. Cambridge, MA; London: Harvard University Press, 2016.

———. 'Mao: Art for the Masses'. *Orientations* 34, no. 9 (November 2003): 64–65.

———. *Poster Power: Images from Mao's China, Then and Now*. London: University of Westminster, 2011.

Evans, Harriet, and Stephanie Donald, eds. *Picturing Power in the People's Republic of China : Posters of the Cultural Revolution*. Lanham, MD; Oxford: Rowman & Littlefield, 1999.

Evans, Harriet, and Stephanie Hemelryk Donald. *China and Revolution: History, Parody and Memory in Contemporary Art*. Sydney: The University of Sydney, 2010.

Farrer, Anne. 'Twentieth-Century Chinese Prints at the British Museum: The Formation and Development of the Collection'. In *Collecting Chinese Art : Interpretation and Display*, edited by Stacey Pierson, 105–18. London: Percival David Foundation of Chinese Art, 2000.

Feaver, William. 'China at the Double: ART'. *The Observer*, 21 November 1976, 29.

Fraser, Ronald. *1968: A Student Generation in Revolt*. London: Chatto & Windus, 1988.

Frazier, Robeson Taj. *The East Is Black: Cold War China in the Black Radical Imagination*. Durham & London: Duke University Press, 2015.

Galimberti, Jacopo, Noemi de Haro García, and Victoria H.F. Scott. 'Introduction'. In *Art, Global Maoism and the Chinese Cultural Revolution*, edited by Jacopo Galimberti, Noemi de Haro García, and Victoria H. F. Scott, 1-13. Manchester: Manchester University Press, 2019.

Gao, Yuan. *Born Red: A Chronicle of the Cultural Revolution*. Stanford, CA: Stanford University Press, 1987.

Gentz, Natascha, and Peiming Yang, eds. *Poster Art of Modern China, Exhibition Catalogue, the University of Edinburgh*, 2014.

Gerth, Karl. *Unending Capitalism: How Consumerism Negated China's Communist Revolution*. Cambridge: Cambridge University Press, 2020.

Ginsberg, Mary. 'Revolutionary Art at the British Museum'. *Transactions of the Oriental Ceramic Society* 71 (2006-2007): 33–43.

———. *The Art of Influence: Asian Propaganda*. London: British Museum Press, 2013.

Gittings, John. 'A Thousand Cuts'. *The Guardian*, 2 May 1974, 14.

———. 'Excess and Enthusiasm'. In *Picturing Power in the People's Republic of China: Posters of the Cultural Revolution*, edited by Stephanie Donald and Harriet Evans, 27–46. Lanham: Rowman & Littlefield Publishers, 1999.

———. 'Reporting China since the 1960s'. In *China's Transformations : The Stories beyond the Headlines*, edited by Lionel M. Jensen and Timothy B. Weston, 285–302. Lanham, MD; Plymouth: Rowman & Littlefield, 2007.

———. 'The World Is Their Prize'. *The Guardian*, 8 May 1971, 2.

Gleadell, Colin. 'Sale of Revolutionary Chinese Art at Bloomsbury Auctions'. *The Telegraph*, 27 October 2009, http://www.telegraph.co.uk/culture/art/artsales/6447181/Sale-of-revolutionary-Chinese-art-at-Bloomsbury-Auctions.html.

Gosking, Nigel. 'Mao's Marvels'. *The Observer*, 30 September 1973, 36.

Gray, John. 'It's Not an Exaggeration to Compare Methods of New "woke Movement" to Mao's Red Guards'. *Daily Mail Online*, 18 July 2020. https://www.dailymail.co.uk/debate/article-8537583/JOHN-GRAY-not-exaggeration-compare-methods-new-woke-movement-Maos-Red-Guards.html.

Greene, Felix. *The Wall Has Two Sides: A Portrait of China Today*. London: Cape, 1963.

Greene, Graham C. 'Foreword'. In *The Art of Calligraphy in Modern China*, edited by Gordon S. Barrass, 7. London: British Museum, 2002.

Gregg, Melissa, and Gregory J. Seigworth. 'An Inventory of Shimmers'. In *The Affect Theory Reader*, edited by Melissa Gregg and Gregory J. Seigworth, 1–28. Durham & London: Duke University Press, 2010.

Gregor Benton and Edmund Terence Gomez. *The Chinese in Britain, 1800-Present: Economy, Transnationalism, Identity*. Basingstoke: Palgrave Macmillan, 2008.

Grosz, Elizabeth. 'The Thing'. In *The Object Reader*, edited by Fiona Candlin and Raiford Guins, 124–38. London; New York: Routledge, 2009.

Hardie, Alison. 'Art for the Masses: Revolutionary Art of the Mao Zedong Era, 1950-1976'. *IIAS Newsletter*, March 2002, 39.

Hare, David. *The Asian Plays*. London: Faber & Faber, 1986.

He, Weimin, and Shelagh Vainker. *Chinese Prints 1950-2006 in the Ashmolean Museum: 1950-2006*. Oxford: Ashmolean Museum, 2007.

He Zhenggu 何政谷. 'Tan Hongse Shoucangpin Zhong Ciji de Meili 谈红色收藏品中瓷器的魅力[On the Charm of Porcelain Red Collectibles]'. *Wenwu Jianding Yu Jianshang* 文物鉴定与鉴赏 10 (2011): 34–35.

Helle, Roger. 'America's Coming Cultural Revolution'. *The Patriot Post*, 22 July 2020. https://patriotpost.us/articles/72316-americas-coming-cultural-revolution-2020-07-22.

Hellstein, Valerie. 'Abstract Expressionism's Counterculture: The Club, the Cold War, and the New Sensibility'. Museum of Modern Art Conference New

Perspectives in Abstract Expressionism, 2011. http://www.moma.org/momaorg/shared/pdfs/docs/calendar/Hellstein2.25.11MoMApaper.pdf.
Hensman, Charles Richard. *China: Yellow Peril? Red Hope?* London: SCM Press, 1968.
Hill, Katie. *The Political Body: Posters from The People's Republic of China in the 1960s and 1970s.* London: University of Westminster Chinese Poster Collection, 2004.
Ho, Denise Y. *Curating Revolution: Politics on Display in Mao's China.* Cambridge: Cambridge University Press, 2018.
Ho, Denise Y., and Jie Li. 'From Landlord Manor to Red Memorabilia: Reincarnations of a Chinese Museum Town'. *Modern China*, July 2015, 1–35.
Honig, Albert M. *China Today: Sin or Virtue?* Hicksville, NY: Exposition Press, 1978.
Hooper, Beverley. *Foreigners under Mao: Western Lives in China, 1949-1976.* Hong Kong: Hong Kong University Press, 2016.
———. *Inside Peking: A Personal Report.* London: Macdonald and Jane's, 1979.
Horn, Joshua Samuel. *Away with All Pests: An English Surgeon in People's China, 1954–1969.* London: Paul Hamlyn, 1969.
Howard, Roger. *The Tragedy of Mao in the Lin Piao Period and Other Plays.* Colchester: Theatre Action Press, 1989.
Huan, Chen. 'Political Exhibitionism'. *The Guardian*, 27 September 1973, 3.
Hubbert, Jennifer. '(Re)Collecting Mao: Memory and Fetish in Contemporary China'. *American Ethnologist* 33, no. 2 (2006): 145–61.
Hung, Ruth Y. Y. 'Red Nostalgia: Commemorating Mao in Our Time'. *Literature Compass* 12, no. 8 (2015): 371–84.
James, Nicholas Philip. *John Dugger: Ergonic Sculpture and Other Works.* London: Cv Publications, 2011.
Jang, Scarlett. 'The Culture of Art Collecting in Imperial China'. In *A Companion to Chinese Art*, edited by Martin J Powers and Katherine R. Tsiang, 47–72. Chichester: Wiley Blackwell, 2016.
Jenkins, Roy. 'How China Sees the World'. *The Observer*, 9 December 1973, 13.
Jenner, Delia. *Letters from Peking.* Oxford: Oxford University Press, 1967.
Jensen, Marc G. 'John Cage, Chance Operations, and the Chaos Game: Cage and the "I Ching"'. *The Musical Times* 150, no. 1907 (1 July 2009): 97–102.
Johnson, Hewlett. *Searching for Light: An Autobiography.* London: Joseph, 1968.
———. *The Upsurge of China.* Peking: New World Press, 1961.
Jongh, Nicholas de. 'Tenth Struggle'. *The Guardian*, 20 September 1976, 8.
Karl, Rebecca E. *Mao Zedong and China in the Twentieth-Century World: A Concise History.* Durham: Duke University Press, 2010.
King, David. *Red Star over Russia: A Visual History of the Soviet Union from the Revolution to the Death of Stalin.* New York: Abrams, 2009.
———. *Russian Revolutionary Posters.* London: Tate Publishing, 2015.
———. *The Commissar Vanishes: The Falsification of Photographs and Art.* New Edition. London: Tate Publishing, 2014.
———. *Trotsky: A Photographic Biography.* Oxford; New York: Wiley-Blackwell, 1986.

King, Richard, ed. *Art in Turmoil : The Chinese Cultural Revolution, 1966–76*. Vancouver: UBC Press, 2010.
Kirkby, Richard. *Intruder in Mao's Realm: A Foreigner in China during the Cultural Revolution*. Hong Kong: Earnshaw Books, 2016.
———. 'Sex in Mao's China: How a Foreign Barbarian Blushed'. *South China Morning Post*, 24 November 2016. https://www.scmp.com/magazines/post-magazine/long-reads/article/2048586/sex-maos-china-how-foreign-barbarian-blushed.
Knight, Frida. 'Exhibition in Miniature'. *China Now*, 39, February 1974, 11–12.
Knight, Sophia. *Window on Shanghai: Letters from China, 1965–67*. London: André Deutsch, 1967.
Kraus, Richard Curtis. *The Cultural Revolution: A Very Short Introduction*. Oxford; New York: Oxford University Press, 2012.
Laing, Ellen Johnston. *Art and Aesthetics in Chinese Popular Prints : Selections from the Muban Foundation Collection*. Ann Arbor: University of Michigan Press, 2002.
———. 'Chinese Peasant Painting, 1958–1976'. *Art International* 27, no. 1 (1984): 2–12, 40, 48, 64.
———. *The Winking Owl: Art in the People's Republic of China*. Berkeley, CA; London: University of California Press, 1988.
Landsberger, Stefan. *Chinese Propaganda Posters : From Revolution to Modernization*. Amsterdam: Pepin, 1995.
Landsberger, Stefan, Duo Duo, and Anchee Min. *Chinese Propaganda Posters : From the Collection of Michael Wolf*. Köln: Taschen, 2008.
Landsberger, Stefan, and Marien van der Heijden. *Chinese Posters : The IISH-Landsberger Collections*. Munich: Prestel, 2009.
Landsberger, Stefan R., Anchee Min, Michael Wolf, and Duo Duo. *Chinese Propaganda Posters*. Köln; London: Taschen, 2011.
Langkjær, Michael A. 'From Cool to Un-Cool to Re-Cool: Nehru and Mao Tunics in the Sixties and Post-Sixties West'. In *Global Textile Encounters*, edited by Marie-Louise Nosch, Zhao Feng, and Lotika Varadarajan, 227–37. Oxford & Philadelphia: Oxbow Books, 2014.
Lanza, Fabio. 'Global Maoism'. In *Afterlives of Chinese Communism*, edited by Christian Sorace, Ivan Franceschini, and Nicholas Loubere, 85–88. Canberra: ANU Press, 2019.
———. 'Making Sense of "China" during the Cold War: Global Maoism and Asian Studies'. In *De-Centering Cold War History: Local and Global Change*, edited by Jadwiga E. Pieper Mooney and Fabio Lanza, 147–66. London: Routledge, 2013.
———. *The End of Concern: Maoist China, Activism, and Asian Studies*. Durham: Duke University Press, 2017.
Larsen, Darl. *Monty Python's Flying Circus: An Utterly Complete, Thoroughly Unillustrated, Absolutely Unauthorized Guide to Possibly All the References : From Arthur 'Two-Sheds' Jackson to Zambesi*. Lanham, MD; Plymouth: Rowman & Littlefield, 2008.
League of Socialist Artists. *Manifesto & Theses on Art*. London: League of Socialist Artists, 1977.

Lee, Christopher J. *Making a World after Empire: The Bandung Moment and Its Political Afterlives*. Athens: Ohio University Press, 2010.
Leese, Daniel. 'Mao the Man and Mao the Icon'. In *A Critical Introduction to Mao*, edited by Timothy Cheek, 219–39. Cambridge: Cambridge University Press, 2010.
Lent, Adam. *British Social Movements since 1945: Sex, Colour, Peace and Power*. Basingstoke: Palgrave, 2001.
Levinson, Paul. *Digital McLuhan: A Guide to the Information Millennium*. London; New York: Routledge, 1999.
Li, Jie, and Enhua Zhang, eds. *Red Legacies in China: Cultural Afterlives of the Communist Revolution*. Cambridge, MA; London: Harvard University Press, 2016.
Li Yingjun 李迎军. 'Cong Zhongshan Zhuang Kan Chuangtong Fushi Wenhua de Jicheng Yu Chuangxin 从中山装看传统服饰文化的继承与创新 [The Cultural Inheritance and Innovations of the Chinese Tunic Suit]'. *Yishu Sheji Yanjiu* 艺术设计研究 1 (2010): 34–37.
Li, Zhengling, Junwei Ning, and Israel Epstein. *David and Isabel Crook in China*. Beijing.: Foreign Language Teaching and Research Press, 1995.
Lifton, Robert Jay. *Thought Reform and the Psychology of Totalism: A Study of 'Brainwashing' in China*. Chapel Hill, NC: University of North Carolina Press, 1989.
Liscomb, Kathlyn Maurean. 'Social Status and Art Collecting: The Collections of Shen Zhou and Wang Zhen'. *The Art Bulletin* 78, no. 1 (March 1996): 111–36.
Living in China: Twenty Authors from Abroad. Beijing: New World Press, 1979.
Lovell, Julia. *Maoism: A Global History*. London: The Bodley Head, 2018.
Luard, David E. T. *Britain and China*. London: Chatto & Windus, 1962.
Lucie-Smith, Edward. *Art in the Seventies*. Oxford: Phaidon, 1980.
MacCabe, Colin. 'Class of '68: Elements of an Intellectual Autobiography 1967–81'. In *Theoretical Essays: Film, Linguistics, Literature*, 1–32. Manchester: Manchester University Press, 1985.
MacFarquhar, Roderick, and Michael Schoenhals. *Mao's Last Revolution*. Cambridge, MA; London: Belknap, 2006.
Malik, Sarita. *Representing Black Britain: Black and Asian Images on Television*. London: SAGE Publications, 2002.
Marwick, Arthur. *The Sixties : Cultural Revolution in Britain, France, Italy, and the United States, c.1958–c.1974*. Oxford: Oxford University Press, 1998.
Marxist-Leninist Organisation of Britain. 'More Police Violence against Chinese'. *Red Front: For Working-Class Power for a Socialist Britain!*, 1:1, October 1967, 23.
McEwen, John. 'Art'. *The Spectator*, 4 December 1976, 31.
Mcmahon, Robert J., ed. *The Cold War in the Third World*. Oxford; New York: Oxford University Press, 2013.
McNally, Anna. 'Not Just Curious Objects: The China Visual Arts Project Archive'. *Journal of Design History* 31, no. 4 (2018): 383–394.
Merewether, Charles. 'Introduction: Art and the Archive'. In *The Archive*, edited by Charles Merewether, 10–17. London: Whitechapel, 2006.

Miles, Barry. *London Calling: A Countercultural History of London since 1945*. London: Atlantic Books, 2010.
Miller, Daniel. 'Consumption'. In *Handbook of Material Culture*, edited by Christopher Y. Tilley, 341–54. London: SAGE, 2006.
———, ed. *Material Cultures: Why Some Things Matter*. London: UCL Press, 1998.
Mitter, Rana. 'China and the Cold War'. In *The Oxford Handbook of the Cold War*, edited by Richard H Immerman and Petra Goedde, 124–40. Oxford: Oxford University Press, 2013.
Mittler, Barbara. *A Continuous Revolution: Making Sense of Cultural Revolution Culture*. Cambridge, MA: Harvard University Press, 2012.
Moniot, Drew. 'James Bond and America in the Sixties: An Investigation of the Formula Film in Popular Culture'. *Journal of the University Film Association* 28, no. 3 (Summer 1976): 25–33.
Muensterberger, Werner. *Collecting: An Unruly Passion: Psychological Perspectives*. Princeton, NJ; Chichester: Princeton University Press, 1994.
Needham, Joseph. 'A Question of Values Part 1: Be the Man for Others'. 29, *China Now*, February 1973, 5-7.
Neville, Richard. *Playpower*. London: Paladin, 1971.
Olslager, Lorelies. 'On the Reporters Anthony Grey Leaves Behind'. *Daily Mirror*, 8 October 1969, 15.
Overy, Paul. 'A Stroll Round Pompeii'. *The Times*, 23 November 1976, 11.
Owen, Nick. 'Workers of the World, Unite! The Cultural Revolution Comes to the Ashmolean Museum'. *Culture24* (blog), 26 September 2011. http://www.culture24 .org.uk/art/painting%20%26%20drawing/art364858.
Pagani, Catherine. 'Chinese Material Culture and British Perceptions of China in the Mid-Nineteenth Century'. In *Colonialism and the Object: Empire, Material Culture and the Museum*, edited by T. J. Barringer and Tom Flynn, 28–40. London: Routledge, 1998.
Pang, Laikwan. *The Art of Cloning: Creative Production during China's Cultural Revolution*. London & New York: Verso, 2017.
Pierson, Stacey. *Collectors, Collections and Museums : The Field of Chinese Ceramics in Britain, 1560–1960*. Bern; Oxford: Peter Lang, 2007.
———. 'From Market and Exhibit to University: Sir Percival David and the Institutionalization of Chinese Ancient History in England'. In *Collecting China: The World, China, and a History of Collecting*, edited by Vimalin Rujivacharakul, 130–37. Newark: University of Delaware Press, 2011.
Qin Jie 秦杰. *Hongse Shoucang* 红色收藏 *[Red Collections]*. Nanchang, Jiangxi: Jiangxi Renmin Chubanshe, 2007.
Rank, Michael. 'Chinese Posters of Revolution and Reform'. *China Review*, no. 16 (Summer 2000): 32–35.
Revolutionary Communist Party of Britain (Marxist-Leninist). 'Cornelius Cardew His Life and Work'. Encyclopedia of Anti-Revisionism On-Line, 5 November 1986. https://www.marxists.org/history/erol/uk.hightide/cardew-2.htm.
Reynolds, Anthony. 'Revisiting the Convoy Route'. *China in Focus*, no. 2 (1997): 16.
Reynolds, Tony. 'China Days'. *China in Focus* 9 (Winter 2000): 17–18.

———. 'Tony Reynolds'. *Cotteridge Quaker Meeting*, no date. http://www.cotteridge.quaker.eu.org/new_page_11.htm#contents.
Richards, Sam. 'The Rise & Fall of Maoism: The English Experience', 2013. http://www.marxists.org/history/erol/uk.firstwave/uk-maoism.pdf.
Rifkin, Adrian. 'The Chinese Exhibition at the Warehouse Gallery'. *Artscribe* 5 (February 1977): 17.
Robinson, Joan. *The Cultural Revolution in China*. Harmondsworth: Penguin, 1969.
Rose, Gillian, and Divya Praful Tolia-Kelly. 'Visuality/Materiality: Introducing a Manifesto for Practice'. In *Visuality/Materiality: Images, Objects and Practices*, edited by Gillian Rose and Divya Praful Tolia-Kelly, 1–11. Farnham: Ashgate Publishing, 2012.
Rothwell, Michael D. *Transpacific Revolutionaries: The Chinese Revolution in Latin America*. New York: Routledge, 2013.
Rowlands, Michael, Stephan Feuchtwang, and Lisheng Zhang. 'Rupture and Repair: A Museum of the Red Age Confronts Historical Nihilism'. In *Ruptures*, edited by Martin Holbraad, Bruce Kapferer, and Julia F. Sauma, 52–69. London: UCL Press, 2019.
Sayle, Alexei. *Stalin Ate My Homework*. London: Sceptre, 2010.
Schiller, Justin G. '1964: The Little Red Book'. *The New Antiquarian*, 30 October 2014. http://www.abaa.org/blog/post/1964-the-little-red-book.
Schrift, Melissa. *Biography of a Chairman Mao Badge: The Creation and Mass Consumption of a Personality Cult*. New Brunswick, NJ: Rutgers University Press, 2001.
Scott, Maureen, and Mike Baker. *Essays on Art and Imperialism*. London: League of Socialist Artists, 1976.
Seltman, Muriel. *What's Left? What's Right?: A Political Journey via North Korea and the Chinese Cultural Revolution*. Kibworth Beauchamp, Leicestershire: Matador, 2014.
Shah, Alpa, and Judith Pettigrew, eds. *Windows into a Revolution: Ethnographies of Maoism in India and Nepal*. London & New York: Routledge, 2018.
Shepherd, Michael. 'East and West'. *Sunday Telegraph*, 29 November 1976.
Shipley, Peter. *Revolutionaries in Modern Britain*. London: Bodley Head, 1976.
Snow, Edgar. *Red Star over China*. London: Victor Gollancz, 1938.
Spalding, Frances. *British Art since 1900*. London: Thames and Hudson, 1986.
Spee, Clarissa von. 'Introduction: Printing the Pictorial in China—Historical and Cultural Contexts'. In *The Printed Image in China : From the 8th to the 21st Centuries*, edited by Clarissa von Spee, 14–25. London: British Museum, 2010.
———. *The Printed Image in China: From the 8th to the 21st Centuries*. London: British Museum, 2010.
Spence, Jonathan D. *The Chan's Great Continent: China in Western Minds*. New York: W. W. Norton & Company, 1999.
Stewart, Susan. *On Longing: Narratives of the Miniature, the Gigantic, the Souvenir, the Collection*. Durham, NC: Duke University Press, 1993.
Stott, Robin. 'New Medical Care'. 36, *China Now*, November 1973, 12-14.
Strong, Roy. *The Roy Strong Diaries, 1967–1987*. London: Phoenix, 1997.

———. 'The Victoria and Albert Museum—1978'. *The Burlington Magazine*, CXX, no. 902, May 1978, 272-278.
Su, Yang. *Collective Killings in Rural China during the Cultural Revolution*. Cambridge: Cambridge University Press, 2011.
Sullivan, Andrew. 'You Say You Want a Revolution?' *Intelligencer*, 26 June 2020. https://nymag.com/intelligencer/2020/06/andrew-sullivan-you-say-you-want-a-revolution.html.
Sullivan, Michael. *Art and Artists of Twentieth-Century China*. Berkeley; LA; London: University of California Press, 1996.
Sun, Wei. 'British Museum Reopens China Gallery'. *Global Times*, 17 December 2017. http://www.globaltimes.cn/content/1080654.shtml.
Swann, Peter C. 'Introduction'. In *Chinese Paintings of Today: An Exhibition of Works Collected and Presented by Collet's Chinese Gallery*, edited by Mary Shen and Sheila Dorrell, 1–3. London: Collet's Chinese Gallery, 1964.
Szonyi, Michael, and Hong Liu. 'New Approaches to the Study of the Cold War in Asia'. In *The Cold War in Asia: The Battle for Hearts and Minds*, edited by Michael Szonyi, Hong Liu, and Yangwen Zheng, 1–10. Leiden: Koninklijke Brill NV, 2010.
Tang, Xiaobing. *Visual Culture in Contemporary China: Paradigms and Shifts*. Cambridge: Cambridge University Press, 2015.
Tate. 'Inside the Home of Collector David King – Picture Essay'. Accessed 2 June 2020. https://www.tate.org.uk/whats-on/tate-modern/exhibition/red-star-over-russia/inside-home-collector-david-king.
Terrill, Ross. *800,000,000: The Real China*. Harmondsworth: Penguin Books, 1971.
The Art Fund, 'The Art Fund in 2013/14: Annual Report'. London, UK: The Art Fund, 2013. https://www.artfund.org/assets/about-us/annual-report/art-fund-review-digital-double-2013.pdf.
The Fine Arts Collection Section of the Cultural Group under the State Council of the People's Republic of China, ed. *Peasant Paintings from Huhsien County*. Peking: Foreign Languages Press, 1974.
The Guardian, 'Politicians Interview Pundits: George Osborne and Andrew Marr'. 26 September 2009, http://www.theguardian.com/media/2009/sep/26/george-osborne-interviews-andrew-marr.
The Leveller. 'A Short Guide to Maoists in Britain'. 20 (November 1978). http://www.marxists.org/history/erol/uk.firstwave/shortguide.htm.
The Observer. 'China: The Greatest Enigma of Our World'. 28 September 1969.
Tilbury, John. *Cornelius Cardew (1936–1981): A Life Unfinished*. Matching Tye, Essex: Copula, 2008.
Tilley, Christopher Y. 'Objectification'. In *Handbook of Material Culture*, edited by Christopher Y Tilley, 60–73. London: SAGE, 2006.
Tisdall, Caroline. 'Art Controversies of the 70s'. In *British Art in the 20th Century: The Modern Movement*, edited by Susan P. Compton, 83–88. Munich; New York: Prestel-Verlag, 1986.
———. 'Avant-Garde to All Intents'. *The Guardian*, 25 August 1972, 8.
———. 'Chinese Agitscape'. *The Guardian*, 15 December 1972, 15.

———. 'Record of Achievement'. *The Guardian*, 17 November 1976, 10.
Tuchman, Barbara W. *Notes from China*. New York: Collier books, 1972.
Unger, Jonathan. 'The Cultural Revolution at the Grass Roots'. *The China Journal* 57 (2007): 109–37.
University of Oxford News & Events. 'Sullivan Collection of Modern Chinese Art Bequeathed to the Ashmolean', 13 December 2013. https://www.ox.ac.uk/news/2013-12-13-sullivan-collection-chinese-art-bequeathed-ashmolean.
Vainker, Shelagh. *Chinese Paintings in the Ashmolean Museum Oxford*. Oxford: Ashmolean Museum, 2000.
———. *Modern Chinese Paintings: The Reyes Collection in the Ashmolean Museum, Oxford*. Oxford: Ashmolean Museum, 1996.
———. 'The New Galleries of Chinese Art'. *Arts of Asia* 41, no. 3 (2011): 102–13.
Vanke, Francesca. 'Degrees of Otherness: The Ottoman Empire and China at the Great Exhibition of 1851'. Edited by Jeffrey A. Auerbach and Peter H. Hoffenberg, 191–206. London & New York: Routledge, 2016.
Varutti, Marzia. *Museums in China: The Politics of Representation after Mao*. Woodbridge, Suffolk: The Boydell Press, 2014.
Wain, Peter. *Mao: Art for the Masses: Revolutionary Art of the Mao Zedong Era, 1950–1976*. Edinburgh: National Museums of Scotland, 2003.
———. 'Mao Zedong and Art'. In *Mao: Art for the Masses: Revolutionary Art of the Mao Zedong Era, 1950–1976*, 4–9. Edinburgh: National Museums of Scotland, 2003.
———. *Miller's Chinese & Japanese Antiques Buyer's Guide*. Tenterden: Miller's, 1999.
Walden, George. *China: A Wolf in the World?* London: Gibson Square, 2008.
———. *Lucky George: Memoirs of an Anti-Politician*. London: Allen Lane, 1999.
Walder, Andrew G. *Agents of Disorder: Inside China's Cultural Revolution*. Cambridge, MA: Harvard University Press, 2019.
———. *Fractured Rebellion: The Beijing Red Guard Movement*. Cambridge, MA; London: Harvard University Press, 2012.
Walker, John A. *Left Shift: Radical Art in 1970s Britain*. London: I.B. Tauris, 2002.
Walsh, David. 'Uncovering the Truth about Trotsky and the Russian Revolution "Continues to Run My Life": A Conversation with the Remarkable David King'. *World Socialist Web Site*, 4 December 2008. http://www.wsws.org/en/articles/2008/12/king-d04.html.
Wang, Helen. *Chairman Mao Badges: Symbols and Slogans of the Cultural Revolution*. London: British Museum Press, 2008.
———. 'Icons of Revolution. Mao Badges Then and Now'. British Museum, 2008. https://www.academia.edu/1098957/Icons_of_Revolution._Mao_badges_then_and_now_exhibition_text_.
Watson, William. *The Genius of China: An Exhibition of Archaeological Finds of the People's Republic of China Held at the Royal Academy, London*. London: Times Newspapers, 1973.
Waugh, Auberon. 'Another Voice'. *The Spectator*, 21 May 1976, 6.

Waugh, Thomas. 'How Yukong Moved the Mountains: Filming the Cultural Revolution'. *Jump Cut: A Review of Contemporary Media*, no. 12/13 (December 1976): 3–6.

Westad, Odd Arne. *The Global Cold War: Third World Interventions and the Making of Our Times*. New Edition. Cambridge; New York: Cambridge University Press, 2007.

Whitfield, Roderick. 'Landmarks in the Collection and Study of Chinese Art in Great Britain'. In *Europe Studies China: Papers from an International Conference on The History of European Sinology*, edited by Ming Wilson and John Cayley, 202–14. London: Han-Shan Tang Books, 1995.

Widgery, David. *The Left in Britain 1956-68*. Harmondsworth: Penguin Books, 1976.

Williams, Emily. 'Collecting the Red Era in Contemporary China'. *Made in China* 2, no. 3 (2017): 78–83.

———. 'Red Collections in Contemporary China: Towards a New Research Agenda'. *British Journal of Chinese Studies* 11 (2021): 71–90.

Williams Morris Gallery. 'Exhibitions: Cultural Revolution: State Graphics in China from the 1960s to the 1970s', 2019. https://www.wmgallery.org.uk/whats-on/exhibitions-43/cultural-revolution/past/2019.

Wilson, Christopher. 'Reputations: David King'. *Eye*, Summer 2003. http://www.eyemagazine.com/feature/article/repuations-david-king.

Wilson, David M. *The British Museum: A History*. London: British Museum Press, 2002.

Wilson, Verity. 'Celebrating Twenty-Five Years in the Far Eastern Collection of the Victoria and Albert Museum'. *Orientations* 26, no. 10 (November 1995): 52–63.

Winchester, Simon. *Bomb, Book and Compass: Joseph Needham and the Great Secrets of China*. London: Penguin, 2009.

Wolin, Richard. *The Wind from the East: French Intellectuals, the Cultural Revolution, and the Legacy of the 1960s*. Princeton, NJ; Woodstock: Princeton University Press, 2010.

Wong, Natalie Siu Lam. 'On the (Re)Emergence of Cultural Revolution Imagery in China, Hong Kong and Singapore in the 21st Century'. University of Westminster, 2010. Unpublished Thesis.

Wood, Frances. *Hand-Grenade Practice in Peking: My Part in the Cultural Revolution*. London: Slightly Foxed, 2011.

Woodward, Ian. *Understanding Material Culture*. Los Angeles: SAGE Publications, 2014.

Workers' Institute Party Committee. 'Workers' Institute Successfully Conducts Vigorous Programme to Uphold Chairman Mao's Revolutionary Line Amidst the Mass Upsurge in Britain—A Report', 31 March 1977. https://www.marxists.org/history/erol/uk.hightide/wi-report.htm.

Worsley, Peter. *Inside China*. London: Allen Lane, 1975.

Woudhuysen, James. 'David King: Graphic Designer, Ranged Left'. *Blueprint* 2, no. 11 (1984): 34–38.

Wright, Patrick. *Passport to Peking: A Very British Mission to Mao's China*. Oxford: Oxford University Press, 2010.

Wu, Yiching. *The Cultural Revolution at the Margins: Chinese Socialism in Crisis.* Cambridge, MA: Harvard University Press, 2014.

Yan, Geng. *Mao's Images: Artists and China's 1949 Transition.* Wiesbaden: J.B. Metzler, 2018.

Yang, Jisheng. *The World Turned Upside Down: A History of the Chinese Cultural Revolution.* Translated by Stacy Mosher and Jian Guo. New York: Farrar, Straus and Giroux, 2021.

Zhang Liguo 章利国. 'Shoucang Lilun Xianzhuang he Zhongguo Shoucangxue de Yiyi ji Yanjiu Fanwei 收藏理论现状和中国收藏学的意义及研究范围 [The present situation of collecting theory and the significance and research scope of Chinese collecting science]'. *Rongbaozhai* 荣宝斋 08 (2010): 250–55.

———. 'Wenhua Chuancheng Shoucang You Xue - Lue Shuo Shouna Gai Shoucang Xue 文化传承收藏有学 - 略说收纳该国收藏学 [Cultural Heritage and Collection Study: A Brief View of Collection in China]'. *Meishu* 美术 11 (2018): 106–10.

Zharkevich, Ina. *Maoist People's War and the Revolution of Everyday Life in Nepal.* Cambridge: Cambridge University Press, 2019.

Zheng, Shengtian. 'Searching for the "Lost Chapter" in the History of Contemporary Chinese Art'. In *Art of the Great Proletarian Cultural Revolution, 1966–76*, edited by Scott Watson and Shengtian Zheng, 8–15. Vancouver: Morris and Helen Belkin Art Gallery, 2002.

'Zhongguo Gongchandang Jianshi' Bianxie Zu 《中国共产党简史》编写组 ["A Brief History of the Chinese Communist Party" Writing Group]. *Zhongguo Gongchandang Jianshi* 中国共产党简史 *[A Brief History of the Chinese Communist Party].* Beijing: Renmin Chubanshe, Zhonggong Dangshi Chubanshe, 2021.

Zhongguo Shoucangjia Xiehui 中国收藏家协会 [China Association of Collectors]. 'Quanguo Hongse Bowuguan, Zhanlanguan, Jiating Shoucangguan, Diyiji 全国红色博物馆，展览馆，家庭收藏馆，第一集 [All China Red Museum, Exhibition Hall and Home Collection Hall, Volume 1]'. *Zhongguo Hongse Shoucang* 中国红色收藏 6 (2017).

Zhonghua Renmin Gongheguo Wenhuabu 中华人民共和国文化部 [Ministry of Culture of the People's Republic of China]. 'Wenwu Cangpin Dingji Biaozhun 文物藏品定级标准 [Rating Standards for Cultural Relic Collections]'.

Zhonghua Renmin Gongheguo Wenhuabu 中华人民共和国文化部 [Ministry of Culture of the People's Republic of China], 5 April 2001. http://www.lawinfochina.com/display.aspx?lib=law&id=1829&CGid=.

Zorza, Victor. 'Thoughts of Mao Take Root in Britain'. *The Guardian*, 30 May 1967, 8.

Index

Ahmed, Sara, 11
AHRC. *See* Arts and Humanities Research Council (AHRC)
'Aid China' campaign, xviii
Ali, Tariq, 7
alternative Marxist traditions, 8–9
Althusser, Louis, xxvn16, 46n79
antiques, 62, 67, 72, 91, 93, 100, 102
Arendt, Hannah, 87
'Art for Whom?' exhibition (1978), Serpentine Gallery, 32–33
Arthur M. Sackler Gallery, Smithsonian Institution, 113
'Art in China in the 1960s and 1970s' exhibition (2011–2012), Ashmolean Museum, 129
artistic inspiration from 1970s China, 46–49
'Artists' Liberation Front, 46
'The Art of Influence: Asian propaganda' exhibition (2013), British Museum, 124
Arts and Humanities Research Council (AHRC), 137
Arts Council of Great Britain, 38
Artscribe, art magazine, 31
Ashmolean Museum, xiii, xxiii, 125–27, 129–33; Chinese painting collection, 126–27; donation, 126; Eastern Art Paintings Gallery, 129; *guohua* paintings, 126; Khoan and Michael Sullivan Gallery for Chinese painting, 129; Mao-era collection, 125–27, 129–33; modern ink paintings collection, 126; purchases, 126; temporary exhibitions at, 129–33; twentieth-century collection, 125–27
Asian Art Museum, San Francisco, 113
auctions, 99–100; Bloomsbury Auctions, 98, 100–101, 118, 122, 128, 134; Christie's, 100; Sotheby's, 100

badges, Chairman Mao, xii–xiii, xix, xx, 5, 18, 74–77, 88–93, 98–99, 101–6, 118, 121, 123–25, 130–31, 140, 150; alternative materials (bamboo, 74; ceramic, 74; plastic, 74)
Badiou, Alain, xxvn16
Balakrishnan, Aravindan, xvi
Balakrishnan, Chanda, xvi
Bandung Conference (1955), xv
Barbrook, Richard, 7–8, 23
Barclay, Craig, 114
Barrass, Gordon, 117, 121, 134
Baudrillard, Jean, 75
Belk, Russell, 87

Bell, James, 12
Benjamin, Walter, 98
Bijur, G. V., 44
Billingham International Folklore Festival, Stockton-On-Tees, 38
Bishop, Bill, 103–4
Blofeld, Ernst Stavro, 19–20
Bloodsworth, Denis, 6
'blue ant' trope, xvii, 6, 15, 18
Bolinder-Müller, Verena, 114
Bolton, Andrew, 117
Bond, James, 19–20
bookshops for Maoist objects, 23–24, 44–45, 96, 98; Arthur Probstain's, 44–45, 50; Banner Books, 44; Collet's, xv, 44–45, 44n68, 62, 126; Gwanghua, 45, 134; Hanshan Tang books, 98, 114; New Era Books, 23–24
Brett, Guy, 37–39
Britain, xvi, 3–25; Chinese material culture in, 14–24, 57–78 (circulation, 14–15; Mao suit as fashion, 21–24; Mao suit in television and film, 15–21; cultural interest in China (artistic inspiration from 1970s China, 46–49; cultural interest in 1970s China, 44–46; imperial, 42–44); fanaticism, connotations of, 6–7; Mao-era political art and artefacts, collections of, 113–41; Mao's China in, 3–25, 48–50 (as alternative socialist modernity, 7–11; Cultural Revolution, affective power of, 11–14; as 'problem nation', 5–7); Marxist–Leninist groups in, 10–11; students in China, 68–76
British Art World, xxii, 25, 31, 34–35, 39–42, 46, 48–49
British Library, London, 72, 100, 114
British Museum, xiii, xxiii, 115–18, 123–25; displays, Mao era, 123–25; donations, 116–18; historical objects, 115–16; purchases, 118; twentieth-century material collection, 116–18

British sinology, 67
Britons in China, 68–76
Brooke, Penny, 74–77, 118
Buchli, Victor, 57
'Buddha Ballet', 46
Buddhism, 43, 46
Burton, Anthony, 115

Cage, John, 43
Callahan, William, 11, 14
cancel culture, 149
Cardew, Cornelius, 43–44
Carey, Frances, 116
Carnaby Street, London, 21–24
Carr, J., 118
ceramic yoghurt pot, 68–70
Chairman Mao. See Mao Zedong
Chairman Mao badges. See badges
Chairman Mao badges: symbols and slogans of the Cultural Revolution (Wang), 102
The Champions, 16
Chen Jian, 6
China: anti-colonial positioning, 8; anti-imperial positioning, 8; British conception of, xviii, xxii, 3–25; British cultural interest (artistic inspiration from 1970s China, 46–49; cultural interest in 1970s China, 44–46; in imperial China, 42–44); British students in, 68–76; communism of, 12–13; Cultural Revolution in, xi, 3–25, 31–50; culture in Britain, xix; descriptions of, xvii; encounters with objects in, 66–68; as esoteric culture, xviii; foreigners, 67–68; from Hong Kong, 62–66; Mao-era, xiv–xviii, xxiii, 3–25; material culture in Britain, 14–24, 57–78 (circulation, 14–15; Mao suit as fashion, 21–24; Mao suit in television and film, 15–21); model as alternative socialist modernity, 7–11; in Monty Python, 16; old *versus* new, 43; photographs of, 18–19;

porcelain of, xviii, 86, 99–100; as problem nation, 5–7; relationships with objects, xx–xxi; revolutionary appeal, 7–8; as sinister, 18; socialism of, 8–11; tradition of collecting, 87; viewing through objects, xvii–xx; visual culture, 4–5, 14–15, 57, 66–68, 115, 123, 127, 135–37, 140, 150, 154; Western views of, xvii

'China and Revolution: History, Memory and Parody in Contemporary Art' exhibition, University of Sydney, 137

China Pictorial, 18, 36, 47–48

China Reconstructs, 18, 36

China Visual Arts Project Archive. See University of Westminster

Chinese art in France, xiii

Chinese Cartoons, xviii

Chinese Central Academy of Fine Arts, 87

Chinese Communist-as-villains, 19–21

Chinese Drawings, xviii. *See also* paintings

Chinese films, films about China, 44

Chinese National Museum, 151

Chinese People's Liberation Army, xvi

Chinese woodblock prints, 114

Chinese Woodcuts, xviii

Clore, Vivien, 12–13

clothing, 18–24, 48; Mao cap, 23; Mao jacket, 93; Mao suit, 5, 14–24

Clunas, Craig, 37, 45, 67, 73

Cold War, 5–8, 19, 60, 65

Cole, Henry, 115

collection of objects: in China, 87–89; definition, 86; European tradition of, 87; as form of private engagement, 85–89; individual, 85–106; legacies of engagements with, 149–56; literature on, 86; public, 113–41; social and cultural value of, 87–88; understanding, 86–89

Collier, John, 79n29

Communism, 12–13, 17, 41

Communist Party of China (CCP), xix, 4, 36, 150–51

Communist stores, 62

Confucianism, 43

Cork, Richard, 32–33, 40–41

Cradock, Percy, 61

Cribb, Joe, 118

'Criticise Lin Biao Criticise Confucius' (批林批孔 *piLin piKong*) campaign, 35, 91, 134

Croizier, Ralph, 37

Crook, Paul, 88–92, 133

Cultural Revolution, 4–5; affective power of, 11–14; in British popular culture, 3–25; childhood collecting in, 89–92; in China, xi, xix, xxivn2; collections in Britain, xiii–xiv; exhibitions on, 37–38, 45, 114, 123–24, 136, 129–32, 136–39, 152–53; Huxian peasant paintings and, 35–37; idealising, 31–50; material culture, xxi–xxiii, 14–24, 57–78 (circulation, 14–15; Mao suit as fashion, 21–24; Mao suit in television and film, 15–21); objects, xxiii, 57–78 (bookshops for, 44–45; as collectable, 86; encounters with, 66–68; future of, 154–56; global journeys of, 85–106; identities, 57, 86; individual collections, 85–106; internet collections, 101–5; legacies of engagements with, 149–56; public collections, 113–41; relationships with, xx–xxi; viewing through, xvii–xx)

'Cultural Revolution: State Graphics in China in the 1960s and 1970s' exhibition (2011–2012), Ashmolean Museum, 129

Dallas, Ian, 21–22

Daoism, 43

Davin, Delia, 8, 77–78

dazibao (大字报 big character poster), 47, 59

de Haro García, Noemi, xvi
Deleuze, Giles, 11
Deng Xiaoping, 4, 50, 134
Denton, Kirk, 151
Derrida, Jacques, 152
Diamonds Are Forever, 19–20
Dobrogoszcz, Tomasz, 16
Donald, Stephanie, 137
'Down with American Imperialism! Down with Soviet Revisionism!' poster, 90
Dugger, John, 34, 45–48
Dutton, Michael, 12, 153–54
Dyer, Christopher, 118

eBay, 103
emotions, 11–14
Evans, Harriet, 67–72, 131, 134, 137
'Exploring East Asia' gallery, National Museum of Scotland, 129

Fan, Jianchuan, 151
Fanshen (Hare), 44
Farrer, Anne, 115–17
Feaver, William, 40
Fernbach, David, 9, 13
festival poster, London's Classic Cinemas, 45
First Opium War (1839–1842), xviii
Folkestone exhibition, 137–38
Foreigners in China, 67–68
Foreign Languages Press, 31, 36, 67
Foucault, Michel, xxvn16
'Four Olds', 4
Fourteenth Arts Festival, Bromsgrove, 38
Freer Gallery of Art, Smithsonian Institution, 113
French Maoism, xxvn16
Friendship Store (友谊商店 *Youyi shangdian*), 89
Fu Baoshi, 62

Galimberti, Jacopo, xvi
'Genius of China' exhibition, Royal Academy, London, 43

Gerth, Karl, 108n23
Ginsberg, Mary, 116, 118
Gittings, John, 23, 62–66, 127, 133; as China watcher, 63–66; on Chinese communism, 65; interest in Chinese arts and culture, 62–64; on Maoist project, 65–66; political and cultural change, insight into, 64–65
global Maoisms, xiv–xvii
'global sixties', xx
Goldman, Jerry, 17
Gray, John, 150
Great Leap Forward (1958–1961), xix
The Great Learning (Pound), 43
Gregg, Melissa, 11
Grey, Anthony, 64
Grosz, Elizabeth, 74
Guardian, 23, 40, 65
Guatarri, Félix, 11
Gulbenkian Museum of Oriental Art, Durham, 44

Hadley, Janet, 37
Hare, David, 44
Harrison Hall, Jessica, 123
Hensman, Charles, 5
Herdan, Innes, 37
Heseltine, Lady Anne, 123–24
He Weimin, 126–27, 129
Hill, Katie, 134
Hinton, William, 44
The History of the Tenth Struggle (Howard), 44
Hong Kong, xvii, xxivn2, 62–66
Honig, Albert, 68
Hooper, Beverley, 68–69, 92
Horniman Museum, London, 114
Hornsey Art College, 33–34
Howard, Roger, 44
Howells, Kim, 9, 33
How Yukong Moved the Mountains (film), 44
Hughes, Carol, 50
Hung On You boutique, London, 21–22
Huxian exhibition, xxii, 32, 34–35, 37–44, 48–50

Huxian peasant painters, xxi–xxii, 35–39
Huxian peasant paintings, 31–37, 50, 77; Brett's description of, 38–39; and British Art World, 39–42; coverage in, 39–42; Cultural Revolution and, 35–37; exhibition, xxii, 32, 34–35, 37–44, 48–50; global exhibitions, 37–38; Great Leap Forward and, 35; reviews on, 39–42; Socialist Education Movement and, 35; at Warehouse Gallery, 40

I Ching (易经 *Yijing*, Book of Changes), 43
'Icons of Revolution: Mao badges then and now' exhibition, British Museum, 123
IISH-Landsberger Collection, Netherlands, 153
imperial Chinese culture and aesthetics, 42–44
individual acquisition/collection of objects, 57–78, 85–106; Brooke, Penny, 74–76; Crook, Paul, 89–92; Evans, Harriet, 68–72; Gittings, John, 62–66; King, David, 95–99; Kirkby, Richard, 92–95; Twist, Clint, 101–5; Wain, Peter, 99–101; Wain, Susan, 99–101; Walden, George, 58–62; Wood, Frances, 72–74
ink paintings, 62–63, 113, 125–26, 129, 132
International Exhibition of Chinese Art, London, xviii
internet collections, 101–5
Irvine Sellers, 21
Ivens, Joris, 44

Jenkins, Roy, 10
Jianchuan Museum Cluster (建川博物馆 *Jianchuan bowuguan*), Anren, Sichuan, 151
Jiang Qing, 4, 35–37
Johnson, Boris, 149–50

'Joseph Hotung Gallery', British Museum, 123
July, Serge, xxvn16

Karl, Rebecca, xvi
Kerr, Rose, 67, 139, 152
'Khoan and Michael Sullivan Gallery', Ashmolean Museum, 129
King, David, 95–99; anti-colonial sympathies, 99; China visit, 98–99; Chinese objects, collection of, 95–99; Chinese periodicals, collection of, 96–97; functions of collection, 98–99; interest in Communist movements, 96; posters, collection of, 96–97; self-identity, 98; Soviet material, collection of, 95–96; 'Trotsky: the Conscience of the Revolution', 96
King's Road, London, 21–24
Kirkby, Richard, 69, 92–95, 126–27; collection, 93–95; posters collection, 93–94; small booklets collection, 94–95; *Urbanization in China: Town and Country in a Developing Economy, 1949–2000 AD*, 93
Knight, Sophia, 13
Korean War (1950–1953), xix
Kwan, Simon, 120, 152

Laing, Ellen, 36, 134, 153
'Lambeth Slavery Case' (2013), xvi
Landsberger, Stefan, 155
Langkjær, Michael, 15, 22
Lanza, Fabio, xv–xvi, xvii–xviii
League of Socialist Artists, 34
Lent, Adam, 10
Levinson, Paul, 155
Li Fenglan, 37
Lin Biao, 131
Little Red Book, xi–xii, xix, 5, 16, 18–19, 23–24, 45–46, 95, 99, 118
Liu Shaoqi, 61
Liu Yiqian, 107n4
Liu Zhide, 37

'Long Live the Victory of the People's War' (人民战争胜利万岁 *renmin zhanzheng shengli wansui*) poster, 96–97
'Looking East' gallery, National Museum of Scotland, 129
Loridan, Marceline, 44
Lovell, Julia, 7
Luke, Keye, 16

MacLuhan, Marshall, 155
'Mao: Art for the Masses: revolutionary art of the Mao Zedong era, 1950–1976' exhibition, (2003–2004), National Museum of Scotland, 130
'Mao: From Icon to Irony' exhibition (1999), Victoria & Albert Museum, 123
Mao badges. *See* badges
Mao cap, 23
Mao-era China, xiv–xvii, xviii, xxiii, 3–25; as alternative socialist modernity, 7–11; Cultural Revolution, affective power of, 11–14; material culture, xxi–xxiii, 4–5, 14–24, 57–78, 115, 123, 127, 135–37, 140, 150, 154 (circulation, 14–15; individual collections, 85–106; Mao suit as fashion, 21–24; Mao suit in television and film, 15–21; public collections, 113–41); objects, xxiii, 57–78 (bookshops for, 44–45; as collectable, 86; encounters with, 66–68; global journeys of, 85–106; identities, 57, 86; individual collections, 85–106; internet collections, 101–5; legacies of engagements with, 149–56; public collections, 113–41; relationships with, xx–xxi; viewing through, xvii–xx); as 'Problem Nation', 5–7
Maoisms, xiv–xvii, 8–11, 15–17; total saturation of, 16–18
Maoists: guerrillas in Nepal, xi; movements, xiii; in United Kingdom, xii–xiii

Mao papercuts, 58–59, 117
'
Mao suit, 5, 14–15, 150; the Beatles, 23; in British context, 15; as fashion, 21–24; in James Bond films, 19–20; as shorthand for conformity/totalitarianism, 18, 20; as shorthand for evil, 19–21; in television and film, 15–21; in West, 15
Mao Zedong, xiii–xiv, xix, 3–4, 14, 36, 46, 117, 130
Marr, Andrew, 23
Marxist–Leninist groups, 10–11, 14, 34, 43
material culture, xxi–xxiii, 4–5, 14–24, 57–78, 115, 123, 127, 135–37, 140, 150, 154; circulation, 14–15; engagements with, 57–78; individual collections, 85–106; Mao suit as fashion, 21–24; Mao suit in television and film, 15–21; public collections, 113–41
Mauricio, Jose, 126
McCullin, Donald, 96
McElney, Brian, 114
McEwen, John, 40
McKillop, Beth, 67, 141
McLoughlin, Kevin, 127
McNally, Anna, 134–36, 141
Medalla, David, 34, 46–48
Merton, Anna, 133–34
'Microcosm' exhibition, Krauss gallery (London), 46
Miller, Daniel, xx, 57
Mind Your Language (television), 16
Moniot, Drew, 19
Monty Python, 16
Monty Python's Flying Circus (television), 16
The Most Dangerous Man in the World (film), 16–17, 19
Muban Foundation, London, 114
Mungan, Christina, 118
Murck, Alfreda, 117
Musée Cernuschi in Paris, France, xiii
Musée Guimet in Paris, France, xiii

Museum für Asiatische Kunst in Berlin, Germany, xiii
Museum of East Asian Art, in Bath, 114
Museum of Fine Arts in Boston, US, xiii

Narbeth, Colin, 118
National Art Gallery, Beijing, 35
National Film Theatre, London, 44
National Museum of Scotland (NMS), xiii, xxiii, 100, 127–33, 139–40; Art Fund for, 128; curator, 127; 'Exploring East Asia' gallery, 129; 'Looking East' gallery, 129; Mao-era objects collection, 127–33; purchases, 128; temporary exhibitions at, 129–33
Needham, Joseph, 10, 43
Nehru, Jawaharlal, 22–23
'Nehru' jackets, 22–23
New China Bookstores (新华书店 *Xinhua shudian*), 64, 89, 91, 93
NMS. *See* National Museum of Scotland (NMS)

objects, Mao-era, xxiii, 57–78; bookshops for, 44–45; as collectable, 86; encounters with, 66–68; future of, 154–56; global journeys of, 85–106; identities, 57, 86; individual collections, 85–106; internet collections, 101–5; legacies of engagements with, 149–56; public collections, 113–41; relationships with, xx–xxi; viewing through, xvii–xx
Observer, 6
Oriental Museum, Durham, 114
Overy, Paul, 40

paintings, xix, 93, 116–17, 126–27; *guohua*, 126; Huxian, 31–37, 50, 77; ink, 62–63, 113, 125–26, 129, 132; *xieyi*, 116
pamphlets, 59

papercuts, 58–60, xix; with anti-imperialist themes, 59; Cultural Revolution, 58–62; with image of five key Marxists, 117; 'Up to the Mountains and Down to the Countryside Movement', 62–63; Walden, George, 58–59
Peck, Gregory, 16–18
periodicals, xix
photographs, 18–19
Picturing Power in the People's Republic of China: Posters of the Cultural Revolution (Evans and Donald), 137
Pierson, Stacey, xviii, 116
PLA plimsolls, 93
Playpower (Neville), 9
'The Political Body: Posters from the People's Republic of China in the 1960s and 1970s' exhibition (2004), University of Westminster, London, 114, 137
porcelain of China, xviii, 86, 99–100, 128; cup, 86; vase with Chairman Mao painted, 128
portraits, 18
'Poster Power: Images from Mao's China, Then and Now', University of Westminster, London, 138
posters, xix, 62, 89; 'Down with American Imperialism! Down with Soviet Revisionism!', 90; Maoist, 17, 40, 49, 75, 77, 88; propaganda, xiii, 124–26, 150–52, 155; value of, 61–62
Pound, Ezra, 43
Powell, Rupert, 101
Prometheus (film), 20
propaganda, 124; artistic diversity of, 124; goal of, xiii, 124; Maoist, 17, 40, 49, 75, 77, 88; pejorative interpretations of, 126; posters, xiii, 89–91, 93–94, 114, 117–18, 121–22, 126–28, 133–39, 150–51, 155–56

'Propaganda: Power and Persuasion' exhibition (2013), British Library, London, 114
Pryce, Jonathan, 20
public collection of objects, 113–41; Ashmolean Museum, 125–27, 129–33; British collections in comparative context, 113–15; British Museum, 115–18, 123–25; National Museum of Scotland, 127–33; University of Westminster, 133–39; Victoria and Albert Museum, 118–25

Qi Baishi, 77–78
Qin Cao, 129
Qing dynasty, xiii, xviii
Qin Jie, 152

Rainey, Michael, 21–23
Rand, Michael, 96
Rank, Michael, 77, 118
Rawson, Dame Jessica, 117–18
Rawson, Phillip, 44
'reading the walls' practice, 64
Red Collecting, 150–54
Red Guards, 4; armbands, xi, 18; groups, 4; headband, 114; publications, 64; rubber dolls, 63; suits, 21–22; violence, 6–7
Red legacies, 150–54
Red Star Over China (Snow), 8, 58
Reyes, Angelita Trinidad, 126
Reynolds, Anthony, 123
Rifkin, Adrian, 31–33, 40
'The Road to Rejuvenation', National Museum of China, Beijing, 151
Robinson, Joan, 9
Rongbaozhai studio, Beijing, 63
Royal Doulton, 100

SACU. *See* Society for Anglo-Chinese Understanding (SACU)
Sartre, Jean-Paul, xxvn16
Sayle, Alexei, 13–14, 45
Schiller, Justin, 99
Schrift, Melissa, 103
Scott, Maureen, 23
Scott, Ridley, 20
Scott, Victoria H. F., xvi
Seigworth, Gregory, 11
Sendero Luminoso, xv
Shanghai Propaganda Poster Art Centre, 151
Sheng Guanxi, 118
Shepherd, Michael, 40–41
Sheringham, Michael, 50
Shipley, Peter, 11
Sino-British relations, xii, 5–11, 60, 64, 66–67, 123–24, 156
Sino-Western engagements, xvii
Sloane, Hans, 115
Smith, Cecil Harcourt, 115
Snow, Edgar, 8, 58
social realism, 34
Society for Anglo-Chinese Understanding (SACU), 10, 23, 37–38, 43, 44, 46, 63–64, 93, 133
souvenir, 71–72, 75–75
Soviet Union, 5–8; revisionism in, 9
Sparrow, John, 10
SPECTRE (Special Executive for Counter-Intelligence, Terrorism, Revenge and Extortion), 19–20
Spence, Jonathan, xvii
stamps, 93, 110n64
Stewart, Susan, 71, 75, 153
A Stitch in Time (1968–1972, Medalla), 47
Stott, Robin, 10
Sullivan, Khoan, 126
Sullivan, Michael, 126
Sun Yatsen, xxi, 14
Swann, Peter, 126

Teague, Ken, 114
Thompson, J. Lee, 16–17
Tian'anmen, 4, 6, 124
Tilley, Christopher, 77
Tisdall, Caroline, 40
Tomorrow Never Dies (film), 20

Trump, Donald, 149
'T.T. Tsui Gallery', Victoria & Albert Museum, 123
Twist, Clint, xi–xii, xix, 101–5
Twitter Maoism, 150

United Kingdom, Maoists in, xii–xiii. *See also* Britain
University of Westminster, xxiii, 133–39; building collection, 133–36; changing functions, 136–39; China Visual Arts Project, 133–39; Chinese Poster Collection, 137; Crook donation, 133; donations to, 133–34; exhibitions, 137–39
'Up to the Mountains and Down to the Countryside Movement' papercut, 62–63
Urbanization in China: Town and Country in a Developing Economy, 1949–2000 AD (Kirkby), 93

Vainker, Shelagh, 117, 127
Victor, Pierre, xxvn16
Victoria and Albert Museum, xiii, xxiii, 115–18, 139–40; displays, Mao era, 123–25; twentieth-century material collection, 118–23
Vietnam War, 7–8, 65
visual culture, 4–5, 14–15, 57, 66–68, 115, 123, 127, 135–37, 140, 150, 154
von der Berg, Christer, 114

Wade, Nigel, 127
Wain, Peter, 88, 99–101, 127–28, 130
Wain, Susan, 99–101, 127–28

Walden, George, 58–62, 68; Cultural Revolution China and, 58–62; Mao's China, critical perspective on, 60–62; memories, 59–60; papercuts, 58–60
Walker, John, 46–47
Wang, Helen, 102, 118
Wang Zhuangling, 99
washbasins, 72–73
Wasserstrom, Jeffrey, 137
Waugh, Auberon, 6, 12
Williams Morris Gallery, London, 129
Wilson, David, 116
Wood, Frances, 67, 69, 72–74
woodblock printmaking, 114
woodblock prints, 126
Woodward, Ian, 74
Workers' Institute of Marxism-Leninism-Mao Zedong Thought, xvi
Worsley, Peter, 8

xiaorenshu (小人书), 93
Xi Jinping, 154
Xinhua, news agency, 18, 23–24, 44
Xu Shiyou, 131

Yan'an, 123–24
Yang Peiming, 151
'Yangtze River Bridge' (painting), 48
Yangtze river bridge, Nanjing, 128, 132

Zao Wou-Ki (Zhao Wuji), 37
Zhang Hongxing, 141
Zhang Liguo, 87
Zheng Shengtian, 152
Zhou Enlai, 4, 36

About the Author

Emily R. Williams is an assistant professor in the Department of China Studies at Xi'an Jiaotong-Liverpool University, Suzhou, where she teaches on modern Chinese history and society. Her research focuses on the art and material culture of the Maoist period, its legacies in contemporary China, and the collection of this material in China and the United Kingdom.

CPSIA information can be obtained
at www.ICGtesting.com
Printed in the USA
BVHW092046150222
629155BV00003B/18